THE ARTS OF FRIENDSHIP

The Idealization of Friendship in
Medieval and Early Renaissance Literature

BY

REGINALD HYATTE

E.J. BRILL
LEIDEN · NEW YORK · KÖLN
1994

The paper in this book meets the guidelines for permanence and durability of the Committee on Production Guidelines for Book Longevity of the Council on Library Resources.

PN
682
.F74
H93
1994

Library of Congress Cataloging-in-Publication Data

94-3014
CIP

ISSN 0920-8607
ISBN 90 04 10018 0

PRINTED IN THE NETHERLANDS

THE ARTS OF FRIENDSHIP

BRILL'S STUDIES
IN
INTELLECTUAL HISTORY

uxori Mariæ, alteri mi

TABLE OF CONTENTS

FOREWORD

Friendship has been a perennial topic of learned debates, treatises, and literary imaginings in Europe since the beginnings of Greek philosophy. From among the vast and varied body of writings on the subject, the present study limits itself to texts that deal with a single, major facet of the topic—perfect friendship of the virtuous and wise. Whereas two other main areas or aspects of the topos—ordinary friendships and the bad—are of particular interest in the field of social history, literary representations of perfect friendship tend towards the mythical, transcendent, and, oftentimes, antisocial in asserting themselves as superior countermeasures to social norms and authoritative correctives to substandard aberrations. Even in the texts in the final chapter below which propose social ideals of civic-minded, virtuous friendship in a contemporary context, ideality—society as it should be—belies, if not denies, social reality, and the writers clearly trust more in the virtues of rhetoric and a story convincingly told than in history.

While addressing itself to the sublime side of the topic, the study in the literary development of an idea further restricts its scope to Latin, French, and Italian writings of the twelfth through mid-fifteenth centuries. These linguistic and temporal bounds, though undeniably arbitrary, have the singular advantage of containing the most plentiful and varied comprehensive developments on ideal friendship outside classical Greek and Latin literature. The study does not aim to be an encyclopedia of all types and variations of the ideal within its restricted scope. It concentrates on several primary works composed in a wide variety of genres. The texts have been selected on the basis of the diversity that their definitions or models offer and, also, of their correspondences among themselves as illustrations of a few major kinds of the ideal. After a preliminary survey of Greek and Roman notions of *philia* or *amicitia* and its perfection, three chapters are organized around three categories of ideal friendship—Christian, chivalric, and humanistic. These categories delimit the most important and diverse areas of interest and activity in medieval and early-Renaissance theories and representations of excellent friendship, and at the same time they emphasize interrelationships among the texts in each grouping.

The study is comparative in its approach, and it takes its literary and ethical measures for comparison from the texts. The selected writings themselves are fundamentally comparative, since their principal strategy for establishing the authority of their representations of model contemporary friends lies in situating them on a par with or, frequently, above time-honored, traditional standards. The Christian and humanistic works usually perform this self-authorizing comparison through explicit or implicit reference to textual standards of ancient Greek and Latin *amicitia perfecta* or biblical archetypes of Christian friendship, but in the chivalric fictions, intratextual reference to the narrative's male-female lovers serves to confirm the excellence of its knightly comrades' mutual affection. In the second chapter on several correlative aspects of ideal Christian friendship or love, the study compares theoretical principles in religious treatises with narrative representations of perfect Christian friends and lovers. It defines here, as in the other chapters, the extent to which writers admitted woman into their idealized domain of *amicitia* and the roles which they prescribed for her. The third chapter discusses in French fictions two types of superior chivalric friendship and the cooperation or antagonism between knights' mutual love and their love of woman. In one type, the romance ideal of chivalric friendship derives its referential principles and authority from the codes of *fine amor*, to which it is assimilated, and in the other, a secular model with an otherworldly extension, two knightly companions' perfect oneness in nature and sentiment serves as the measure for the imperfection of love of woman. The concluding chapter provides a close reading of three late-medieval and early-Renaissance vernacular works in which the humanist writers, bypassing biblical, patristic, and medieval literary tradition on perfect friendship, put side by side ancient or antique-style textual model friends and their own contemporary measures and representations. While presenting the princely court, the merchant-class family, and woman's authoritative voice as contemporary conveyors of virtuous friendship, the writers rival in the vernacular ancient rhetorical excellence. Rhetoric, the art of persuasive argument and a demonstration of the author's own virtue, is a major component in these updated arts of perfecting friendship.

I would like to thank Professors Barbara C. Bowen of Vanderbilt University and Norman S. Grabo and Jane Ackerman of the University of Tulsa, each of whom read parts of the manuscript and suggested courses of revision. A version of the section on the *Prose Lancelot* was printed earlier in *Neophilologus*. I am grateful to the editors of the journal for granting me permission to publish an expanded redaction here. I owe a special debt of gratitude to the University of Tulsa, which offered me a generous research grant in 1988. And to the Camargo Foundation, which afforded me the opportunity to complete this monograph in Cassis, France, and to Michael Pretina, Foundation Director, for his kind and constant attention to our peace of mind during the 1991 Persian Gulf War, sincere thanks.

CHAPTER ONE

THE PRE-CHRISTIAN POLEMIC ABOUT THE THEORY AND PRAXIS OF FRIENDSHIP

Many of Italy's and France's humanistic writings of the later Middle Ages and Renaissance reintroduced the ancient Greek and Roman concepts of virtuous *amicitia* from their sources, the ancient texts, and accommodated them to the intellectual spirit of their age. Classical philosophers had claimed that only the man of virtue and wisdom could attain to true friendship. Late-medieval and Renaissance writers reestablished the ancients' man of virtue, the excellent friend, who represents the paragon of human perfectibility, if not of perfection itself, compatible with Christian ethics. Ending a millenary tradition of the conversion of Aristotelian-Ciceronian *amicitia perfecta* to Christian spiritualized friendship and love, three late-medieval and Renaissance humanists—Giovanni Boccaccio, Laurent de Premierfait, and Leon Battista Alberti—who will be discussed in the final chapter took a new approach in the vernacular to the ancient ideal. First, they bypassed for the most part patristic and medieval literary tradition on perfect friendship and returned directly to the source texts. Then, they placed side by side classical versions of model friends and their own updated measures of perfection in idealized projections of contemporary, lettered friends, some of whom are active in political life. In their collateral—and most optimistic representations of ancient and contemporary prototypes, they emphasized the extension of the moral authority of true and honorable friendship into social, political spheres.

Frequently, medieval and Renaissance writings present a sharp contrast between the private, contemplative individual and the active political person. Illustrative of this attitude in the mid-fourteenth century is Francesco Petrarch's praise of Cicero's solitary philosophical pursuits and his decrial of what he judged to be Cicero's fruitless political struggles.[1] Many other

---

[1] Hans Baron, "Cicero and the Roman Civic Spirit in the Middle Ages and Early Renaissance," *Bulletin of the John Rylands Library* 22 (1938): 86-88. See Petrarch's letters, *Rerum familiarium libri*, trans. Aldo S. Bernardo, 3 vols. (Albany and Baltimore: State University of New York Press and the Johns Hopkins University Press, 1975-1985), bk. 24, letters 2-4. In judging

Italian and French writers promoted, however, the active civic life as a stimulus to individual creative, philosophical powers, and they viewed virtuous friendship as the ancients had represented it, as an essential component of the philosopher's goal of the greatest happiness, the *summum bonum*. These writers attempted to reconcile the concepts of private friendship and political association, and they often insisted, as had the ancients, that harmonious relations among individual citizens are the foundation for a harmonious state. Much of what they wrote was based upon readings of the same Greek and Roman authors whom their medieval predecessors had studied, but their point of view was new and very different. In order to evaluate the magnitude of this deviation from tradition in late-medieval and Renaissance attitudes, it is necessary first to outline the various ancient notions of *amicitia* and its perfection.

Friendship held a key place in pre-Christian philosophy since it served as the subject of a long-running debate among the ancients as to its nature and ends and, most importantly, the end of philosophy itself, the supreme happiness, in which *amicitia* plays a large part. There is no single, unanimously accepted definition of perfect friendship among the ancients. While they generally agreed on its fundamental qualities of virtue, wisdom, and beneficence, they often disagreed on the definition of each of these and their value in respect to one another; and it is sometimes the case that the ancient philosophical models of perfect friendship belie common usage, as when they posit a single friend, a large fellowship, or an indefinite number of unrelated individuals as the unit of *amicitia perfecta* instead of the commonly accepted pair or very small group.

A hotly disputed question among the ancients is whether theory has precedence over practice, or praxis over ideality. One camp sees the highest friendship as the exclusive property of the godlike, wholly self-sufficient sage while the other finds friendship's highest value in its application in social and political practice. Most agree, however, in recognizing two sorts of friendship different from and inferior to the ideal—the ordinary and the false. Unlike the eternal, exceedingly rare ideal, the ordinary is temporary and can be observed almost anywhere; the false, which is not friendship at all, is equally widespread. The Romans often devote a large part of their works to these two familiar species. The extant Greek writings on friendship usually concentrate on the ideal, the domain of the wise

---

his own life, Petrarch considered wasted the time spent in service to the state.

and virtuous, and their references to the other two seem to serve mainly to suggest the nature of the ideal, which some philosophers consider transcendent and ineffable, by representing what it is not.

The classical concepts of *philia* and *amicitia*, both the ordinary species and the elusive ideal, cover a much broader area of meaning than that defined or suggested by modern usage of 'friendship.' For the sake of illustration, it is possible to construct a composite image of the person in relation to humankind and to the physical universe that encompasses nearly the whole range of ancient concepts. The following description of friendship and its perfection based on Greek and Latin writings does not pretend to encapsulate any single theory but serves only to indicate the vast territory that the term covered in the ancient world and, at the same time, the extremely narrow confines of perfect friendship.

The area which friendship covers can be pictured as a pyramid, the base of which represents the harmonious cosmos, and the apex, a few, two, or even a single man or a single-minded community. While the pyramid includes an ever decreasing number of friends as it approaches its peak, it also groups hierarchically, from bottom to top in order of increasing worth, four categories corresponding to four sources of *philia*: nature, necessity or usefulness, pleasure, and virtue-wisdom. Concord, the principle of peaceful relations on the universal level, covers the broad base, and it brings into harmony the elements, celestial movements, and the cosmos as a whole. Just above the base begins animal and human friendliness in creatures sharing a natural affinity because they are of a similar species or the same family and they occupy a common territory. This section of the pyramid includes the mutual love of animal or human family members based upon nature—common species, common blood.

Further from the base is a human sort of friendship with its sources in nature and necessity. Humans in a common territory make 'friendly' agreements of nonaggression among themselves to create social units, tribes, city-states, or political parties within a state for their collective good and protection. Moreover, they make nonaggression pacts with neighboring groups or states in order to protect their territorial or political privileges. Such political concord is a rational response to the need to assure one's own safety and that of the group. Here affection plays a small part or none.

Still further from the bottom, the necessity-based segment continues as it comprises individuals who, for the sake of self-preservation and social, financial, or political advantage, form particular alliances with other individuals in their social unit. Mutual affection may result from such friendship, but it is not the source. That the ordinary or even superior person needs allies, friends, to succeed in society is a principle that the ancient philosophers do not deny. The parties to such a relationship may be equal in status, wealth, and influence, or they may be very unequal, as in the case of some patrons and clients. Although the Greeks and Romans possessed special terms which could be used to distinguish need-based sociopolitical alliances from affective relationships, they did not always draw a sharp linguistic line between the two. In fact, the distinction is often so blurred that by the time of the late Roman Republic, the various terms for the political alliance of equals, an unequal cliental relationship, and affective affinity are applied to all three interchangeably.[2] Because this sort of friendship has its source in a person's need of another's assistance, when the need disappears, the partnership tends to dissolve. All such relationships make up what the ancients sometimes call ordinary friendships, sometimes, when they compare them to *vera amicitia*, the base kind.

Immediately above need-based associations is another sort, also called ordinary or base, which has its source in pleasure or congeniality. The partners feel affection for one another, but the true object of their inclination is not a person but the mutual indulgence in their similar likes. They feel pleasure in their fellowship because they enjoy sharing the object of their predilection. If, however, one or both change tastes, the source of mutual affection disappears, and with it friendship. Some ancient writers rank this class below the utility-based kind, and others do not even mention it.

Finally, at the apex, *amicitia perfecta*. It is difficult, if not impossible, to synthesize the ancient philosophers' conceptions of it, for they disagree on many important points. Yet they generally agree on the following fundamentals: perfect friendship exists only between virtuous men who love virtue in one another for its own sake; *amici veri* are like a single soul in two (or, sometimes, more) bodies; they have all possessions in common, and their affection is reciprocal; their characters, tastes, and opinions are in complete agreement; while growing closer to one another in intimacy,

---

[2] J. Hellegouarc'h, *Le vocabulaire latin des relations et des partis politiques sous la République*, Collection d'Etudes Anciennes, 2nd rev. ed. (Paris: Les Belles Lettres, 1972), pp. 41-62.

they also grow in virtue and wisdom that benefit others besides themselves; *vera amicitia*, one of the greatest gifts of the gods to man, is worth pursuing and even dying for; it requires a long period of maturation and testing; it lasts for a lifetime or even beyond life; and finally, there are exceedingly few, if any, living examples to which to refer. True friendship has as its primary object not another person but perfect wisdom, goodness, and beauty, which are essentially friendly, benevolent, and beneficent. True friends love these qualities, which they see reflected in their partners.

One subject of disagreement among ancient philosophers is the relationship between true and ordinary friendships, especially in regard to the part that utility plays. Many ancients consider *vera amicitia* as a prerequisite to the ends of wisdom and happiness, and they—namely, Plato, some Stoics, and the Epicureans—claim that the virtuous seek friendship because of its usefulness in their quest for the ultimate, godlike happiness. Others—Aristotle and Cicero—make a sharp distinction between the sources of ordinary friendships, utility and pleasure, and that of the ideal, which begins with virtue, and they view true friendship as an end in itself, worth pursuing for itself, therefore disinterested. But even these latter describe *vera amicitia* as the means by which the virtuous man improves his character and approaches the perfect wisdom; and their attribution of both pleasure and usefulness as necessary concomitants of the ideal has led one modern scholar to charge their notions with at least a strong hint of self-interest.[3] On both sides of the ancient debate, however, utility is a necessary characteristic of virtue, since one proves his virtue through usefulness to friends. In the present day it is often assumed that the best friends are purely disinterested and that friendship and influence, political, social, or financial, make a dirty mixture.[4] Such presumptions of utopian altruism do not correspond to what the ancients say about *amicitia*. In ancient philosophy there is a good sort of self-interestedness and a bad type. The virtuous man recognizes his moral betterment as a benefit of good friendship, but while gladly accepting this advantage, he does not seek friends

---

[3] Jean-Claude Fraisse, *Philia. La notion d'amitié dans la philosophie antique* (Paris: J. Vrin, 1974), pp. 392-94.

[4] Francesco Alberoni, an Italian sociologist, notes that in Italy today 'friendship' carries negative connotations because it is associated with favoritism and underhanded influence—*L'amitié*, trans. Nelly Drusi (Paris: Ramsay, 1985), pp. 7-8.

only for this end. In virtuous friendship, the high degree of self-interest motivated by self-love is matched by the good things that each friend wishes and does for his partner. On the other hand, a person motivated by the bad sort seeks friends primarily for self-promotion, financial, social, or political advancement, or for pleasure; he uses others as means to an end, while the virtuous person views others as both means and ends in themselves. Moreover, at the highest level of *amicitia* the essential characteristics of the lower or common levels persist and are even intensified—the higher the level, the greater the friends' mutual pleasure and utility. *Amicitia perfecta*, the peak, is in fact not disjoined from the lower levels, which in themselves are imperfect because they include only a part or parts of the ideal; it is perfect, for it encompasses all the parts—natural, social, and political concord, utility, pleasure, wisdom, goodness, and beauty—in its wholeness.

A second matter of disagreement among ancient philosophers is the degree of goodness and wisdom required in excellent friendship. Some posit the absolute degree, godlike perfection itself, while others propose relative degrees, such as universally acclaimed virtue and practical wisdom. Moreover, not all ancient writers believe that goodness and wisdom are of equal importance there.

A third source of disagreement is the question of how many partners may participate in *amicitia perfecta*. Those who maintain that true friends share their everyday experiences speak of a pair or, at most, very few because of the practical limitations of joint living-space, intimacy, and assistance. Those who think of shared experiences and closeness in terms of a self-contained communal unit extend the number indefinitely to include all members of single-minded community. Still others, who do not consider intimacy as a necessary condition of ideal friendship, posit a monothetic unit, the single sage, completely self-sufficient; and since they claim that all true sages, even though they may never have met, are true friends by reason of their likeness—true wisdom is one—these philosophers assume an indefinite extension of the number of perfect friends to include the sum of singular units.

The ancient philosophers' various concepts of friendship and its perfection do not comprise the same segments between the extremes of the harmonious cosmos and *amicitia perfecta* on the pyramid. It seems now expedient to identify the ancient writings on *philia*, to note what parts of the above synthesis include their different definitions, and to specify the extent to which the Middle Ages knew these texts and in what form. The following abstracts, presented in chronological order, are in some cases based on fragments and secondhand reports. Many of the Greek writings mentioned below are lost,[5] and all that is known about them today consists of maxims, isolated phrases, and summaries recorded by Greek and Roman adapters, commentators, biographers, and encyclopedists such as Cicero, Seneca, Xenophon, Proclus, Stobaeus, Plutarch, etc. The most important ancient collection of summaries and fragments from lost works is the Greek *Lives of the Eminent Philosophers* of Diogenes Laertius (fl. ca. 225-250 A.D.), frequently an unreliable source for the history of philosophy, but *melior Diogenes nihilo*! There is no extant medieval Latin version of Diogenes Laertius' text. Nonetheless, Henricus Aristippus may have translated a portion of the *Lives* into Latin in the mid-twelfth century, and parts of a Latin translation of the work served as a source in Hieremias de Montagnone's *Compendium moralium notabilium* of 1285 and the early-fourteenth-century *De vita et moribus philosophorum* of Walter of Burley, who repeatedly refers to Diogenes Laertius' authority.[6]

It must also be noted that the texts abstracted here which have survived as complete works represent a wide variety of genres—philosophical dialogues, treatises, epistles, parallel lives as moral and rhetorical exempla, and personal recollections. The differences among genres influence to some extent the information which each work provides on *amicitia* and its perfection. For example, the two Platonic dialogues on *philia* do not present an exhaustive treatment of the subject, for their dialogue form is more given to questioning and reasoned discourse than to the sort of social observation and definitive conclusions on *philia* presented in Aristotle's *Nicomachean Ethics*, a treatise, and Seneca's many philosophical epistles which offer moral advice to his disciple Lucilius touch on *amicitia* only occasionally and not in a thorough or systematic manner, whereas Cicero's fictional dialogue *Laelius* presents a formal, comprehensive discourse on the topic. Given the problem of genre differences, this writer

---

[5] See, for example, the anthology of 'lost' texts culled from secondhand sources in vol. 2 of *Fragmenta philosophorum graecorum*, ed. and trans. G.-A. Mullachius, Scriptorum Graecorum Bibliotheca, 120 (Paris: A. Firmin-Didot, 1867).

[6] See Valentinus Rose, "Die Lücke im Diogenes Laertius und der alten Übersetzung," *Hermes* 1 (1886): 367-97, and J. T. Muckle, "Greek Works Translated Directly into Latin Before 1350," 2nd part, *Mediaeval Studies* 5 (1943): 110.

has gleaned information differently from each work. In the Platonic dialogues he has tried to follow the direction of Plato's thought, but in Aristotle's treatise he has outlined conclusions for the most part; the summary of *Laelius* concentrates on the form of the discussion and its development as a whole, but the treatment of Seneca's letters does not attempt to present the separate ideas as parts of a coherent system.

Further, the branch of philosophy to which each complete work belongs is perhaps as important as genre in influencing what kind of information on *amicitia perfecta* the text presents. For instance, Plato's *Symposium*, belonging to the branch of metaphysics, aims at the knowledge of the idea of *Philia*; the *Nicomachean Ethics* attempts, except in its last book, to define the moral life and *philia*'s place in it; and although its subject-matter is ethical, *Laelius* belongs to the branch of rhetoric, which is apparent in its exhortative, polemic nature and its emphasis on the main speaker's moral character as a persuasive force. In the following, consideration has been given to the influence that the specific branch has on shaping and limiting a philosophical work's ideals.

Pythagoras (ca. 580-ca. 500 B.C.) is reported to have been the first to maintain that friends have all goods in common and that *philia* is equality (Diogenes Laertius 8,10). It seems, however, that what Pythagoras and his disciples considered to be *philia* was primarily a fellowship of beliefs, a community founded upon adherence to a single doctrine, and then, only incidentally, a personal relationship. The Pythagorean principles of the equality of friends, their joint possessions, and shared beliefs reappear in many Greek writings and in the Latin works on *vera amicitia* which reached medieval readers. The Pythagorean communities of the sixth through fourth centuries admitted women on the same footing as men, and noble birth was not sufficient ground for admission. This does not mean, however, that the mystical communities admitted the low-born. Both noble birth and virtuous character were entrance requirements, but aristocratic blood was considered a condition, not a guarantee, of the virtue required for admission. Later philosophers occasionally viewed women in ways that recall Pythagorean ideas. For example, Antisthenes (ca. 446-ca. 366 B.C.), a student of Socrates and founder of the Cynic school, claimed that "the virtue of man and of woman is the same" (Diogenes Laertius 6,21);

Plato discussed the comparable worth of women and men in *The Republic*, book 5 (454 E-455 E); and Epicurus admitted women into his school of philosophy in Athens. But in general ancient writers barred, either categorically or implicitly, women along with the low-born as candidates for *vera amicitia* and the title of 'sapient and virtuous.'

Although their views disagree fundamentally, the pre-Socratics Heracleitus (ca. 550-ca. 480 B.C.) and Empedocles (ca. 490-ca. 430 B.C.) saw in the action of the elements the universal forces of concord, *hê philia*, and of discord, *to neikos*. For Heracleitus, elemental discord or strife dominates the ever-becoming cosmos and is the source of endless change and renewal. Empedocles maintained that *philia*, 'love' and 'friendship' as well as 'concord' in Greek, continuously alternates with discord in causing like and unlike elements to combine or separate, and thus their alternation gives equilibrium to the cosmos. Only fragments of the writings of Heracleitus and Empedocles have survived, but their views on the physical universe were transmitted to the Middle Ages in works on friendship. In the *Nicomachean Ethics* 8,1 (1155 b 4-8), Aristotle opposes Heracleitus' position that conflict unites to an Empedoclean principle, that like seeks like, and Cicero refers to Empedocles' theory of alternation in *Laelius* 7,23-24. Moreover, Aristotle explains the notions of *philia* and *neikos* in regard to the elements in *On Generation and Corruption* 1,1 (315 a 3-25), which was known in Latin translations from the late twelfth century.[7] Medieval writers frequently speak of the amity and animosity among the elements and relate them to human interaction.

A few precepts on *philia* by two of Socrates' students, Antisthenes and Aristippus, the originator of Cyrenaicism or hedonism, survive, but they

---

[7] There exist two Latin versions of this work from the end of the twelfth century, an anonymous translation from the Greek original and Gerard of Cremona's rendering from the Arabic—L. Minio-Paluello, "Henri Aristippe, Guillaume de Moerbeke et les traductions latines médiévales des *Météorologiques* et du *De generatione et corruptione* d'Aristote," *Revue philosophique de Louvain* 45 (1947): 210.

do not constitute a theory.[8] With Plato and Xenophon, on the other hand, there are the beginnings of a theory. Plato (ca. 427-348 or 347 B.C.) deals extensively with the metaphysics of male love and friendship in *Lysis*, the *Symposium*, and *Phaedrus*. He does not, however, offer a complete analysis of the reciprocal activity of *philia*, nor does he deal with male love-friendship as an ideal in itself but rather as a pale reflection of archetypal *Philia* and as a means to it. He posits love-friendship as a prerequisite for wisdom, or the knowledge of absolute Beauty, hence for the *summum bonum*. The first printing of Marsilio Ficino's Latin translation of Plato's works in 1484 and his commentaries on the *Symposium*, *Phaedrus*, and *Lysis* made Plato's notion of *philia*, with Ficino's own mystical and Christian construction, accessible to a large public. Nonetheless, in the Middle Ages these three dialogues were not known in Latin or vernacular versions.[9] Medieval readers can have known them very imperfectly at best through Diogenes Laertius' chapter on Plato or through Latin authors' allusions to certain ideas in these dialogues, such as Apuleius' *On Plato and His Doctrine* 2,13 and 2,22, Cicero, Seneca, and others.

We will deal here only with *Lysis* and the *Symposium* because together they explain, or at least suggest, the part that *philia* plays as means to the end of wisdom and perfect happiness in Plato's metaphysics. *Lysis*, which is thought to belong to the end of the early period of the Platonic corpus, presents much lively bandying about of various ideas on *philia*, propositions which are taken to their logical conclusions and, for the most part, rejected in the end; yet it contains the basis for the concept of friendship as an instrument. Two of Plato's arguments in *Lysis* either drew fire or gained support from many Greek and Latin writers on *philia*. First, after supposing friendship to have its source in usefulness, Plato's Socrates argues that the truly good man, who is absolutely self-sufficient, has no need of friends. Aristotle and others challenged the assumptions that utility is the source of the best friendship of wise, virtuous men and that absolute self-sufficiency is possible for mortals, but Aristippus and, later,

---

[8] For Antisthenes' ideas on friendship, see Diogenes Laertius 6,11-12. For Aristippus, see Diogenes Laertius 2,91-97.

[9] Plato's dialogues in Latin up to the fifteenth century were limited to Chalcidius' translation of almost half of *Timaeus*, Henricus Aristippus' versions of *Meno* and *Phaedo*, and William of Moerbeke's partial translation of *Parmenides* from Proclus' Greek *Commentaries on the "Parmenides."*

Epicurus supported the first assumption and Antisthenes and the Stoics, the second. If one pushes these two suppositions a bit further than Plato actually does in *Lysis*, they leave the province of everyday *philia* where the dialogue began and enter the immortal realm that Plato treats in some of his later works, as in the *Symposium*: ideal or godlike friendship is not based upon utility, and the truly good man, who has attained the highest wisdom and perfect happiness, is no longer a mortal but a godlike friend.

A second major argument in *Lysis* that subsequent philosophers pondered is that the good, but not perfectly good, man is drawn not to someone like himself as a friend but to something in another person unlike himself which he lacks and wishes to possess. Plato leaves for the most part unanswered the question of precisely what source or force brings two men together as friends or lovers. After rejecting one by one as untenable propositions, because unuseful, the various attractions of like to like, of unlike to unlike, and like to unlike, then of good to good, bad to bad, and good to bad, Socrates accepts as reasonable what seems to be the only remaining possibility: that which is neither good nor bad loves the good. One might interpret the abstruse "that which is neither good nor bad" to be a relatively good man, closer to righteousness than wickedness; and one might understand the good to be either absolute Goodness or a partial reflection of the absolute in another person. Socrates explains that the relatively good man senses his own deficiency in goodness, and he is drawn either to what fully satisfies his want, absolute Good, or to what partially satisfies it, relative goodness, but different from his own, in another man. Further, Socrates posits a certain kinship or suitability of nature (*to phusei oikeion*) as the source of the relatively good man's attraction to goodness. At this point the dialogue comes to an abrupt end as several discussants withdraw, and Socrates does not elucidate what this natural kinship is or how it ties together in *philia* the three components of the Good and two relatively good men unlike in goodness. One suspects that a clear-cut explanation is not provided because this suitability of nature that animates hybrid human-superhuman *philia* is intuitive, suprarational. Socrates' final remark, that the discussants have failed to define *philia*, leaves the matter open to further inquiry and clarification, which he continues in his conversation with Diotima in the *Symposium*.

The ostensible subject of the *Symposium* is erotic love in the form of homophilia, which each of the numerous interlocutors commends in turn. But because of essential characteristics which love, friendship, and homophilia share in both dialogues, the *Symposium* can be considered to continue and complete, often by way of parable, the lessons of *Lysis*, which also dealt in part with homosexual attraction. In interpreting the *Symposium*, one might begin with other kinds of *philia* and still arrive at the same immortal ideal—the perfect love of Beauty, self-sufficiency, god-likeness. In Socrates' discourse in the *Symposium* the role that Eros plays in inspiring what might be labeled 'rational youth-loving,' the highest form of mortal love according to Diotima, may be understood to suggest metaphorically the animating action of mutual need, delight, and rational love of goodness in *philia*. A good man is drawn to a beautiful youth, and he wants, indeed needs, this particular youth to gratify his own desire. This mixture of desire and need—what one scholar calls *"philia* heightened by *eros* into pathos"[10]—is only the first step which the man must surpass in order to arrive at a higher degree and degrees of love, increasingly more general and rational and, in the end, suprarational. Diotima illustrates the various stages through which a relatively good man must pass before becoming absolutely good and self-sufficient, hence totally unneedful. In doing so, she clarifies the paradoxical argument in *Lysis* that although only good men can be friends, the truly good man needs no friends. She reveals the sole objective of all *philia* to be the attainment of immortality, which may take many different forms—offspring, everlasting fame, poetry, invention, law-making—of which the highest form is godlike knowledge of the Beauty that is the cosmos. As A.-J. Voelke observes, Socrates' arguments in both dialogues serve not to define the nature of love-friendship but to explore the metaphysical problem of the relationship between *philia* as an empirical datum and *philia* as an absolute value, between the perceptible world and the knowable universe.[11]

Diotima begins by maintaining that Love or Eros is neither beautiful, wise, and good nor ugly, ignorant, and bad. His moral, physical, and intellectual qualities are situated about halfway between those extremes. She describes him as a great spiritual intermediary, neither immortal nor mortal, who interprets and transports human things to the gods and divine

---

[10] Horst Hutter, *Politics as Friendship. The Origins of Classical Notions of Politics in the Theory and Practice of Friendship* (Waterloo, Ontario: Wilfred Laurier University Press, 1978), p. 64.

[11] Voelke, *Les rapports avec autrui dans la philosophie grecque d'Aristote à Panétius*, Bibliothèque d'Histoire de la Philosophie (Paris: J. Vrin, 1961), pp. 21-24.

things to mortals. According to her, Eros is useful in that he leads man to the greatest happiness. At a very low level, a man who loves beautiful material objects desires in fact what he lacks; when he possesses those things which fulfil his material needs and desires, he is somewhat happy. The love of beauty of mind and good actions leads to a more precious, lasting possession and hence to greater happiness. At the highest level, man desires immortality. To reach this end, a good man starts by seeking a youth who has physical beauty or, preferably, moral and intellectual merit as the instrument whereby he may beget immortal things, such as poetry or good deeds. In the 'vinely' inspired Alcibiades' concluding encomium of Socrates, it is clear that Plato has in mind here a most chaste and rational love of the man for the youth. When the man's desire matures, it loses its particularity, and what began as the love of a beautiful youth becomes love of all beautiful persons, then a desire for superior beauty in conduct, intellect, and the soul, and finally the intuitive knowledge of Beauty itself: "So when a man by the right method of boy-loving [*dia to orthôs paiderustein*] ascends from these particulars and begins to descry that beauty, he is almost able to lay hold of the final secret.... Beginning from obvious beauties he must for the sake of that highest beauty be ever climbing aloft, as on the rungs of a ladder, from one to two, and from two to all beautiful bodies; from personal beauty he proceeds to beautiful observances, from observance to beautiful learning, and from learning at last to that particular study which is concerned with the beautiful itself and that alone; so that in the end he comes to know the very essence of beauty" (*Symposium* 211 B-D). Diotima's mystical, climactic vision goes far beyond the limits of mortal *philia*. Those writing after Plato disagreed on how high human reason and goodness combined with friendship or love might hope to rise in the pursuit of the greatest good.

It is impossible to indicate precisely where on the pyramid described earlier Plato's concept of love-friendship fits, especially when it seeks to transcend mortal confines. Plato is not concerned with formulating a theory of friendship *per se*, and he does not always draw clear distinctions among the various species of the genus *philia*. Of the many different sorts of *philia* discussed in these two dialogues—elemental concord (mentioned in the *Symposium* 186 A-B), parental affection, ordinary friendship and love, homophilia, the exceptional chaste love-friendship of a virtuous man and a becoming youth—Socrates' chief concern is for the godlike sage's love of Beauty, which alone is perfect in itself. In the two dialogues, the limits of *philia* are fluid; they contract or expand as the discussants' attention shifts back and forth from various relative degrees, from particulars, to love of absolute Beauty. At the beginning of *Lysis*, Socrates observes that one of his young companions loves an adolescent, and he gives stock advice on practice in such relationships where Eros and friendship join: lovers-friends are of equal wealth since they share all things, the young man should not flatter his beloved, and *philia* must be reciprocal. Once Socrates begins, however, to investigate the ultimate object of *philia* and posits ideal Beauty, he shifts the discussants' attention from the pair of lovers-friends to a single man's rational and transcendent love of the absolute. Consequent to this shift, all varieties of mortal *philia* take their place—and there remain—at the bottom of the ladder leading to the Ideal. Viewed from the heights of godlike knowledge of Beauty, even the best example of human love-friendship seems imperfect or, indeed, false.

Plato does not provide an explanation of the role of the 'other,' the second equal person in a friendly relationship, and consequently a theory of the reciprocal activity of friendly parties on the way to ultimate happiness is not possible. In Plato's model of rational youth-loving, both parties benefit one another, as Pausanias explains in the *Symposium* 184 C-E. But the loving man and his beloved youth are by necessity not equals in age, knowledge, and the power to do good. Therefore the model does not conform to the kind of friendship described in *Lysis*, where equality is emphasized and the erotic or affective factor plays no significant part, at least after the beginning of the dialogue. One of Socrates' preliminary arguments in *Lysis* is that neither the person who loves nor the beloved is necessarily a friend. It would not seem that an equal other accompanies Plato's true friend of Beauty to the top of Diotima's ladder. As with the Stoic sage who will be discussed presently, Plato's metaphysics leaves one with a paradoxical single friend, the universal *philos* of all good persons, actions, and ideas and the particular friend of none. One of the objectives of most post-Platonic philosophers dealing with the ethics of *philia* is to write the second self into the model of perfect friendship.

The *Memorabilia* of Xenophon (ca. 430-ca. 355 B.C.), which repeat some of the advice given at the beginning of *Lysis*, emphasize the moral content of Socrates' teachings on the activity and value of friendship. A.-J. Voelke sees in book 2, chapters 4-6, the germ of a theory of friendship:[12] according to Xenophon, Socrates taught that the true friend, who possesses the qualities of self-mastery, self-reliance, and firmness of character, alone is capable of beneficence, which he bestows on a man whom he wishes to befriend and who does the same for him; praise of the man whom one hopes to attract as a friend and self-commendation should conform to the truth; and the noble-spirited man is more inclined towards benevolent feelings than towards inimical ones. Voelke might have gleaned other key ideas from the same chapters: although people claim that friendship is a most precious possession, they are generally careless about winning and preserving it; some friends perform more valuable services than others, and one should try to be as useful as possible to his comrades; friends should rival one another in beneficence and provide mutual encouragement and aid in self-improvement; and the qualities of hospitality and scrupulousness should be sought in an associate, and gluttony, idleness, lust, and avarice, shunned. Furthermore, book 1, chapter 2, contains two ideas which, like the others noted above, are found in subsequent ancient works on the topic: a man is his own dearest friend, and a comrade's benevolence has no worth unless he has enough power to realize it in beneficent acts. Character and utility are the threads connecting these precepts. The man who loves himself and therefore strives for virtue—that is, self-reliance, self-mastery, strength of character, and, especially, good deeds—seeks another whose comparable self-esteem and pursuit of virtue will permit them both to give and receive beneficence and thus to grow in virtue.

In reference to the pyramid described earlier, Xenophon's report of Socrates' teachings points to the peak of perfection and, at the same time, the segment defining the association of equals for reason of utility, which comprises a wide range of relationships that have greater or lesser worth according to the degree of usefulness that each friend offers. Xenophon says little about the part played by pleasure and congeniality. Some later philosophers also pass over this part in silence, perhaps because they judge it to be unworthy of serious consideration in the rational pursuit of ultimate happiness, but others elevate it to a level of importance superior to utility. Xenophon's *Memorabilia* were not known in the Middle Ages.

---

[12] Ibid., p. 21.

Nevertheless, some of his precepts on friendship reappear in works by
Cicero and Seneca that were well-known to medieval readers. For example, Cicero puts one of Socrates' sayings recorded by Xenophon in the
mouth of a Roman Stoic in *Laelius* 17,62.

Aristotle (384-322 B.C.) was the first to formulate a complete theory of
friendship in his *Nicomachean Ethics*, books 8 and 9, where he identifies,
defines, and classifies most species of *philia*. An anonymous translator
put part of book 8 into Latin at the end of the twelfth century or the beginning of the thirteenth.[13] Before 1250, Robert Grosseteste, Bishop of
Lincoln, translated the ten books of the *Nicomachean Ethics* into Latin.
His version was revised by an anonymous writer and then again, perhaps,
by William of Moerbeke before 1286.[14] The *Eudemian Ethics*, book 7,
and the *Magna moralia* also contain some of Aristotle's ideas on friendship, but they will not be summarized here.[15] Cicero's *Laelius* and *De
officiis* incorporated many of the views on *philia* from the *Nicomachean
Ethics*, and these three texts in Latin or excerpts from them, along with
several Senecan precepts and, of course, Christian writings, constituted
the canon of *amicitia* for the Middle Ages.

Aristotle bases his theory of friendship in books 8 and 9 of the *Nicomachean Ethics* on the observation of man and woman as active, social
beings. He defines *philia* at its broadest as the mutual goodwill and the
feeling of love or esteem that unite people. Having posited benevolence,

---

[13] Auguste Pelzer, "Les versions latines des ouvrages de morale conservés
sous le nom d'Aristote en usage au XIIIᵉ siècle," *Revue néo-scolastique de
philosophie* 23 (1921): 333-35. The reader will find an early-fifteenth-century
synopsis of books 8 and 9 of the *Nicomachean Ethics* in Appendix B.

[14] *Sancti Thomae de Aquino opera omnia iussu Leonis XIII P.M. edita*, vol.
47, part 1: *Sententia libri ethicorum*, ed. R.-A. Gauthier (Rome: Ad Sanctae
Sabinae, 1969), pp. 203-33. For the scholarly debate over a possible translation or revision by William of Moerbeke, see Vernon J. Bourke, "The *Nicomachean Ethics* and Thomas Aquinas," in *St. Thomas Aquinas, 1274-1974,
Commemorative Studies* (Toronto: Pontifical Institute of Mediaeval Studies,
1974), vol. 1, pp. 240-42.

[15] Bartholomew of Messina translated the *Magna moralia*, now generally
judged to be spurious, into Latin between 1258 and 1266. There is no known
medieval Latin version of all the *Eudemian Ethics*, although books 4-6, which
are identical with books 5-7 of the *Nicomachean Ethics*, and two chapters on
philia from book 7 were translated—Muckle, "Greek Works," p. 107.

affection, and reciprocity as basic to friendship, he excludes inanimates, deities, and elemental harmony, although he mentions Empedocles and Heracleitus. Friendly relationships at this fundamental level may be social concord, as with the reciprocal respect of ruler and subjects, or natural love, as that of husband and wife, parents and children, or brothers for one another. Esteem and goodwill are granted in different degrees to individuals according to their social rank or place in the family. For example, subjects ought to value their ruler more highly than he or she does them.

Ethically excellent friendship, *teleia philia*, is characterized by nearly equal degrees of reciprocal esteem and benevolence and nearly the same good character in both parties, and it ranks first among the various sorts of *philia*: "Excellent friendship is that of good men who are similar in virtue. For they indeed wish good things alike for one another insofar as they are good, and they are good in themselves. Moreover, those who desire good things for their friends' sake are the first of all among friends" (*Nic. Eth.* 8,3; 1156 b 7-11). Aristotle's 'virtue' or 'excellence' requires a few words of clarification here. He explains at length in the earlier books that moral virtue or excellence, of which he identifies many types, is a state of character resulting from the rational choice to pursue the mean between an excess and a deficiency, both of which are vices. For example, the virtue of generosity stands intermediate to the excess of prodigality and the deficiency of avarice; between the extremes of self-indulgence and indifference to pleasure lies temperance. Cordiality or friendliness (*philia*), he explains, is a virtue situated between the deficiency of quarrelsomeness and the excesses of obsequiousness or flattery (*Nic. Eth.* 2,7). These earlier lessons apply to the encomium in books 8 and 9 of excellent *philia*, which encompasses many virtues, such as friendliness, generosity, self-love, piety, beneficence, and magnanimity. Therefore it avoids numerous extremes—e.g., excessive affection, insensibility, and too great or too little desire for utility, pleasure, or fame. The statement that *philia* "is a virtue or implies virtue" (*Nic. Eth.* 8,1; 1155 a 4) invites the question of its status as a virtue in itself or as a consequence of virtue. Commentators have argued that it is one or the other or even both at the same time when viewed from different angles.[16] Suffice it to say that the *Nicomachean*

---

[16] See, for example, St. Thomas Aquinas' arguments for and against *amicitia* as a virtue in vol. 41 of *Summa theologiae, Latin Text and English Translation, Introductions, Notes, Appendices and Glossaries* (London: Blackfriars, 1972), 2a 2ae, question 114, articles 1 and 2, pp. 198-205. It is possible that

Ethics lends itself to various interpretations here, as it does in many other places.

   True friends love one another, but the part that love plays in perfect friendship differs greatly from its operation in ordinary *philia*. Firstly, the true friend, a virtuous man, values good character and deeds in another. His love takes as its object not so much the other person as the other's goodness. Secondly, loving is more important in friendship than being loved precisely because the true friend cherishes goodness above all else, and he manifests his love of goodness through beneficent acts towards another, who reciprocates. Thirdly and most importantly, the true friend loves himself, and he desires his own betterment through self-knowledge, which is essential to wisdom. Self-love, which Aristotle identifies as the desire for the greatest happiness, serves as a motive for seeking friends, for the virtuous man cannot be truly happy without them. The excellent friend sees in his nearly equal partner an alter ego, a mirror of his own virtue and a source of self-knowledge, but the image that he beholds is not static: as he watches his partner improve through his beneficent assistance, he sees the reflection of his own self-betterment, of his increased virtue. The good man needs virtuous friends, for the *summum bonum* that he seeks is an activity in which he exercises his beneficence towards others. Yet the necessary and similar 'other' does not function simply as a passive recipient of beneficence and a reflector of virtue: while he grows in goodness, he too acts ever more beneficently towards his partner. Aristotle does not specify the ultimate degree to which this double-mirror effect of moral betterment and self-knowledge may attain, but he asserts that, given the necessity of friendship especially for the wisest and best, *absolute* self-sufficiency is impossible for man. Thus he rejects the premise that allowed Socrates to deny in *Lysis* that like is drawn to like, and good to good.

   At this point we should examine more closely the earlier comments regarding married partners and brothers in light of Aristotle's definition of excellent *philia*. He maintains that friendship between wife and husband appears to be natural and that it may be based on virtue if both partners are of good character. Since, however, he also claims that woman's virtue and man's differ essentially in nature, one must conclude that even the

---

Aristotle means only to say that the association of bad men cannot be considered *philia*.

best husband and wife (or any man and woman for that matter) cannot be alike in virtue and, therefore, cannot become excellent friends. Furthermore, he classifies married friendship as an unequal relationship in which the husband is, or should be, superior; he compares good marriage to aristocracy, where the better rules. If such inequality is intrinsic in good and friendly relations between wife and husband, it excludes the possibility of excellent *philia*. As for brothers, he notes that they naturally feel affection for one another because of their common source, daily life under one roof, nearness in age, and the same upbringing which favors the formation of similar character in each. He puts fraternal *philia* in the same class as comradeship or mere association, where shared terrain or education or similar circumstances foster affection between men. He does not suggest that because of their natural fondness brothers are more likely than unrelated persons to become true friends. For Aristotle virtuous character, not common blood or upbringing, serves as the base for excellent friendship. As we shall see in the next chapter, the Christian charity that joins monastic brothers to one another is a medieval ideal of fraternal friendship—there, virtue and similar conduct and aims, not common blood and association, define brotherhood.

Aristotle ranks *teleia philia*, which is permanent, as the highest of three species of friendship between equals. The two lesser, common sorts have shared pleasure or usefulness as their chief causes. He notes that the young and the rich tend to form friendships for reason of pleasure and old men and the business-minded, for advantage. Inferior moral worth in one or both parties often characterizes such ordinary relationships. Since utility and pleasure are contingent and unstable, relationships based upon either or both offer at best an improvement in circumstances, and they are likely to disintegrate when one of the parties ceases to be useful or needful or changes character, tastes, or social status. Of these two sorts, Aristotle finds friendship for reason of advantage less stable, and, hence, he ranks it below the other. Yet utility and pleasure are both necessary components of the highest order of *philia* because, first, the true friend needs to demonstrate his usefulness in order to be happy. Second, in all three sorts of friendship, the partners must share their private lives quite frequently in order to cultivate their relationship; therefore, a certain affability and an agreeable nature are essential to the maintenance of that condition. The requirement of intimacy also limits the number of friends to those with whom one can share his private life and thoughts at one time—that is, to

a very few. Similarly, since it would be most difficult or even impossible
to exercise beneficence towards several comrades, especially if they were
to need aid at the same time, a man must limit his friends to a very few.

In respect to the highest category of *philia*, Aristotle deals with an important practical consideration—a test of character.[17] He advises that one
evaluate with great care his partner's stability of character as well as his
moral progress. He indicates that the probationary period is rather long,
but he gives no details as to how or under what circumstances the testing
takes place. If the companion passes the test, then he is accepted without
qualification as a friend for life. On the other hand, if the evaluator observes during the probation that his comrade's character seems unlikely to
improve or actually goes to the bad, he has the obligation, presumably
from self-love, to discontinue their intimacy. Also, if one of the uncom-
mitted partners makes so much progress that he far outdistances the other
in virtue, then they should cease to live on intimate terms. They should
continue, however, to treat one another cordially in remembrance of their
past closeness.

In the end Aristotle's ethics seems ambiguous as regards ideal friendship. He denies in the *Nicomachean Ethics* 1,6 that Plato's theoretical or
knowable Idea has any place in the study of human conduct, and later he
extols the moral activity of virtuous friendship as a necessary part of the
happy life. But he asserts in 10,7-8 that *theôria*, or the intellectual activity of contemplation, alone is perfect happiness and that only it can bring
the philosopher to the highest wisdom and good that he seeks. Within the
whole of the *Nicomachean Ethics*, then, virtuous *philia* is, when viewed
from different angles, an end worth pursuing for itself, means to attaining
the happy life, and, perhaps, not an indispensable component of the happiest life. The ranking of *philia* below *theôria* corresponds to the division
in book 6 between moral or practical virtues and the superior intellectual
or contemplative ones. Although within the ethical domain virtuous
friendship has the highest value as the best activity and the greatest exter-
nal good, that domain is as a whole inferior to the contemplative or metaphysical realm where resides godlike wisdom, the greatest internal good.
Aristotle praises virtuous friendship because, given its position at the
summit of the moral life, it comes closest to the contemplative.

---

[17] Cf. Ecclesiasticus 6,7: "Si possides amicum, in tentatione posside eum, et
ne facile credas ei."

Although it is correct, strictly speaking, to say that there is no specifically spiritual dimension to friendship in the *Nicomachean Ethics*,[18] we
should note that Aristotle's *teleia philia* includes a contemplative component, as a man reaches for self-knowledge and the knowledge of goodness
itself by contemplating his own image, his moral betterment, and a particular aspect of the Good in his alter ego. But it is unclear to what extent
philia based on good character partakes or may partake in the superior activity in the metaphysical sphere. As will be noted later in respect to
Christian *amicitia Dei*, the mystic's contemplation of God is sometimes
enhanced by her or his mutual contemplation with a spiritual friend who
aids and is aided in the pursuit of divine love.

The fragments that survive from the works of Epicurus (341-270 B.C.)
and Zeno of Citium (ca. 333-ca. 262 B.C.) contain a number of ideas on
friendship which the Middle Ages received mainly through the writings of
Cicero, Seneca, and Diogenes Laertius. Epicurus makes the following
claims about friendship, wisdom, and supreme happiness in the apotheg-
matic collections now known as *The Principal Doctrines* and *Vatican
Sayings*: the *summum bonum* is complete security of mind and freedom
from worry, which come from wisdom and friendship; the well-born man
devotes himself to wisdom, a mortal good, and to *philia*, an immortal
one; of all the good things that wisdom can procure for human content-
ment, friendship is the greatest; *philia* ought to be sought for its own
sake, but it has its beginning in utility; and more important than the aid
which one receives from friends is the confidence that he has regarding
their aid.[19] Like many other ancient philosophers, Epicurus viewed *philia*
as a worthy end in itself and, also, as an even more worthy expedient to

---

[18] Brian Patrick McGuire, *Friendship and Community: The Monastic Experience 350-1250*, Cistercian Studies Series, 95 (Kalamazoo: Cistercian Publications, 1988), p. xxx.

[19] These five maxims are found in *The Principal Doctrines* 40, *Vatican Sayings* 78, *Principal Doctrines* 27, and *Vatican Sayings* 23 and 34, respectively.
Diogenes Laertius recorded *The Principal Doctrines* in *Lives* 10,139-54. *The
Vatican Sayings (Gnomologium Vaticanum)* were recovered in 1888. See
translations of both collections in *The Stoic and Epicurean Philosophers. The
Complete Extant Writings of Epicurus, Epictetus, Lucretius, Marcus Aurelius*,
ed. J. Oates (New York: Random House, 1940).

the philosopher's goal of happiness.

Epicurus' sayings reflect a unique concept of friendship, particularly as a consequence of wisdom. First, Epicurus, an atomist, taught that community among men does not come about because of nature. For him man is a social being not by nature but by reason of utility. He makes agreements of mutual nonaggression and assistance with other men in the interest of his own security and betterment. Nor is man naturally courageous: "Courage is not born from nature but from the consideration of what is useful [in the circumstances]; friendship, too, is born from usefulness" (Diogenes Laertius 10,120). Also: "The same knowledge that makes us courageous in the presence of danger by teaching us that it does not last forever, nor even a very long time, teaches, too, that friendship is the best guarantee of security in our precarious position."[20] Epicurus' teachings on the role of utility in *philia* disagree with Aristotelian doctrine. According to Epicurus, since man's position in the world and society is by nature precarious, his need for useful friends is not contingent and temporary but permanent. Therefore, friendship based upon usefulness is permanent, too, provided that the partners always support one another courageously in the face of temporary dangers and that they are even ready to die in coming to each other's aid (Diogenes Laertius 10,120).

A second general consideration which conditions Epicurean *philia* is security of mind as the supreme happiness. Most Epicureans considered an active political life as an obstacle to attaining that goal. This does not mean, however, that they shunned friendship with political leaders. On the contrary, they were sometimes intimates of chiefs of violently opposing factions, but they attempted to maintain their private relationships apart from this ofttimes destructive factionalism. The historian and biographer Cornelius Nepos (ca. 100-ca. 25 B.C.) writes of the Roman Epicurean Atticus in this regard: Atticus was a friend to the political enemies Mark Antony and Cicero, and he did not let Mark Antony's proscription and execution of Cicero alter his amicable association with the former.[21] While advocating a politically neutral approach to friendship, Epicureans considered that security of mind could be nurtured best in the company of like-minded men and women in a somewhat closed community, the garden of Epicurus, under the eye of the master. Their institution of a haven for

---

[20] *Principal Doctrines* 28. Cicero records this maxim in *De finibus* 1,20,68.
[21] Cornelius Nepos, life of Atticus appended to his *Great Generals of Foreign Nations* 25,9,2-25,10,16.

philosophers-friends of both sexes recalls in part Pythagorean communal practices.

Zeno of Citium, founder of the Stoic school, admitted that friendship might lead to happiness, but he did not consider *philia* as an indispensable means to that end. He taught that "a friend and the advantages derived from him are means to good" (Diogenes Laertius 7,96). The question of friendship's usefulness as a way to the *summum bonum* is only marginally relevant to Zeno's philosophy, however, for he was hardly interested in the ordinary or even better than ordinary realm of moral activity. He conceived of *philia*, ideal friendship, as a benefit or attribute of the highest intellectual virtue—in other words, true, godlike wisdom is a precondition for true *philia*. For him the sage lives in complete conformity to nature, the universal reason which governs the cosmos; he has mastered all his impulses and passions, the irrational and, hence, unnatural movements of the soul; he lives according to virtue, which is the same as wisdom. Zeno claimed that this intellectual virtue is itself the *summum bonum* and that nature leads the philosopher towards the goal of virtue, which tends to make the whole of life harmonious (Diogenes Laertius 7,87 and 89). Once the philosopher reaches perfection, he alone acquires all good things: "friendship, freedom, piety, riches, beauty, the arts of kingdom and generalship."[22] True *philia* and the other benefits of perfect virtue belong to the realm of absolute self-sufficiency.

While Zeno maintained the Pythagorean principle that a friend is a second self (Diogenes Laertius 7,23), his concept of the equal other is one of an absolutely self-sufficient other. He divided mankind into two classes, the perfectly virtuous sage or sages and the remainder, vice-ridden fools. He recognized no intermediate order. The wholly virtuous are friends, while the others, vicious by reason of their perverse nature, cannot be. Therefore, Zeno's notion of friendship may be delimited by a point at the apex of the pyramid imagined earlier—and below, absolutely nothing! The early Stoics drew up lists of their Seven Sages, who were, in theory, friends by reason of their sageness. The seven, whose names sometimes

---

[22] Zeno of Citium, *The Fragments of Zeno and Cleanthes*, trans. A. C. Pearson (London: C. J. Clay & Sons, 1891), p. 16 of the introduction.

differ from list to list, were Greeks who lived around the early sixth century B.C. In regard to practice, they cannot have been friends in any ordinary sense of the word, for they lived in different cities or countries.

The early Stoics' ideal of virtue-wisdom obviously has little practical
application in the ethical domain of friendship. In middle and late Stoicism, however, this intellectual objective was sometimes compromised
and transformed, and the result served in large part as the moral basis for
the practical *amicitia perfecta* of the good and wise in Cicero's and
Seneca's writings. Although Zeno recognized no middle grade between the
sage and the fool, he did admit an intermediate class of appropriate activity, *to kathêkon* (plural: *ta kathêkonta*). A sage's acts, called *ta katorthô-
mata*, agree perfectly with universal reason and, thus, are virtuous, and a
fool's acts are illogical and vicious. *To kathêkon*, action which is neither
virtuous nor vicious in itself, is harmonious with nature, such as filial
reverence, or with right conduct, such as dutifulness to friends, or it admits of rational justification.[23] Zeno's followers soon interpreted this
suitable, neutral activity in such a way as to bring it in line with the earlier inaccessible Stoic sageness and to make 'wise friendship' practicable.
The Stoic Chrysippus (ca. 281-205 B.C.) considered the flawless accom-
plishment of all actions comprising *ta kathêkonta*, in full knowledge of
their conformity with nature, reason, and right conduct, as virtuous rather
than merely suitable (cf. *Nic. Eth.* 2,4,3-5; 1105 a-b.) Through the right-
minded fulfillment of ever more *kathêkonta* (what the Latins call *officia*,
'duties' or 'proper conduct'), a man, more sagelike than foolish, demonstrates moral progress. Through the recognition of a relative degree of
virtue, of moral perfectibility, Chrysippus prepared the way for the formulation of a concept of practicable Stoic friendship.

Panaetius of Rhodes (ca. 185-ca. 110 B.C.), the founder of Middle Stoicism who taught in Rome, is reported to have divided the Stoic notion of
virtue into the theoretical, or *virtus contemplativa*, and the practical, or
activa (Diogenes Laertius 7,92).[24] Panaetius' practical virtue is that intermediate stage between godlike sageness and common mortal folly. His
relatively good and prudent man does not possess the sage's absolute self-

---

[23] I. G. Kidd, "Moral Actions and Rules in Stoic Ethics," in *The Stoics*, ed.
John M. Rist, Major Thinkers Series, 1 (Berkeley: University of California
Press, 1978), pp. 247-49.

[24] Diogenes Laertius notes here that Chrysippus and other Stoics recognized
three or four divisions of virtue.

sufficiency or impassivity; he is capable of affection and of aiding and being aided by a friend. Panaetius' writings have not survived, so one can
only speculate about their exact content. It is certain, however, that they
served as one of the sources for Cicero's treatise *De officiis*, and they were
possibly a source for *Laelius*. But there can be no doubt that Cicero altered Panaetius' principles considerably to suit his own ends. It seems un-
verifiable to reconstitute a Panaetian theory of friendship on the basis of
Laelius, as F.-A. Steinmetz has done,[25] for *Laelius* draws from so many
different sources, some of which are lost Greek works, that no single lost
source can be isolated with any certainty from the general mass. It is prudent to do no more than credit Panaetius with having introduced to the
Romans his practicable version of Stoic virtue and, hence, at least the
germ of an alternative notion of Stoic friendship not limited to the Seven
Sages. Even though Cicero offers in *Laelius* two of Panaetius' Roman
students, Laelius Sapiens and Scipio Africanus the Younger, as the
paragon of *amicitia perfecta*, there is good reason to judge that his attempt
at idealizing the practice of friendship by redefining sageness at an intermediate level goes beyond the limits of Panaetius' doctrine and Stoicism
in general. For orthodox Stoics, the practical can serve as nothing more
than a *modus vivendi*. Jean Brun summarizes the orthodox position on
praxis in this manner: since all are either fools or sages, and since it is
impossible to become a true sage because man is incapable of universal
reason, it is better to try to act like less of a fool than more of one.[26] The
example of Epictetus (ca. 55-ca. 135 A.D.), a freedman whose Greek
writings influenced Renaissance thinkers, shows that some later Stoics,
unlike Cicero, did not abandon or extenuate pristine theoretical sageness
because of its obvious inaccessibility, nor did they promote practicable
Stoic friendship to the level of the ideal. In his discourse *On Friendship*,
Epictetus asserts the unconditional supremacy of theoretical virtue-wisdom over the practice of friendship, and he deems all the Aristotelian and
Ciceronian causes and conditions of excellent *philia* to be false ideas regarding true friendship.[27] In middle and late Stoicism, the theoretical and

---

[25] Steinmetz, *Die Freundschaftslehre des Panaitios nach einer Analyse von
Ciceros "Laelius de amicitia,"* Palingenesia, 3 (Wiesbaden: Franz Steiner,
1967).

[26] Brun, *Le stoïcisme*, 8th ed. (Paris: P. U. F., 1980), p. 115.

[27] *On Friendship*, bk. 2, chap. 22, of *The Discourses*. This work was not
known in Latin or vernacular versions in the Middle Ages. In 1450 Niccolò
Pirotti translated into Latin the *Enchiridion*, a selection by Epictetus' student

the practical coexist, but they are by no means coequal. Cicero's *Laelius* produced a bastardized ideal practice, one that the Middle Ages accepted, after selective editing and corrective commentary, as legitimate moral philosophy and, sometimes, a guide in the Christian contemplative's life.

Cicero (106-43 B.C.) composed *Laelius de amicitia* in 44 B.C. In medieval Europe this dialogue was one of the most widely read classical works on *amicitia perfecta* along with Latin versions of the *Nicomachean Ethics* after the twelfth century. Cicero incorporates the whole range of Aristotelian *philia*: natural, social, and political concord and friendship for reasons of utility, pleasure, or goodness. It is clear that books 8 and 9 of the *Nicomachean Ethics* make up *Laelius'* ethical substratum.[28] Cicero synthesizes the theoretical and practical considerations of many other Greek philosophers, too, while formulating a distinctly Roman concept of *amicitia vera*.[29] He very seldom names the Greeks, even when it is obvious that he has a particular philosopher or school in mind, but he names on every possible occasion Romans, especially political figures. He devotes a large part of his treatise to practice as illustrated by Romans who serve in his estimation as models of the wise and virtuous, the amicable, or the bad. For example, Cato the Elder takes precedence over Socrates as a paragon of wisdom (*Laelius* 2,9-10). This Romanization of

---

Arrian of maxims and passages from *The Discourses*—Gerard Verbeke, *The Presence of Stoicism in Medieval Thought* (Washington, D.C.: The Catholic University of America Press, 1983), p. 7.

[28] See R. F. Braxator, *Quid in conscribendo Ciceronis Laelio valuerint Aristotelis ethicon nicomachorum de amicitia libri* (diss. Halle, 1871).

[29] Aulus Gellius reports in *The Attic Nights* 1,3,11 that he believes that Cicero was reading *On Friendship*, a lost treatise by Theophrastus, Aristotle's disciple and successor, while composing *Laelius*. On the basis of Aulus Gellius' statement Gustav Heyblutt conjectures that many of the practical considerations in *Laelius* come from Theophrastus—*De Theophrasti libris peri philias* (diss. Bonn, 1976). As mentioned earlier, F.-A. Steinmetz maintains that a lost work of Panaetius served as the chief source for *Laelius*. On the other hand, it has been argued that, in the first place, a lost Panaetian work could not possibly have been Cicero's source here and, secondly, Cicero apparently did not follow Theophrastus closely at all since Aulus Gellius insists upon the differences between the two texts—*Laelius de amicitia*, trans. Robert Combès, Collection des Universités de France, 3rd ed. (Paris: Les Belles Lettres, 1983), pp. li-liii.

the Greek ideal is one of *Laelius'* original features.

Another distinctive feature in the Latin work is Cicero's encomium of Roman virtue, which Donald Earl defines thus: "Virtue, for the Republican noble, consisted in the winning of personal preeminence and glory by the commission of great deeds in the service of the Roman state."[30] A noble citizen performs these deeds not for their own sake but for the Republic, which recognizes them publicly and eternally through glory. Civic virtue, which is essential for a man to qualify for the title of *amicus verus* in Cicero's dialogue, assumes the subordination of the individual's will and the friends' common will to the higher interests of the state, particularly to concord within the Republic. Medieval Christian writers usually disregard civic or Republican virtue in their treatments of *amicitia perfecta*, but they posit a party other than the state—God—to which virtuous friends submit.

A third feature which distinguishes *Laelius* from the extant Greek works on the subject is Cicero's formulation of the topic on occasion as a legal code in which he promulgates and enumerates the laws of *amicitia*. This characteristic of *Laelius'* form, rather than of its ideas, is a peculiarity which many medieval writers retain and develop in their own treatments of friendship.

Cicero's theory of the highest *amicitia*, of its source, nature, and objectives, relies heavily on the *Nicomachean Ethics*: *amicitia vera* exists only between good men, who are drawn to one another because of their similarity and love of goodness; it conforms to universal nature in that it is like elemental harmony, the love of family members, and social concord; it consists in unanimity on all human and divine matters and perfect mutual benevolence; beneficence strengthens it; pleasure and usefulness accompany the ideal, but they are not its source; and *amicitia perfecta* is a necessary ingredient of the *summum bonum*. As for the summit of the pyramid depicted earlier, Cicero's ideal covers a much larger area than the tiny peak of orthodox Stoic friendship. He follows Aristotle in relegating both pleasure, which the Cyrenaics considered the first cause of all friendship, and utility, its source according to Epicurus and others, to the grade of circumstances attendant upon the ideal. At the subjacent level of ordinary friendships, he identifies the same two factors as sources of impermanent

---

[30] Earl, *The Moral and Political Tradition of Rome* (Ithaca: Cornell University Press, 1967), p. 21.

relationships.

Especially important in the highly charged political context of *Laelius* is the perfect convergence of individual wills. Cicero's declaration that "friendship is nothing other than unanimity [*consensio*], joined with benevolence and love [*caritas*], on all divine and human matters" (*Laelius* 6,20) seems to give equal weight to human or sociopolitical and religious or higher philosophical considerations. This definition is frequently quoted in Christian writings on *amicitia*, where consensus on divine matters has precedence over the earthly. The Roman historian Sallust, Cicero's younger contemporary, epitomizes this perfect convergence of wills in a similar definition which was often repeated in the Middle Ages: "To wish for the same things and not to wish for the same is, certainly, true friendship [*firma amicitia*]."[31]

Cicero notes that Greek tradition offers only three or four pairs of model friends, whom he does not name,[32] and he supplies from Roman history examples of wise and good men who were *amici veri* or would have been, had they found a compeer. His use of Romans from the preceding century rather than contemporaries as models of virtue strongly suggests here, as in his dialogue *On Old Age*, a preoccupation with the supposedly long-lost, native Roman rectitude that other late Republican and early Imperial writers, notably Sallust and Horace, also extol. He identifies as the most prominent features of virtue self-reliance, loyalty, uprightness, justice, generosity, strength of character, and freedom from passion, caprice, and insolence. He argues that a superior relative degree of wisdom, acknowledged by learned men and the Roman forefathers and measured by the experience of everyday life, is sufficient. He contends that if one were to apply absolute wisdom as the measure, all men without exception would have to be rejected. Furthermore, virtue is not a hidden inner quality but something manifest and an object of public acclaim, so that a good man, upon hearing a commendation of another, may be attracted to him, indeed, may begin to love him even before they meet face to face. Thus, a man of virtuous character—that is, publicly acknowledged—attracts and is attracted to his like. Here Cicero accepts as the criterion for virtue "everyday

---

[31] Sallust, *Bellum Catilinae* 20,4.

[32] *Laelius* 4,15. Cicero names the Greek Orestes-Pylades pair only in the context of a contemporary Latin play, 7,24. He mentions these two as well as Theseus and Pirithous in *De finibus*, and he names Damon and Phintias in *De finibus*, *De officiis*, and *The Tusculan Disputations*.

usage in our [Roman] life and our language" (*Laelius* 6,21; Aristotle frequently favors public consensus as a moral standard.) True friends are rivals in virtue, and through their mutual benevolence and beneficence and the convergence of their wills, they help one another attain to ever higher levels of goodness and wisdom. Cicero affirms that the highest levels can be reached only with a friend's aid.

Cicero devotes almost two-thirds of his dialogue to practice, and he attempts to explain how and why some rare relationships last a lifetime and even longer while the rest founder. This part recalls many points in books 8 and 9 of the *Nicomachean Ethics* which deal with a variety of contracts and obligations, such as governmental constitutions, self-interested gifts, loans, beneficence, and material and moral indebtedness. Cicero limits this broad range of contracts and obligations to the narrow confines of the duties of true friendship and formulates a *codex legum amicitiae*. Each of the laws that Cicero spells out is complemented by clauses, subclauses, provisoes, or precedents worthy of a Roman lawyer's pen. For example, his first law states that one should ask a friend to do only what is honorable, and without waiting to be asked, he should perform righteous acts for his companion's sake (*Laelius* 12,40 and 13,44; cf. *Nic. Eth.* 8,8; 1159 b 4.) Nevertheless, one must be willing to risk his own reputation, as long as he does not put himself in danger of utter disgrace, in order to defend and aid a companion accused of wrongdoing. This proviso does not contradict the general law, however, for the *amicus verus*, having already sufficiently assayed his intimate's character, is certain of his integrity. Therefore, he can stake his own honor, within limits, without actually endangering it because he is sure of defending the right. Not only does he rebut all charges of improbity, he does not even allow himself to think for a moment that his partner may be capable of wrongdoing (cf. *Nic. Eth.* 8,4; 1157 a 20.)

Cicero provides examples of Romans who violated this law and of their poor legal defense for their misdeeds. He condemns Gaius Blossius, who defended his support of the political reformer Tiberius Gracchus, a proven traitor in Cicero's eyes, on the grounds of friendship. Their relationship could not be good because Cicero's *bonum* is the patrician cause and prerogative which they tried to subvert. This century-old case reflects Cicero's own battles against such reformers as Catiline, Julius Caesar, and Mark Antony, and it reveals his political disappointments and frustrations during the Republic's twilight. More importantly, it demonstrates the danger that bad political friendships—bad according to the writer's ideology—pose to the harmony of the community. It underlines, in a negative manner, Aristotle's principle that *philia* is the basis of the body politic. How can the state be in harmony—albeit the harmony of opposition—without friendship, and how can friendship flourish in a disharmonious state? This interdependence of the particular and the general good derives from universal harmony, and for Cicero false or bad *amicitia* threatens to destabilize the community, if not the cosmos itself. Some medieval Christian writers extend Cicero's censure of bad political associates to particular friendships among monks because, in part, of the threat that misguided alliances pose to harmony in the cloistered community.

Because *amicitia vera* is a lifelong engagement with solemn obligations, Cicero advises that one test potential friends in large and small matters over a considerable period of time before committing oneself to unconditional confidence and fidelity. While assaying the qualities of honesty, strength of character, loyalty, and frankness, the examiner should not fail to note such secondary traits as sociability and a certain affability of speech and manner which make the sharing of friends' lives and homes possible and pleasant.

Cicero notes that *amicitia perfecta* is best cultivated by men blessed with wealth, power, and high rank. Although he does not specify high or rather high birth as a prerequisite, he clearly implies it. The same conditions are found in the *Nicomachean Ethics*. On the other hand, those who do not possess these qualities are poor candidates for lasting friendship; they have a real need of associates for reasons of defense and aid, and when the need diminishes or disappears, so does their association. "Helpless women" (*mulierculae*)—men who do not enjoy a relatively high degree of self-sufficiency—make up one species of this deficient genus (*Laelius* 13,46; cf. *Nic. Eth.* 9,11; 1171 b 10.) An excess, too, of wealth or power may blind men and bar them as promising candidates. Cicero claims that politicians as a class are the least likely to become true friends. This statement may be understood as a concession to Epicureanism, even though Cicero, frequently an outspoken critic of Epicureans in his own century, dismisses their teachings on friendship as cowardly and inconsistent with the pursuit of virtue in *Laelius* 13,45-48. He dedicates this treatise to his lifelong friend Titus Pomponius Atticus, an Epicurean with whom he studied under an Epicurean. Atticus was an *eruditus* mostly disengaged from political activity. Since, however, almost all of Cicero's

Roman models of the virtuous, sage, and friendly are political figures, one must draw the paradoxical conclusion that although politicians make up the class least likely to earn the title of *amici perfecti*, as individuals they are in fact the main title-holders.

The Laelius-Scipio pair as the embodiment of the ideal does not exist in isolation from society. It embraces many other good but less than perfect alliances. Both men maintained with others friendly relationships which share characteristics with the ideal but rank below it in importance. Cicero makes several observations about these better than ordinary relations (cf. *Nic. Eth.* 8,14 and 9,1-2.) While as a rule one must do everything in his power to benefit all his associates—that is, to increase their virtue, wisdom, and fortune and to improve their status—he must realize that some are incapable, even with the most powerful support, of advancing to the highest level; therefore, he apportions his aid according to each companion's capacity to benefit from it. And although friends rightly regard one another as equals without taking into account their respective stations or means, they should always give preference to long-standing associates over new ones in allocating their affection. In all cases affection must be meted out rationally, since ungoverned fondness—for example, love that cannot bear separation—may hinder an intimate's advancement.

Among the good relationships which do not, however, measure up to the ideal, some become permanently unbalanced because one partner makes too much or too little progress or even loses ground in the pursuit of virtue (cf. *Nic. Eth.* 9,3.) Prudence and the code of friendship govern the course to be followed in this event. If a man has already committed himself after a thorough test of his companion's character, he should by rights remain faithful even if it becomes apparent later that his sworn friend cannot live up to the highest expectations. A commitment is solemn, irrevocable. On the other hand, if there is no commitment, the two should discontinue their intimacy in a manner that permits the association to dissolve, or appear to dissolve, slowly and naturally. Cicero advises against an abrupt cessation which might lead to offense or open hostility and against allowing a partnership abandoned long ago to turn into enmity; he recommends the maintenance of a semblance of amity. This advice perhaps reflects Cicero's and Cato the Younger's reduction in intimacy but continued public display of friendliness after their parting of wills over politics which Plutarch reports in *The Life of Cicero* 34,1-3.

In the dialogue's conclusion, Cicero uses the Laelius-Scipio pair to

summarize *amicitia perfecta*: Laelius was attracted to Scipio because of
his virtue, which remains after his death and will affect the yet unborn;
they shared one roof and table and did battle and traveled together; they
never once caused offense to one another; in private matters they enjoyed
their company and counsel, on public questions, complete agreement, and
in leisure, delight and unflagging eagerness for knowledge.

    The dialogue form and the disposition of interlocutors in *Laelius* consti-
tute a major literary model for medieval writers. Laelius, an elderly sage,
lectures on his friendship with the recently deceased Scipio to two
younger male in-laws, who ask questions and also overcome on occasion
their senior's scruple when modesty prevents him from speaking. Cast as
a three-part discussion at its beginning but soon thereafter reshaped as an
extended monologue, the work takes its form from the Platonic dialogue.
Given *Laelius'* popularity in the Middle Ages and evident imitations of it,
one can claim without exaggeration that it was in large part responsible
for the preservation and propagation of the philosophical dialogue as a
medieval literary genre. Moreover, certain of *Laelius'* dramatic and framing peculiarities have parallels in a special branch of religious friendship
in medieval writings. Several medieval works promote worthy friendship
between spiritual master and disciple. The tendency in some Christian
writings to complement *amicitia inter pares* of the David-Jonathan type
with the unequal master-disciple relationship, a sort of *primus inter pares*,
may have been influenced in part by *Laelius'* dramatic framing. At the dialogue's beginning, Cicero takes great care in preparing the discussion's
elaborate stage-within-a-stage and in defining the relationships among the
speakers. There the master-disciple friendship between Laelius and his
sons-in-law, which is characterized by affection, benevolence, goodness,
and mutual trust, serves as the dramatic frame through which Scipio and
Laelius' *amicitia inter pares* is viewed. Medieval readers would have found
this same construction—the master addresses his friend(s)-disciple(s) on
friendship between equals—in Seneca's letters on *amicitia* to Lucilius. In
the Middle Ages, this dramatic frame reappears in the master-disciple dialogues on Christian friendship by John Cassian and Aelred of Rievaulx.

    Although Cicero, unlike the earlier Greeks, provides concrete examples
of his countrymen as model friends, it would be wrong to credit him with
having verified the social reality of perfect friendship. It is more accurate
to consider him a mythographer of *amicitia vera*. Clearly, Plato's and the
early Stoics' intellectual ideal was impracticable, but was Panaetius' prac-

ticable version of Stoic virtue or the Ciceronian model in fact ever realized in Rome or elsewhere? Cicero names real men as true friends, but they were men from an already distant past. They were legends in his time, and he presents them as moral myths, superior to any found in Greek tradition. He could have chosen to offer as his primary example of *perfecti amici* himself and his friend Atticus to whom he addresses the dialogue— and *Laelius* can be read, at least in part, as the mythologization of their friendship—but he opts for myth-writing over autobiography. In its glorification of a partly historical, partly legendary exemplum, *Laelius* is a sort of secular hagiography. Its many imitators do not, any more than Cicero, confirm the social reality of perfect friendship. Cicero's idealized Laelius, Scipio, and their successors represent aspirations, not realities, of the society in which they are portrayed.

In his *Memorable Acts and Sayings of Romans and Foreigners*, completed in 31 A.D. or later, Valerius Maximus (first cent. B.C.-first cent. A.D.) offers a provocative response to *Laelius*. At the same time, the author presents an extreme view of the highest friendship proven by an exceptional act of fidelity, courage, and self-sacrifice. The act typifies a sort of virtue akin to the hero's self-forgetful bravery in the defense of his country even though the writer, unlike Cicero, does not specifically link patriotism and *amicitia*. Valerius Maximus' work was very widely read in the original Latin and vernacular versions in the Middle Ages, and medieval readers valued it as a mine of ancient anecdotes and ethical exempla.

Book 4, chapter 7, titled "*De amicitia,*" emphasizes the utilitarian: "Since indeed a man's future livelihood may be lost when not under the protection of friendship, such necessary aid should not be accepted lightly."[33] Valerius Maximus offers there some reflections or, rather, commonplaces—for instance, true amity is stronger than the bonds of kinship (a statement which he contradicts in a later chapter), and a friend proves himself to be true or false in hard times. The author is principally

---

[33] Translated from the unnumbered introductory paragraph to this chapter in *Valerii Maximi factorum et dictorum memorabilium libri novem*, ed. C. Kempf, Bibliotheca Teubneriana (Stuttgart: Teubner, 1966), p. 201. P. Constant's French translation listed in the select bibliography gives a different meaning here because his Latin text is punctuated differently.

concerned with rhetorical exempla of the practice of *amicitia*, and he offers nothing resembling a theory. Here, as in the rest of his collection, he groups historical notables, Romans first, then foreigners, usually Greeks, under a common thematic rubric, and he recounts and interprets anecdotes about them which nearly always derive from Latin sources. In what is clearly a rejoinder to Cicero, he identifies as a true friend an historical personage whom Cicero branded as false in *Laelius*, and later (book 5, chapter 5, *"De amicitia fraterna"*), he uses Cicero's model of perfection, Scipio and Laelius, to illustrate the preference for a brother over a friend. Cicero stigmatized the Gracchi and their supporters, particularly Gaius Blossius, as traitors to the Republic and false friends. Valerius Maximus censures the Gracchi, too, if much less vehemently, but argues that Gaius Blossius, who defended the deceased Tiberius Gracchus before a hostile court of inquiry, behaved as a loyal friend in braving mortal danger for the sake of his companion's memory. The argument in favor of Gaius Blossius shows more than the desire to contradict and refute Cicero; it proves that already in the early Empire the interests of friends could be argued independently of community or political interests. A little later, Seneca's letters treat friendship without taking into account politics, government, or patriotism.

Most of Valerius Maximus' many Roman *veri amici* have one ethical feature in common: as proof of complete fidelity to a friend, one dies for him or, at least, braves a life-threatening situation while defending him. This attitude faintly echoes Phaedrus' praise in the *Symposium* 178 E-179 B of the unsurpassed courage of lovers-warriors who prefer death to dishonor in the eyes of the beloved. It also calls to mind Cicero's praise in *Laelius* of the Greek friends Orestes and Pylades, who, as represented in a Latin play, each fought fiercely to die in the other's stead. Nevertheless, it seems improbable that Cicero considered this particular case to be anything more than edifying fiction. Valerius Maximus deems examples which he cites from Greek tradition to be inferior to instances of true *amicitia romana*. The many exempla which he offers of Roman *devotio*, or self-sacrifice, in the name of friendship are not essentially different from the equally numerous illustrations in a chapter on patriotism of the hero's supreme sacrifice for his country's sake. *Fides*, or protection and faithfulness, is with Valerius Maximus as with all the ancients a primary and unconditional duty of friendship. Aristotle, for example, claimed that the virtuous friend might give his life for a comrade's sake (*Nic. Eth.* 9,8). Valerius Maximus' representations of *amicitia perfecta* are unique in that he identifies a single act of *fides* as its chief characteristic and end and as proof, often at the cost of life, of virtue in the sense of valor. He maintains in principle that friendship is a private matter between men, apart from interests of the Republic or the Empire; yet he provides almost exclusively as examples of *amici veri* political figures whose fidelity to an intimate is evinced at some crucial and sanguinary moment in the history of the state. As W. Martin Bloomer notes, his illustrations of the practice of heroic friendship conform to the demands of declamatory performance in his time. Besides providing a stock of nearly one thousand exempla on rhetorical topics, including *amicitia*, from which students of declamation might draw, his illustrations are themselves models of the ways in which historical anecdotes can be shaped for exciting delivery.[34] Given that his scenes of courageous friendship clearly aim to persuade, even astonish, through dramatic effect, it is hardly surprising that they offer nothing resembling a coherent theory of *amicitia*.

Valerius Maximus' concept of *amicitia* is different from the other, philosophical ideals in this chapter. His perfect friendship is not directed outside itself or above itself—for example, as a quest for knowledge of the Good. Contained within itself, it aims at its spectacular self-confirmation, and nothing more. In a later chapter on chivalric friendship, we will examine medieval fictions with similarly dramatic cases of heroic friendship with no higher aim than itself and no greater virtue than self-sacrifice that transcends prudence and reason.

As the final example of *vera amicitia romana* in his chapter "On Friendship," Valerius Maximus offers himself and his patron, the late Sextus Pompeius, who was consul in 14 A.D. and proconsul in Asia in 24/25 A.D. The author, who served as Sextus Pompeius' secretary, says that he owes all his good fortune to him and that he found in him a source of strength in prosperity and of calm in troubled times. He compares his patron and himself to the friends Alexander the Great and his second-in-command Hephaistion. Given the respective status of the two Romans, one is tempted to dismiss this example as a literary convention—the writer pays in hyperbole a debt to his Maecenas. On the other hand, there are linguistic and cultural grounds for accepting, at least in part, the au-

---

[34] Bloomer, *Valerius Maximus and the Rhetoric of the New Nobility* (London and Chapel Hill: University of North Carolina Press, 1992), pp. 1-2.

thor's claim to the title of *amicus verus*. In the Roman language and society, literary patronage was an established form of *amicitia* with the same code, nomenclature, and duties, including *fides*, as in other sorts of friendship, such as political alliance, *clientela*, and affective friendship. Peter White notes that in the early Empire, the period during which Valerius Maximus wrote, "the same sort of language is used in speaking of friendships with literary figures as for other forms of *amicitia*," and "whether a man is superior, equal, or inferior in standing to another, both are called *amici*, and the relationship itself is *amicitia*."[35] This language of equality blurred social distinctions in what was sometimes an unequal relationship between artistic patron and protégé. Nonetheless, in respect to the concept, and not the nomenclature, of *amicitia*, Valerius Maximus does more here than follow a 'status-neutral' linguistic code, one already established in the Republican period, which named friendly parties as peers, regardless of their socio-economical standing. If one understands his exemplum to indicate the elevation of the literary patron-protégé relationship to the status of *amicitia perfecta* which he illustrated earlier in the chapter, then his claim seems bold and unconventional. Rarely does one find similar instances of the idealization of *amicitia* between unequal partners as, for example, with Leon Battista Alberti's ideal of friendship between prince and merchant-class courtier in his dialogue *Dell'amicizia* which will be studied in the concluding chapter.

L. Annaeus Seneca (ca. 4 B.C.-65 A.D.) is the last pagan Latin author to deal extensively with ideal amity.[36] Several of Seneca's *Letters to Lu-*

---

[35] White, "*Amicitia* and the Profession of Poetry in Early Imperial Rome," *Journal of Roman Studies* 68 (1978): 78 and 80. Horace's *Epistles* give a practical guide of conduct for the poet who wishes to win and maintain the friendship of a powerful patron, *potens amicus*. See the study by Ross S. Kilpatrick, *The Poetry of Friendship. Horace, Epistles I* (Edmonton: University of Alberta Press, 1986), especially pp. 43-55 on the poet's duties in *Epistles* 1,17 and 1,18. Barbara K. Gold, *Literary Patronage in Greece and Rome* (Chapel Hill: University of North Carolina Press, 1987), analyzes what poets, especially Horace and Propertius, and their patrons wrote about one another.

[36] Two short letters of Pliny the Younger (7,20 and 7,28) discuss *amicitia*, but they are not important enough to treat in this chapter. The title of the following 1722 Paris edition is misleading: *Œuvres de Mr. de Sacy, de l'Académie Françoise: contenant les Lettres de Pline le Jeune, Le Panegyrique*

cilius, well known in the Middle Ages, contain reflections on friendship that have *Laelius* as a reference point, and they often cite Laelius, Scipio, and Cato the Elder, the main speaker in Cicero's dialogue *On Old Age*, as models of wisdom, goodness, and right conduct (see *Letters* 7,6; 11,10; 25,6; 95,72; 104,21.)

A listing of Seneca's ideas on *amicitia* in his letters will show, first, his exclusive interest in ethics and, second, his debt to Cicero: one tests a man's character thoroughly before accepting him as a friend in unconditional confidence (*Letter* 3,2-3); *vera amicitia* lasts a lifetime and is worth dying for (6,2); true friends share all that they possess, and they are two spirits joined with equal zeal in the love of *honesta*, the good (6,3); before befriending another, a man must first be a friend to himself (6,7; Seneca cites here the Stoic Hecaton, a disciple of Panaetius); the loss of a close friend does not overly upset the sage (9,5; cf. *Laelius* 3,10); the wise man finds pleasure in making friends (9,6); *amicitia* based on usefulness will eventually dissolve, but Seneca wants associates to whom he can be useful (9,8-10); friendship should be sought for itself alone (9,12); even though the sage is self-reliant, he still needs *amici*, and he wants as many of them as possible, for Nature calls man to man and away from solitude (9,15-17); the sage regards his intimates as equal or even superior to himself (9,18; cf. *Laelius* 19,69-70); *amici* attend to one another's interests (48,2); absence does not alter the essence of *amicitia*, for the heart, not the body, assures its possession (55,11); the sage needs friends in order to exercise his virtue and beneficence, and they can help invigorate him in this necessary exercise (109,1-2); no matter how wise a man may be, he still needs counsel, and daily collaboration with intimates facilitates his life (109,14-15). Seneca suggests to Lucilius that since character, not birth or social standing, determines goodness, he may find a friend even among his slaves (47,16). This advice reflects Stoic doctrine, which taught that all men and women, too, are intrinsically equal.[37] The suggestion did not prove sound in practice, for one learns in a later letter that the slaves whom Lucilius thought to have befriended fled.

---

de Trajan par le même Pline, Et le Traité de l'Amitié. Louis de Sacy, not Pliny the Younger, is the author of this treatise on friendship.

[37] Cf. *Nicomachean Ethics* 8,11 (1161 b 3), where master and slave *per se* are said to be incompatible as friends due to their dissimilarity, just as a craftsman cannot be a friend to a tool; but in so far as they are both men, it is possible for them to experience friendship in the general sense of social concord if they agree to behave with justice towards one another.

In spite of the frequent allusions to Cicero, Seneca's conception of friendship is fundamentally different from his predecessor's. Seneca's sage practices friendship as an exercise of virtue, but his virtue is not Cicero's. While making no attempt to conceal his debt to Cicero, Seneca states that he wishes to make his letters to Lucilius more intimate and philosophical than those of Cicero to Atticus by not talking about politics. Thus, the political essence of Cicero's Republican virtue and *amicitia* is absent from Seneca's epistles. The separation of friendship from politics in the letters probably bespeaks a social reality in his time—namely, the powerlessness of personal alliances, whether philosophical or political, to influence for the better the course of Nero's Empire.

Jean Brun's evaluation of Seneca's Stoicism as "indulgent, affadi et prêt à beaucoup de concessions" is fair if one compares it to early Stoic doctrine or Epictetus' writings.[38] One might suspect, however, that this diluted and concessive character of his Stoicism contributed to its early and lasting acceptance by Christian thinkers. If 'God-loving' were substituted for 'wise' and 'good,' and 'charity' for 'beneficence' in the ideas from Seneca's letters listed above, one would have the germ of John Cassian's and Aelred of Rievaulx's dialogues on Christian friendship as a product of reason and faith.

To close this introduction, we should note several circumstances about the transmission to the Middle Ages of ancient texts dealing with ideals of *amicitia*. Each of these factors contributed to making the medieval view of the ancient concepts somewhat different from our own understanding of them. First, seen as a whole from the present-day perspective, the corpus of Greek and Latin works and fragments represents a continuing and unresolved polemic on friendship's inception, nature, and ends. For the Middle Ages, however, the classical tradition represented unanimity. Obviously, this view was conditioned by the available texts limited to ethics—the *Nicomachean Ethics*, the Latins just mentioned, and perhaps some excerpts from Diogenes Laertius. The principal works on the metaphysics of *philia* by Plato, the early Stoics, and others were not known in the Middle Ages. Cicero reviewed and refuted in *Laelius* many of the arguments of

---

[38] *Le stoïcisme*, p. 21.

the early Stoics, the Epicureans, and the Hedonists. Yet a medieval reader of his dialogue might not have even suspected the existence of these Greek schools or their long-running and unsettled polemic because Cicero did not name them. Furthermore, the fundamental agreement among Aristotle, Cicero, and Seneca on questions of friendship and its perfection would seem to carry weight as canonic authority in the Middle Ages.

Secondly, the concern for codifying friendship apparent in many medieval tracts may have resulted in part from the reading of ordered excerpts from Aristotle and the Romans in florilegia. In the thirteenth or fourteenth-century florilegium *Auctoritates Aristotelis*, books 8 and 9 of the *Nicomachean Ethics* are reduced to sixty-two maxims listed under the book-number heading.[39] In this form they look not like an ethical treatise but a legal digest. The observation applies likewise to the listings from Seneca's *Letters to Lucilius* in the same florilegium. Because of this radical reformatting of the *Nicomachean Ethics* in many different medieval collections, the reader is given the impression that *philia* has its fixed laws, just like Aristotelian physics or logic which were also reduced to the florilegium format, and its fixed and proper form, the digest. Of course, *Laelius*, with its frequent references to supposed laws, had a great deal to do with the codification of *amicitia* in the Middle Ages—that is, medieval writers imitated Cicero's method.

A third circumstance which colored medieval perception of the ancient texts is language. Most of these works were read in Latin throughout the Middle Ages. The first French translation of *Laelius*, for example, is from the early fifteenth century, and the translator intended it to be read alongside the Latin text. Such key words in *Laelius* and Seneca's letters as *caritas, benevolentia, beneficium, virtus, officium, sapientia,* and many others take on a Christian cast from the medieval reader's bias. The Christian connotations of these terms were of course inconceivable in the late Republican and early Imperial context, and they are incompatible with it. The fact remains, however, that the form of these Latin words did not change in the Christian period, and it is probable that most medieval readers, when encountering them in Cicero and Seneca, saw there meanings not irreconcilable with Christian thought. How 'user-friendly' these two pagan Latin texts were to medieval readers because of the similarity in

---

[39] *Les "Auctoritates Aristotelis," un florilège médiéval*, ed. Jacqueline Hamesse, Philosophes Médiévaux, 17 (Louvain: Publications Universitaires, 1974), pp. 242-46.

terminology to their own ecclesiastical vocabulary! For this linguistic reason, it is hardly surprising that Christian writers singled out both texts, or parts of them, from the pagan corpus at an early date, well before the fall of Rome, and accepted them as moral authorities. No doubt the speaker Laelius' preliminary discussion on the immortality of the soul (*Laelius* 4,13-14) prepared the way for a warm reception or, rather, a receptive revision by the Christian reader. The Church Father John Cassian, usually disdainful of pagan book learning, did not hesitate to embrace *Laelius*. Throughout the medieval period, the Ciceronian-Senecan terminology of *amicitia vera* persisted in large part as the basic vocabulary of *amicitia christiana* and also of secular sorts of friendship in Latin and vernacular works. The pagan terminology persisted, but its semantic content was radically altered.

Nonetheless, it is by no means true that medieval *usage* of the pagan Latin idiom of friendship is invariably fraught with religious connotation, with Christian interference. Medieval epistles are especially rich in the Ciceronian-Senecan vocabulary of *amicitia*. Yet this wealth of frequently repeated Ciceronian or Senecan phrases and professions of faithful friendship is often sterile epistolary convention that cannot be taken at face value. The same *amicus, caritas, benevolentia, fides*, and *virtus* are addressed to intimates, superiors, inferiors, and even strangers and less than friendly associates, which is also the case in Cicero's correspondence. In the numerous medieval collections of model friendship letters for imitation, the *amicus* not infrequently is inexistent—for example, a deceased historical personage—or imaginary. In this polite practice of the literati, oftentimes Ciceronian-Senecan vocabulary and formulas are reproduced for urbanity's sake and stylistic color. One may detect a sincere expression of friendship in medieval epistles more often than not *in spite* of such formulas.

One might draw attention to a final factor—tradition—which helped inform the view that medieval writers on Christian friendship were the continuators and perfecters of the ancients' virtuous *amicitia*. Classical philosophers' belief in the natural predisposition of the good and the wise to *amicitia* and, also, the exalted status which they attributed to its rare ideal manifestation are almost universally shared by medieval authors on the topic. The Latin works on *amicitia* which the Middle Ages received asserted that friendship contributes fundamentally to the good life and that its ideal embodiment is possible. The Greek texts that found their way, little by little, in Latin versions to medieval Europeans did not contradict these assertions. While producing and adding to their own corpus on *amicitia*, religious writers of the Middle Ages maintained much the same beliefs as they redefined true friendship on a spiritual plane. In this continuity of values and consciousness of tradition, they could conceive of themselves as true friends of the giants of antiquity.

CHAPTER TWO

IDEALS OF CHRISTIAN FRIENDSHIPS IN THE TWELFTH AND THIRTEENTH CENTURIES: *AMICITIA DEI*, FRATERNAL CHARITY, AND THE PROBLEM OF SPIRITUAL FRIENDSHIP AND LOVE

Can a woman or man be God's friend?

Ancient philosophers spoke of unidirectional human love of the Good: the sage strives to know immortal goodness. But the Good and even the best mortal are qualitatively incompatible, and the Good does not reciprocate the sage's love. Therefore, as Aristotle claimed, there can be no friendship with deities. Plato described the sage's loving activity as ascending, through the mediation of Eros, to a knowledge of the Good in an attempt to become like it, but he did not suggest that absolute goodness itself might take an active part in drawing the sage up to the highest level.

In Christian doctrine the three persons of the Trinity, bound together by perfect love, enter into a direct relationship with mortals, and, so, Christian friendship takes on a spiritual dimension not imagined by the philosophers discussed in the preceding chapter. In writing on Christian charity, St. Thomas Aquinas (1225-1274) defines a particular aspect of *amicitia christiana*:

> Charity signifies not only love of God, but also a certain friendship with Him; which implies, besides love, a certain mutual return of love, together with mutual communion, as stated in the *Nicomachean Ethics*, book 8.... Now this fellowship of man with God, which consists in a certain familiar colloquy with Him, is begun here, in this life, by grace, but will be perfected in the future life in glory.[1]

What Thomas Aquinas names charity in a particular relationship between God and an individual has a heavenly aspect and an imperfect earthly one which prepares a mortal for the afterlife, where the perfect communion between the Creator and the created that preceded the Fall is restored. In this

---

[1] *Summa theologiae*, first part of part 2, question 65, article 5, in *Basic Writings of Saint Thomas Aquinas*, ed. Anton C. Pegis, 2 vols. (New York: Random House, 1945), vol. 2, p. 503.

life, friendship with God, as illustrated in writings on saints' raptures and
their direct but intermittent communion with celestial beings or God, is
necessarily imperfect and transient; due to the great disparity between the
Creator and the fallen mortal and the consequent, very limited degree of reciprocity, the term 'friendship' applies in a lesser degree to what this One-
to-one relationship is than to what it will be in eternity.

While Christian charity involves a particular relationship between the
One and one, it also includes the totality of particulars on both heavenly
and earthly levels. Through their particular, perfect love of the One, the
heavenly hosts of angels and blessed souls love one another. They follow
the One's will in loving what It loves. This heavenly aspect of charity as
mutual love of like spirits arising from God's love is mirrored on earth in
the harmonious relationship among mortal friends of God, especially in
the monastic community where all hearts and minds are directed towards
the One. In Western Christian writings—and also experience—from about
the beginning of the fifth century, the God-mortal relationship is usually
mediated through the community of Christians, in most cases the
monastery. Writings on community-mediated fraternal charity among fellow Christians on earth assume it, as with the "certain return of love" between a mortal and spiritual beings, to be only preparation for and a faint
reflection of its celestial counterpart, 'true friendship' and mutual charity
in the heavenly community.

Of special interest in this chapter are three variables of monastic life
that are determined in large part by an order's rules and the character of a
monastery's or order's leader and other members. First, brothers or sisters
in a religious house are expected show their love almost equally to one
another—*almost* is in large part dependent, aside from individual character
and inclinations, on the degree to which monastic rules, the abbot or
abbess, and custom deny, permit, or encourage individual religious to
form close friendships with another or others in their cloister. Behind this
denial, permission, or encouragement lies a judgment on the value of
preferential friendship in the religious' pursuit of salvation and in the
community's quest of heaven-like harmony. Second, in the monastery's
vertical-horizontal mixing of paternal authority-love, filial obedience-love,
and fraternal love among those in the same house, one always finds spiritual mentoring: a community member serves as another's spiritual guide
and confidant. A third variable is the degree of fraternal love that a community's members are permitted or expected to show to those outside the

cloister. Among others, these three conditions point to avenues, or im-
passes, of monastic friendships, and the first two particularly enter into
writings on varieties of idealized spiritual friendship which often show the
influence of Aristotle, Cicero, and Seneca.

Brian P. McGuire's *Friendship and Community: The Monastic Experience 350-1250* studies thoroughly the writings on friendship and its practice (or, as is often the case, of writing as the practice of friendship) in
Christian communities. He notes that aristocratic, Aristotelian-Ciceronian
amicitia vera was frequently viewed with suspicion in monasteries up to
the mid-eleventh century with its revived interest in ancient models of
friendship which "can and must be linked with the new schools and their
interest in classical texts."[2] Even though the works of Aristotle, Cicero,
Seneca, and other ancients exercised a great influence on Christian writings through the mid-eleventh century, before that time the classical ideals
of friendship were devalued, often being regarded as worldly temptation or
potential causes of communal disharmony. An overview of McGuire's
conclusions on the most important writers on monastic friendships in
chapters two through five of his study, which cover the period from the
beginnings of monasticism through the early-twelfth century, would be
useful in providing background for the present chapter. One must note,
however, that McGuire's main subject is the historical experience and
context for friendships that might be inferred from texts, not ideal representations of Christian friendship. He maintains that individual friendships in that long period can be understood solely inasmuch as they are
integrated into community life, which took its textual ideal from the description in Acts 4,32 of the first Christian community's shared heart,
spirit, and possessions. As Dom Jean Leclercq has observed, for St. Augustine, one of the founders of Western monasticism, the City of God is
an ideal of a universal *societas amicalis*, or friendly society, where all are
united by Christian charity, of which friendship is the active expression.[3]
The essence of Christian friendship within the community resides in the
double bond between God and the person and between persons brought together by God's love.

McGuire notes that in the beginnings of monasticism in the East, St.

---

[2] *Friendship and Community*, Cistercian Studies Series, 95 (Kalamazoo:
Cistercian Publications, 1988), p. xxix.

[3] J. Leclercq, "L'amitié dans les lettres au Moyen Age," *Revue du Moyen Age
latin* 1 (1945): 401.

Pachomius (ca. 290-346) taught the equal love of monastic brothers for one another while he strongly discouraged close friendships among them. Disapproval of particular friendships pervailed in much of monastic writing until quite recently. Already in the West at that early time, Christian authors had begun to 'convert' Cicero's *amicitia perfecta*: writing on the duties of friends in the Christian community, St. Ambrose (ca. 334-397), who considered Christ and His Father as model friends, replaced Cicero's Roman *amici veri* with biblical examples in the concluding chapter of his *De officiis ministrorum*. For St. Augustine (354-430), who personally placed high value on particular friendships, there is only one sort of *vera amicitia*, of which the source is God, Who reaches out through the Holy Spirit to offer humans charity and grace. Through these gifts men, having become friends of God, may become *veri amici*. To Augustine's ideas of God as friendship's source and the friends' spiritual intimacy as a way to the knowledge of God one may trace the roots of the ideal of spiritual friendship which was elaborated much later. This early period saw, too, the development of spiritual guardianship between equal friends and a master-disciple sort which had their beginnings in Eastern monastic practices (McGuire, chapter two). Later we will examine briefly a master-disciple dialogue on friendship among monastics by St. John Cassian (ca. 365-435), another of the founders of Western monasticism, who derived much from Eastern tradition. His ideas were influential in the rule of St. Benedict written in the first half of the sixth century.

McGuire credits the Venerable Bede (ca. 672-735), who in his historical works frequently used the word *amicitia* for worldly political alliances and kinship, with the first use of the term *spiritualis amicitia* to name a close friendship between two religious. Several letters exchanged between Saint Boniface (ca. 675-754) and nuns prove that, at least in epistles and at a distance, religious men and women of the time could claim to be friends in spirit. Quite often, too, their *amicitia* involved political interests. In the Carolingian period, from about 770 to 850, McGuire notes among a small elite participating in a cultural revival many letters and poems which illustrate "the tradition of secular friendship for political advantage, the classical view of friendship in purely human terms, and the christian platonic conception that friendship is a path to the Good" (page 116), the last especially in the letters of Alcuin (ca. 732-804) and the poetry of Strabo (809-849). Whether or not one agrees with McGuire's belief that the high-flown rhetoric of Carolingian religious writers often expresses sincere friendship, an important point in his study here is that their sustained enthusiasm for earlier literature, as evidenced in their collecting manuscripts, both broadened the range of their notions of monastic friendship and enriched their literary expression of it. Nevertheless, except for Carolingian writers' relative lack of interest in male-female bonds, nothing indicates that their extraliterary practices of *amicitia* differed significantly from those which one might infer from the writings of Bede, Boniface, and others in the preceding period (McGuire, chapter three).

From around 850 to 1050 McGuire finds no writer who devotes special attention to monastic friendship, and the word *amicitia* seldom has religious connotations. Monastic rules and writings describe collective life which excludes the experience or expression of close friendship as undesirable—even as a threat to the soul—in the cloister. In this period of the renewal of asceticism which McGuire calls "the eclipse of monastic friendship," Gerbert of Aurillac (ca. 938-1003), who became Pope Sylvester II, expresses the practice of *amicitia* in his correspondence for social and political purposes and for acquiring manuscripts. McGuire notices, however, rare instances of Gerbert's Christianized Ciceronian idealization of friendship, which originates in God's proclamation of the eternal law of *amicitia* and produces harmony in the cloister, the state, and the world. Written evidence of close friendships among religious in this time exists, but it is slight (McGuire, chapter four).

The period from about the mid-eleventh to the early-twelfth century saw a burgeoning of collections of letters and the beginnings of hagiography dealing with close friendships. Intense literary activity in cathedral schools and the active educational role that monasteries assumed from the end of the tenth century helped prepare this renewed interest in *amicitia*, which gradually became a main theme of monastic writing and life. In a collection of letters from the cathedral school at Worms which date mostly from the second quarter of the eleventh century, there are many examples of epistles which combine or juxtapose classical and Christian concepts of *amicitia* and which "make friendship into an ideal that can fit into any kind of collective way of life" (p. 188). In one letter a bishop advises a nun that he finds no reason why men and women should not be friends. By the late-eleventh century there is substantial evidence of male-female religious friendship or love, as in Goscelin of Saint Bertin's *Liber confortatorius* (1082-1083) on the subject of his love for Eve, a nun and, later, recluse with whom he passionately hoped to be reunited in heaven.

McGuire credits Anselm of Bec (1033-1109) and his acquaintances with a veritable revolution in the expression of monastic friendship: "Anselm's vocabulary of friendship has from the start a completeness not seen since the writings of Saint Augustine or the letters of Alcuin. Every possible nuance of *amicitia* is exploited in order to describe the bond, and there is almost no dimension of spiritual intensity left untouched" (p. 212). In his letters he advises distant friends that each, by looking into his own soul, can know what is in Anselm's. This inwardness of his notion of friendship is linked to the monastic community of friends joined as a whole by common conduct and spiritual pursuit: because of the similarity of monastic brothers in spirit, Anselm esteems very highly the general condition of loving within the community, which becomes a loving entity in itself, and he values very much less the personal bond of love between any one brother and another. In the anonymous *Life of Gundulf*, composed between 1114 and 1124, close friendships—in particular, that between Anselm and Gundulf who converse on divine love—play a new, central role that will become prominent in subsequent hagiography, as in the late-twelfth-century *Life of Christina of Markyate* which we will examine presently (McGuire, chapter five).

Latin writers in the twelfth and thirteenth centuries use, among other terms, *amor, caritas, dilectio, affectus, intellectus,* and *amicitia* to name the same or different aspects of a personal relationship to God, love of humankind, friendship of fellow Christians, and spiritual friendship or love between two Christians or among a very few. However, certain writers seem to avoid using *amicitia* to name Christian love or friendship, perhaps because of the term's worldly connotations, and they apply it principally to social and political alliances and kinship. Some authors discussed in the present chapter frequently quote in their discussions of Christian *amicitia* the *Nicomachean Ethics, Laelius, De officiis,* and Seneca's letters. As will be seen shortly, St. Aelred of Rievaulx (ca. 1110-1167) adapts Cicero's *amicitia perfecta*, which aspires to goodness and practical wisdom, to Christian love in his treatise *Spiritual Friendship*, and he is most careful to point out the spiritual shortcomings and limits of truth in his classical source. He collates passages and models from *Laelius* with biblical and patristic writings that complete Cicero's ideas, that show them as beginnings which Christian truth brings to the ends of God's love and love of fellowmen. Aelred's system of reading Cicero is similar to biblical typology, the exegetical process which, in its simplest terms, sees in persons or things in the Old Testament foreshadowing of the New Testament, the sacraments, or the *eschaton*.[4] In this sense, for a sympathetic medieval Christian reader or writer, selected classical works or passages contain an element of truth when interpreted in the light of Scripture.

Essential to the various ideals and representations of Christian friendships are the respective activities of the divine and the mortal parties in the relationships. The Greek and Latin writers discussed in the first chapter of the present study emphasized human activity: the sage struggles to know himself and the greatest good. Interaction between two or among a few good men serves as an aid in these pursuits. In Christian friendships, however, the Absolute always plays the dominant, active role of the sole originator and sustainer of true *amicitia*. Mortals are not reduced to passivity, however, for they exercise free will in choosing whether to respond to God's love and in what ways. Christian writers maintain that divine gifts operate as gentle persuasion in encouraging a mortal to reciprocate God's love with reason and affection. Thomas Aquinas, speaking of the reciprocity of charity, says:

> By this opinion it is not denied that the Holy Spirit, Who is Uncreated Charity, exists in man who has created charity, or that He moves man's soul to the act of love, as God moves all things to their own actions to which they are inclined by their own proper forms. And thus it is that He disposes all things sweetly, because to all things He gives forms and powers inclining them to that which He Himself moves them; so that they tend toward it not by force, but as if it were by their own free accord.[5]

Thus God and mortals are coactors, albeit unequal ones, in the unfolding of Christian love. The early-thirteenth-century French romance *The Quest of the Holy Grail* indicates that God metes out charity—that is, the "created charity" in the passage above—according to individuals' different capacities for benefiting from it, for responding to divine love and con-

---

[4] This sort of Christian complementary reading of profane authors is not uncommon. Around 1124 Conrad of Hirsau in his *Dialogus super auctores* supplies Christian meanings for Aesop's fables and argues for preserving what can be interpreted as good and profitable in profane poetry—Jean Leclercq, *Monks and Love in Twelfth-Century France. Psycho-Historical Essays* (Oxford: Clarendon Press, 1979), pp. 41-42.

[5] *On Charity (De caritate)*, trans. Lottie H. Kendzierski, Mediaeval Philosophical Texts in Translation, 10 (Milwaukee: Marquette University Press, 1960), article 1, p. 22.

forming their will to divine volition. In this sense grace is not a cause of
human action or reaction but an aid to free will.

In the idea of *amicitia* between God and mortals, it is assumed that mortals, in responding fully to God's love, come closer to Him and become
His friends. Another assumption is that God requites their love on earth
and in paradise. Proof of God's love on earth takes the forms of visions,
spiritual messengers, miracles, and special signs, all of which serve to
make the mortal more fervent in her or his love, more eager to enjoy
God's company in the afterlife. One gift which God may offer as encouragement to fervent love is a human friend. Spiritual friendship—that is,
two or a few mortals' confident love of one another for the sake of God
Who joined them in spirit—is represented or rationalized in some of the
twelfth and thirteenth-century texts which we will examine as an earthly
aid to the attainment of ever-greater benefits of divine love. In his dialogue on spiritual friendship, Aelred of Rievaulx claims that there are
thousands of pairs of Christian martyrs who, through faith in Christ, were
willing to sacrifice themselves for friendship.[6] In comparison, the classical ideals, once prized because rare, are disappointing if one considers the
quantity of those who can be called 'true' friends—few Romans, less
Greeks, and no women. From this one might conclude that the multitude
of flesh-and-blood Christian friends gives proof to the superabundance of
God's love.

This chapter will concentrate on three interrelated aspects of Christian
friendship in this world theorized and represented in Latin and French writings of the twelfth and thirteenth centuries: *amicitia Dei*, friendship of the
monastic community as a whole, and spiritual love or friendship of two
or a very few virtuous Christians. The reader may fault the study for
skimming over more than a millennium that separates Seneca from St.
Bernard of Clairvaux. Although many Christians and pagans mention
ideal friendships in that interval, they wrote very little on the subject *per
se* and nothing so comprehensive as the twelfth-century works of Bernard
of Clairvaux and Aelred of Rievaulx. This chapter will go back, however,
from time to time to works by earlier Christians to clarify positions in
the twelfth and thirteenth-century texts. In this chapter I have chosen the
writings of the Cistercians Bernard of Clairvaux and Aelred of Rievaulx as

---

[6] *Spiritual Friendship*, trans. Mary Eugenia Laker, Cistercian Fathers Series,
5 (Kalamazoo: Cistercian Publications, 1977), 1,28, p. 57.

the basis for much of its discussion of ideals of Christian friendships. Their works represent ideologies specific to their century and religious order that do not always reflect the views on *amicitia christiana* in other centuries or even other orders in their own time. For example, Aelred's strong argument for preferential Christian friendship, *amicitia spiritualis*, is the result of a long tradition of textual reflection dating back, at least, to St. Augustine; but the practice that he proposes as a model represents an avant-garde monasticism, quite apart from mainstream contemporary practices. Another of the twelfth-century examples examined here, the correspondence of Peter Abelard and Heloise, is certainly not entirely orthodox—for example, Heloise's first two letters express attitudes on erotic love that one would hardly think typical of a twelfth-century abbess. It must be argued in defense of the limited approach taken in this chapter that these works offer on the whole clear and intimate views into the fervent—and, often, disputational—spirit that animated Christian friendships and love in their age. In spite of their occasional eccentricities, these texts contain certain basic assumptions regarding Christian *amicitia* that are shared by almost all medieval writers on the topic.

Of no small interest here is the admission, at last, of woman into the domain of perfect friendship of the virtuous and the Good. Gender is, in principle, relatively unimportant in Christian *amicitia* as long as the partners are chaste; and because women on the path to heavenly glory reject the traditional household and marriage dominated by males, they operate, in practice, outside the social context assumed in classical *amicitia*. In theory, the Christian context affords woman equal footing with men in sublime friendship. But in practice—that is, in the texts usually composed by men—one often encounters traditional distrust of sexuality that makes *amicitia christiana* between religious man and woman seem much more of an intellectual and literary construct than a reality. Nonetheless, as Jean Leclercq maintains, the twelfth century, with its new religious orders, gives evidence of quite positive attitudes towards woman expressed in monastic writings on love between man and woman, but women are seen at a distance, as a preferred symbol for love for God.[7] In this chapter we will examine several illustrations of reserved, indeed, refined male-female models of love and friendship.

The texts discussed in this chapter include a wide variety of genres—

---

[7] Leclercq, *Monks and Love*, pp. 23 and 106.

hagiography, dialogues, epistles, chivalric romance, treatises, and popular pious tales. The kind of information on ideals of Christian friendships and love that each work provides is influenced to some extent by its genre. For example, from treatises and, sometimes, dialogues and letters of spiritual instruction we have taken for the most part theoretical principles for which the other texts provide practical illustrations. As for these illustrations, we have gleaned examples of miracles and supernatural communication relative to *amicitia Dei* mostly from hagiography and pious tales, since one of the main objectives of these genres is to publish saints' miracles. These same texts provide illustrations of saintly conduct and dealings with others which the writers offer as moral models for emulation. Aelred's dialogue, like Cicero's *Laelius*, presents a comprehensive example of the practice of true friendship between two men. In the epistolary exchange between Abelard and Heloise, we have concentrated on the dialogic tension between two competing, mutually exclusive models of love in the first four letters, and we have attempted to interpret the letters' resolution of this conflict through prescriptive gender roles. Finally, the French Arthurian romance *The Quest of the Holy Grail* offers for the following discussion spiritual fictions, or 'semblances,' of practice in several varieties of spiritual friendship and female-male love which stand in opposition to fictions of the Round Table's futile, this-worldly companionship and chivalric love.

God's love is primary to *amicitia christiana*. It is a precondition and, at the same time, the goal of Christian love of fellowmen in general, fraternal friendship among those in a religious community, and spiritual love or friendship between individuals. God favors mortals with His love and grace even before these are merited. Mortals gain merit and reciprocate after the fact by loving God and fellow humans. In one of his Latin letters, St. Bernard of Clairvaux (1090-1153) maintains that God, in first loving all mortals, gives them the reason and power to love Him in return and that those who requite His love receive even more of it:

> Let no one who loves God have any doubt that God loves him. The love of God for us precedes our love for Him and it also follows it. How could He be reluctant to love us in return for our love when He loved us even when we did not love Him? I say He loved us. As a pledge of His love you have the Holy Spirit, and you have the faithful witness to it in Jesus,

Jesus crucified. A double and irrefutable argument of God's love for us. Christ died and so deserved our love. The Holy Spirit works upon us and makes us love Him. Christ has given us a reason for loving Himself, and the Holy Spirit the power to love Him. The one commends His great love to us, the other gives it.... Loved we love in return, and loving we deserve to be still more loved.[8]

Above and beyond the divine gift of love bestowed on all, God singles out some men and women as recipients of special favor or gifts to quicken their love and bring them closer to Him. St. Paul's conversion on the road to Damascus exemplifies this favor, the loving action of God Who chooses and seizes a single heart. In commenting upon Paul's testimony concerning his conversion—to wit, that moment when he was caught up into paradise, where he heard arcane words which man is not permitted to speak (2 Corinthians 12,2-4)—St. Cyprian (third century) says that Paul arrived "at such splendor [claritas] as to become a friend of God [amicus Dei]."[9] Cyprian's use of amicus Dei means in this context the chosen one's being drawn up by and to God, a taste of paradise, and, also, the supernatural powers that Paul received as additional gifts from his infinitely superior friend through the Holy Spirit.

Amicitia Dei is the reciprocal love of God and a mortal. After God touches a mortal, the responsive man or woman attempts to know, with additional divine aid, the heavenly source of affection. In one of his letters, Bernard speaks of four steps of loving God that culminate in the face-to-face contemplation of God in the afterlife:

> At first a man loves himself for his own sake. He is flesh and is able only to know himself. But when he sees that he cannot subsist of himself, then he begins by faith to seek and love God as necessary for himself. And so in the second stage he loves God, not yet for God's sake, but for his own sake. However, when, on account of his own necessity, he begins to meditate, read, pray, and obey, he becomes accustomed little by little to know God and consequently to delight in Him. When he has tasted and found how sweet is the Lord he passes to the third stage, wherein he loves God for God's sake and not for his own. And there he remains, for I doubt whether the fourth stage has ever been fully reached in this life by any man, the stage, that is, wherein a man loves himself only for God's sake. Let those say who have experienced it; I confess that to me it seems impossible. It will come about, doubtless, when the good and faithful servant shall have been brought into the joy of his

[8] *The Letters of St. Bernard of Clairvaux*, trans. Bruno Scott James (Chicago: Henry Regnery, 1953), letter 109, pp. 162-63. Cf. John 4,7-21.

[9] Cited by Peter Brown, *The Making of Late Antiquity* (Cambridge: Harvard University Press, 1978), p. 119, note 31.

Lord and become inebriated with the fulness of the house of God. For he will then be wholly lost in God as one inebriated and henceforth cleave to Him as if one in spirit with Him, forgetful, in a wonderful manner, of himself and, as it were, completely out of himself.[10]

In comparing the development described in this passage to Aristotelian-Ciceronian *amicitia*, one can see that Bernard's steps coincide in part with the hierarchical division of the classical model and transcend it. The partial correspondence is not fortuitous, for, as Jean Leclercq has noted, Bernard frequently quotes terms or formulas from *Laelius* in his writings. According to Leclercq, Bernard transforms classical *amicitia perfecta* by replacing Ciceronian virtue with love of God.[11] The first stage that Bernard mentions is self-love, which the ancients considered a prerequisite to *amicitia*. The second and third steps coincide with Aristotle's classification of ordinary friendships—that is, those based on necessity or utility and on pleasure, sweetness. Commentators on the final step in Bernard's ladder point out that even though Bernard speaks of the soul's cleaving to God in heaven "as if one in spirit with Him," he does not mean that the soul merges with God or becomes God, but only that it becomes *like* or *as if* one spirit with God. In Aristotelian-Ciceronian *amicitia perfecta*, the friends become so similar in virtue and wisdom that they are *like* a single mind and spirit in two bodies.

Perfect friendship between a mortal and God at the top of Bernard's ladder is not fully realized in a man's or woman's lifetime. Nevertheless, on earth the friend gets occasional glimpses of the divine, and God manifests His love by supernatural signs. Let us look now at a literary example which illustrates the highest this-worldly stage of *amicitia Dei*. In the incomplete Latin *Life of Christina of Markyate*, composed in the second half of the twelfth century by an anonymous writer who probably knew the English recluse Christina (ca. 1096-ca. 1156), the titles "amica Dei" and "amica Jhesu Christi" are accompanied in the narrative by miracles and visions that illustrate the effects and intermittent illuminations of

---

[10] *Letters of St. Bernard*, letter 12 (ca. 1125), pp. 46-47. This letter is number 11 in the Latin edition of Bernard's epistles. See, also, the four steps of love in Bernard's *De diligendo Deo* (written between 1126 and 1141), chapters 8-10: *Treatises II: The Steps of Humility and Pride. On Loving God*, trans. M. Ambrose Conway, Cistercian Fathers Series, 13 (Kalamazoo: Cistercian Publications, 1980), pp. 115-21. Bernard appended most of this letter to *On Loving God*, pp. 125-32.

[11] *Monks and Love*, pp. 62-63.

God's friendship on earth.[12] In the first instance in which Christina is called "amica Dei" (pages 118-19), because of her devotion to God, He decides to show all just how great her merit is in His sight. He sends St. Margaret in a vision to a woman suffering from epilepsy, and the heavenly messenger instructs her to go to Christina, who cures the woman with water blessed in the Trinity's name; during the blessing and cure, Christina sees the spirit of an apostle near the patient (120-21). Through the Virgin Mary, sent in another vision, God cures His *amica* of her own malady, a sort of paralysis (122-23). In this context God gives the living *amica Dei* supernatural gifts, through the medium of spiritual beings, as signs of His love. In another instance the hagiographer calls Christina "amica Jhesu Christi" when the archfiend tries to defeat her through lustful temptation, evil thoughts, and rumors about unchastity (130-31; see pp. 114-19 for a description of her struggle with devil-sent lust.) Here she overcomes the devil's power through Christ's friendship. Such examples are typical of the effect of *amicitia Dei* in saints' lives: God shows His friendship in this world through rewards and aid, beyond the grace granted to all, for those who merit extra gifts because of their proven love or their potential for responding to divine love.

The fourteenth-century collection of Latin prose stories about St. Francis of Assisi (ca. 1182-1226) and his associates, *The Little Flowers*, tells of similar and other supernatural benefits accorded to God's friends: speaking in tongues, miraculous healing, and the driving out of demons as gifts of the Holy Spirit, apparitions of Christ, the Virgin, saints, and angels, levitation, telepathy, communication at a distance, etc. For example, in regard to Brother Silvester, one of Francis' companions, *The Little Flowers* reports that "the Holy Spirit made him remarkably deserving of divine communications, and he conversed with God many times," and he "spoke with God as one friend to another, as Moses did" (see Exodus 33,11.) Brother Giles, another of Francis' companions, and St. Louis of France conversed by means of telepathy during a visit.[13]

---

[12] *The Life of Christina of Markyate, A Twelfth Century Recluse*, ed. and trans. C. H. Talbot (Oxford: Clarendon Press, 1959). Subsequent references appear in the text with page numbers within parentheses.

[13] *The Little Flowers of St. Francis. First Complete Edition. An Entirely New Version with Twenty Additional Chapters*, trans. Raphael Brown (Garden City: Image Books, 1958), chapters 16 (p. 74), 1 (p. 41), and 34 (pp. 122-23), respectively. Brother Hugolino of Monte Santa Maria (or of Monte Giorgio) composed the Latin original of *The Little Flowers* after 1327, and an

Peter Brown maintains that Christians of the third and fourth centuries made similar claims of the extraordinary benefits of *amicitia Dei* in order to demonstrate the superiority of certain friends of God over pagan religious rivals and, hence, the superior power offered by Christianity.[14] Proof of miracles remains in the present day an essential criterion for canonization in the Catholic Church. And in the United States today, many media evangelists claim to possess some of the same God-given powers found in the New Testament and early and medieval hagiographic accounts, such as the power to defeat the devil, the gift of seeing events that are happening elsewhere or will happen, divine visions and conversations, and the ability to read the secret thoughts of others, to convert unbelievers, and to intercede between mortals and God. It is interesting to note that St. Clare, another of St. Francis' friends, was designated the patron saint of television in 1958 because of her supernatural experience in communication at a distance.[15]

The Christian explanation of miracles associated with *amicitia Dei* runs counter to the rationalism of classical philosophy. Ancient philosophers show some interest in prodigies, but they usually explain—for example, Cicero in his *On Divination* 2,49-69—exceptional phenomena as natural accidents. In *amicitia Dei*, however, miracles are visible signs by which God manifests His love. Christian miracles have, therefore, a rational basis in God's will. Moreover, Christian miracles have an authoritative textual basis in the Bible: miraculous occurrences which serve to confirm *amicitia Dei* in saints' lives and popular pious tales can be traced for the most part to similar events recorded there.

On earth *amicitia Dei* is necessarily accompanied by the Christian's spiritual love or *amicitia* for mortals in general, which we will call 'fraternal charity.' Christ's two divine commandments are to love God and to love one's neighbor as oneself. In following these commandments, the Christian responds to the same divine love in two aspects—first, God's charity or love for each mortal, and second, His love of all. God grants the unmerited gift of grace to all. Christians therefore imitate God in granting

anonymous translator made an abridged Italian version around 1370-1385.

[14] *Making of Late Antiquity*, p. 64.

[15] *Little Flowers*, chap. 35, pp. 123-24.

their spiritual love and goodwill, fraternal charity, freely to all, good and bad, friends and enemies. Ancient philosophers wrote of humans' general (but not spiritual) love for their species as a natural tendency,[16] yet for these same philosophers it would be irrational and perverse to love wicked or foolish persons. But Christ, Who loved the sinner, taught precisely this. By granting charity to all, a Christian gains merit in God's sight, since theology teaches that this is how God loves.

Nevertheless, just as God finds some mortals more worthy of His love because of their capacity to respond and, consequently, grants them special favor beyond what others receive, so do Christians sometimes love in greater or lesser degrees according to an estimate of the recipient's openness to love and her or his goodness. In paradise divine love, or the Holy Spirit, binds together the Trinity, the orders of angels, and the select community of blessed souls. But there, too, those in the celestial hierarchy and the blessed closest to the Trinity are the most fully loved. Fraternal charity on earth mirrors this heavenly concord and, also, heaven's gradations of affection. In the historical development of Christianity, fraternal charity took on a special, rather closed form in the institution of the monastic community, a microcosmos of universal spiritual love, a proving ground for charity, and a preparation for the heavenly community. St. Bernard relates charity within the monastery to the perfect peace and love of paradise: "It is [charity], the mother of angels and men, who brings peace not only on earth, but even in heaven. It is she who brings God to men and reconciles men with God. It is she ... who makes those brethren with whom you once 'broke sweet bread' [in the monastery] to live together in concert."[17] Monastic charity, the sort of fraternal charity limited to those in one's house, flourishes in individual humility, and central to its perfection is the acceptance by one and all of the community's code of conduct, laws, and distribution of authority. In written monastic rules most elements of competition and distinction among the rank and file which are sources of interpersonal friction in the world outside are excluded. The religious community is conceived ideally to be a single body and spirit, a whole unit of monastic friendship, and God especially favors

---

[16] For example, Cicero might have been thinking of the *Nicomachean Ethics* when he wrote of "ista caritas generis humani" as a natural human tendency in *De finibus* 5,23,65.

[17] *Letters of St. Bernard*, letter 2, p. 10.

its united prayers.[18]

From the earliest writings on the cloister, monastic charity, or love for
brothers in one's house, was treated as an obligation deriving from, yet
distinct from, fraternal charity, or love for humanity. St. John Cassian
(ca. 365-435) writes on the theory and practice of monastic charity in his
sixteenth conference or dialogue in Latin titled "On Friendship," which
dates from around 426.[19] The conference is modeled on *Laelius'* dialogue
structure, and many of Cicero's ideas are 'completed' in and accommodated
to a specific context, the monastic rule of Saint Augustine. Cassian distinguishes between fraternal charity, or *agapê*, owed to all, whether good
or bad, and *diathesis*,[20] 'partiality' or 'affection' and 'virtuous disposition'
that exist among a limited number of persons alike in good conduct
(chapter XIV). In the dialogue Christ's preferential affection for John the
Evangelist illustrates *diathesis*, beyond His love for the other disciples.
As Cassian describes *diathesis*, it is not, however, one brother's preferential affection for another above all others but his partiality to each and all
brothers in his community. A monk has an obligation to cultivate *diathesis* with his monastic brothers, but not with those outside the cloister,
especially if they are not good Christians: "The word of the Gospel most
significantly expresses it by saying: 'Every one who is angry with his
brother shall be in danger of the judgment.' And so though we ought according to the rule of truth to regard every man as a brother, yet in this
passage one of the faithful and a partaker of our mode of life is denoted by
the title of brother rather than a heathen" (chapter XVII, p. 456). Cassian's advice on the cultivation of *diathesis* concentrates on not getting
angry at one's brothers, on not provoking others to anger, and on assuag-
ing anger. The practice of patient, humble silence favors *diathesis*. In his

----

[18] The Church as a whole is typically represented as a single physical and
spiritual being, the bride of Christ—for example, in the twelfth-century commentaries on the Song of Songs and Psalm 44 which Jean Leclercq studies in
Monks and Love, pp. 29-57, 114-15, and 138.

[19] Conference 16 in *The Conferences*, trans. Edgar C. S. Gibson, in *Sulpi-
tius Severus, Vincent of Lerins, John Cassian*, vol. 11 of *A Select Library of
Nicene and Post-Nicene Fathers of the Christian Church, Second Series* (New
York: The Christian Literature Company, 1894), pp. 450-60.

[20] Hélène Pétré did not include *diathesis* in her study of the Latin terminology of Christian charity from the beginnings through St. Augustine, *Caritas.
Etude sur le vocabulaire latin de la charité chrétienne*, Spicilegium Sacrum Lovaniense, Etudes et Documents, fasc. 22 (Louvain: Spicilegium Sacrum Lovaniense, 1948). In the New Testament, *agapê* also signifies God's love.

guide on monastic conduct, Cassian discourages alliances that, by becoming cliques, might disturb communal harmony, but he is not unfavorable to carefully disciplined friendships that do not threaten to result in dissension or factionalism.

Communal concord achieved through a self-contained, carefully regulated sort of monastic charity is an ideal in Christian writings that has its textual source in the Acts of the Apostles' description of the first Christian community. It is closely tied to the ideal of *amicitia Dei*, upon which it depends and towards which it tends: the peaceful religious community provides a proper context for praying to God. Like *amicitia Dei*, the closed community of charity that is the monastery demands the individual's devoted attention and free submission of the individual will to superior volition—the order's rule and authority. Following Christ's teaching on the correction of fellow Christians in Matthew 18,15-18, most monastic rules prescribe the expulsion of repeatedly disobedient and, hence, discordant brothers or sisters. Accordingly, Bernard advises an abbot to try first to bring a disobedient brother back into line through kindness, rebuke, and even punishment, and if these fail, then, in an act of charity to the community, to turn him out of the monastery as he would a heathen and a publican: "Do not have any fear that by thus preserving the peace of all at the cost of one, you will be acting contrary to charity. The malice of one brother can easily disturb the unity of the whole…. The godless ought not to be left in the domain of the just, else the just will stretch out their hands to wickedness. Better that one should perish than the unity of all."[21] One may assume that this advice applies as well to particular friends and factions which disturb the unity of monastic charity.

In his Latin prose treatise *The Mirror of Charity* (early 1140s), Aelred of Rievaulx, an acquaintance of Bernard of Clairvaux, represents monastic charity as spiritual circumcision which amputates all vices, sources of care and deviation from love of God and one's brothers in the monastery. By removing lust, anger, arrogance, and melancholy, monastic charity

---

[21] *Letters of St. Bernard*, letter 103, p. 150. This advice repeats St. Augustine's injunction—*The Rule of St. Augustine*, trans. Raymond Canning (London: Darton, Longman, and Todd, 1984), section 4,9, p. 18. St. Francis of Assisi's *Rule of 1221*, chap. 19, and *First Rule of the Third Order* (1221), chap. 7, deal with expulsion—*St. Francis of Assisi, Writings and Early Biographies. English Omnibus of the Sources for the Life of St. Francis*, ed. Marion A. Habig and trans. Raphael Brown, Benen Fahy, et al. (Chicago: Franciscan Herald Press, 1973), pp. 46 and 174.

opens the path to God through peaceful prayer.[22] According to the testimony of a novice which Aelred reports, the good life in the monastery
consists of the absence of quarrels, anger, fraud, litigation, the tumult of
the world, consideration for rank and birth, personal property, and rebel-
liousness.[23] For Aelred, fraternal charity—love for all mortals, good and
bad alike—is a limited source of joy on earth. While the charitable find
delightful and beneficial their love for good Christians, loving their enemies and sinners is only a more or less painful trial of their own virtue.
Aelred notes that Scripture orders the faithful to love all neighbors *as*
themselves, not *as much as* themselves.[24] He advises monastics to share
out their affection and goodwill among others according to what is due to
each: Christ comes first, then spiritual friends, followed by deserving
friends and kin, next those distant and less deserving, and the wicked and
enemies get what remains.[25] Aelred's comments on monastics' unequal
distribution of charity apply to specific groups ranked according to their
spatial and spiritual relationship to the cloister: the brothers in one's
house are spiritual friends, those in other monasteries, seculars, and lay
Christians outside are granted less love, and the ungodly and hard-hearted
are the least deserving. In illustrating monastic charity, Aelred cites, however, examples of preferential, one-to-one friendship in Paul and Philemon's spiritual love and in Jonathan's 'rational' love—that is, conceived
through the observation of virtue—for David.[26] As for the latter pair, one
might note that the ideal of the first Christian community's single heart
and soul in Acts 4,32 is prefigured typologically by the bonding of
David's and Jonathan's souls in 1 Samuel 18,1. In his praise of the superior benefits, delights, and love that come from life in the harmonious
community, Aelred lays the groundwork for his argument which attributes
high spiritual value to the close friendship of a very few within the cloister in his later work, *Spiritual Friendship*.

---

[22] *The Mirror of Charity*, trans. Elizabeth Connor and introduced by Charles
Dumont, Cistercian Fathers Series, 17 (Kalamazoo: Cistercian Publications,
1990), part 1, chap. 17, pp. 114-15.

[23] Ibid., part 2, chap. 17, pp. 192-200.

[24] Ibid., part 3, chap. 37, pp. 290-94.

[25] Ibid., part 3, chap. 38, pp. 294-96.

[26] Ibid., part 3, chaps. 12, pp. 242-43, and 39, p. 297.

Amicitia spiritualis is a preferential affection that joins two or a few Christian friends through the medium of God's love. Here the primary conditions are love of God, humble self-love, and charity towards others, to which is added the spiritual love, originating from God, of another for reason of her or his Christian goodness or capacity for virtue. For St. Augustine there cannot be true friendship on earth unless both parties are joined through God's love, "for true it is not but in such as Thou bindest together, cleaving unto Thee by that love which is shed abroad in our hearts by the Holy Ghost, which is given unto us."[27] Spiritual friends aid one another in discovering God and in meriting His love; they reflect, face-to-face, their love of God and of fellow mortals in an intimate manner. The few medieval writers who praise *amicitia spiritualis* deal with its value as a means to the ends of love of God, fraternal charity, and concord in a religious community or fellowship. Along with *amicitia spiritualis*, this section will discuss spiritualized *amor* between man and woman as another means to those ends.

Spiritual friendship is a late development as a formal concept, although the term *spiritualis amicitia* first appears in the writings of the Venerable Bede (ca. 672-735).[28] Christian commentators on the close friendship of monastics often warn against the spiritual dangers that it may present, such as the love of this world in the love for another flesh-and-blood being, the vices of quarreling, sexual contact, and grumbling, or factionalism in the monastic community. As Aelred warns, friendship, or the inward attachment to another, is potentially the most dangerous of affections, and although it may be useful and good, it must be used with extreme caution.[29] In early works Christian friendship for spiritual ends is not a clearly articulated concept. For example, St. Ambrose (ca. 334-397) adapted to a Christian context in his Latin treatise *The Duties of the Clergy* (*De officiis ministrorum*) many of Cicero's precepts from *De officiis* and *Laelius*, but he did not draw a clear link between Christian friendship based on mutual love of virtue and obligations and the ends of loving God and fraternal charity.[30] The first complete development of the

---

[27] *The Confessions of St. Augustine*, trans. J. G. Pilkington (New York: Liveright Publishing, 1943), 4,4,7.

[28] McGuire, *Friendship*, p. 94, notes that Bede uses "spiritualis amicitiae foedere copulatus" to describe the friendship between St. Cuthbert and a hermit.

[29] *Mirror of Charity*, part 3, chap. 25, p. 260.

[30] See Ambrose's adaptation of Cicero in *Duties of the Clergy*, in *St. Am-*

concept is Aelred of Rievaulx's Latin dialogue *Spiritual Friendship* (begun in 1147 or later and completed before his death in 1167). Aelred finds many worthwhile ideas in *Laelius*, provides scriptural and patristic evidence which supports them, and defines the activity and benefits of his hybrid *amicitia*, wherein the Ciceronian ideal is wholly recast and completed according to Christian spiritual teachings and monastic practices.

Aelred claims that in embracing a Christian friend, he is embracing Christ. While concentrating on the mutual love of two or a few individuals through Christ, he maintains throughout his treatise the larger, if limited, scope of monastic charity. The discussants in Aelred's dialogue are monks. The first sentence of book one states the three-party nature of spiritual friendship: "Here we are, you and I, and I hope a third, Christ, is in our midst."[31] This is not, however, the formula for monastic charity reduced to the minimum. Aelred distinguishes monastic charity from spiritual friendship in an important way. He describes the delight he experiences in the cloister because of the love that he and all the brothers share. But this love is different in nature from *amicitia spiritualis*, which includes "the secrets of friendship, which consists especially in the revelation of all our confidences and plans" (3,83). With Aristotle and Cicero, it will be recalled, *amicitia perfecta* necessarily includes intimacy and the unqualified exchange of confidence.

The problem that Aelred poses in the prologue and the beginning of the first book is that of a Christian reading of *Laelius*. He considers Cicero's treatise a source of delight for Christian readers, but it lacks "the sweetness of the honeycomb of Holy Scripture" (1,7) since Cicero "was unacquainted with the virtue of true friendship" (1,8), which begins, continues, and ends in Christ. The problem for Aelred then is to provide an enlightened reading wherein spiritual love corrects and completes the Ciceronian model. Aelred maintains the three Aristotelian categories of *philia* but redefines the third and highest form, friendship of good men similar in

---

brose, *Select Works and Letters*, trans. H. De Romestin, vol. 10 of *A Select Library of Nicene and Post-Nicene Fathers of the Church, Second Series* (Grand Rapids: W. B. Eerdmans, 1955), book 3, chap. 22, pp. 87-89. For an anthology of Latin patristic writings on Christian friendship, see *Agostino di Ippona. L'amicizia cristiana. Antologia dalle opere e altri testi di Ambrogio di Milano, Gerolamo et Paolino di Nola*, ed. L. F. Pizzolato (Turin: Paravia, 1973).

[31] *Spiritual Friendship* 1,1. Subsequent references to book and chapter in Mary E. Laker's translation (see note 6) are given within parentheses.

virtue, in terms of Christian virtue: "Carnal [friendship] springs from mutual harmony in vice; the worldly is enkindled by the hope of gain; and the spiritual is cemented by similarity of life, morals, and pursuits among the just" (1,38). Such similarity clearly implies the monastic community as spiritual friendship's context. He redirects Ciceronian *amicitia vera* heavenward:

> For spiritual friendship, which we call true, should be desired, not for consideration of any worldly advantage or for any extrinsic cause, but from the dignity of its own nature and the feelings of the human heart, so that its fruition and reward is nothing other than itself. Whence the Lord in the Gospel says: "I have appointed you that you should go, and should bring forth fruit," that is, that you should love one another. For true friendship advances by perfecting itself, and the fruit is derived from feeling the sweetness of that perfection. And so spiritual friendship among the just is born of a similarity in life, morals, and pursuits, that is, it is a mutual conformity in matters human and divine united with benevolence and charity. (1,45-46)

One should note that Aelred, in writing of spiritual friendship's intrinsic desirability and its reward as itself, does not mean to indicate that it is wholly self-contained or self-sufficient or that it is an end in itself. Later he maintains that this personal relationship contributes directly to the whole community's spiritual perfection and to *amicitia Dei*. The partners are compatible because of similar character, good conduct, and spiritual goals. The second half of the last sentence cited above is a quotation from *Laelius* 6,20, which reads "est enim amicitia nihil aliud nisi divinarum humanarumque rerum cum benevolentia et caritate consensio" ("for friendship is nothing else than an accord in all things, human and divine, conjoined with mutual goodwill and affection.") St. Augustine, in quoting the same Ciceronian definition in his letters, interpreted it to mean that there can be no consensus between men on earthly matters unless first they agree perfectly on divine or spiritual ones.[32] In other words, only those with orthodox religious beliefs can be true friends, and they agree on human matters because their tastes and opinions are formed by those beliefs. Aelred accepts the Ciceronian definition only on this condition and with the further qualification of the term *caritas* as the exclusion of every vice (1,47).

---

[32] Harald Hagendahl, *Augustine and the Latin Classics*, Studia Graeca et Latina Gothoburgensia, 20, 2 vols. (Göteborg: Elanders Boktryckeri Aktiebolag, 1967), vol. 1, pp. 94-96, and vol. 2, pp. 523-24.

The principal virtues that maintain *amicitia spiritualis* are those moral characteristics from Plato's *Symposium* 196 B-197 B and the *Nicomachean Ethics* which Cicero recalls in his *De inventione* 2,53 and *De officiis* 1,5 and 3,33: prudence or wisdom, justice, fortitude, and temperance (1,49 and 2,49). Although Aelred does not gloss the four virtues in Christian terms here, in another work, *Jesus at the Age of Twelve*, he explains that they are forms of charity practiced under different circumstances.[33] In *The Mirror of Charity* he glosses the four as specifically Christian virtues which aid the highest virtue, charity, wherein they find their perfection.[34] In medieval literature these four often appear accompanied by the theological virtues of faith, hope, and charity, as with their personification in canto 29 of Dante's *Purgatorio*.

In the second book, Aelred's standard for measuring goodness in spiritual friends tends towards the Ciceronian 'middle-to-high' grade rather than absolute perfection. Aelred repeats the commonplace that only the good can be friends (2,41). His definition of 'good' is important as it relates to Cicero's practical standard:

> I am not cutting 'good' so finely as do some who call no one 'good' unless he is lacking no whit in perfection. We call a man 'good' who, according to the limits of our mortality, "living soberly and justly and godly in this world," is resolved neither to ask others to do wrong nor to do wrong himself at another's request. (2,43)

The first sentence recalls Cicero's objection to impractical standards of perfection in wisdom and goodness. The last part of the second sentence also recalls Cicero. But the heart of the definition indicates a Christian measure, according to St. Paul, of sobriety, righteousness, and piety that appears much more within human reach than even Cicero's scaled-down Stoic standard. Aelred does not aim at the highest level of saintliness in his evaluation of candidates for spiritual friendship. He allows for the inclusion of many more good friends than could possibly be admitted according to Cicero's measure of goodness.

As mentioned earlier, the description of the first Christian community in the Acts of the Apostles 4,32—"cor unum et anima una"—represents the ideal of the monastic community. In describing spiritual friendship, Aelred uses the same words: "And thus, friend cleaving to friend in the spirit of Christ is made with Christ but one heart and one soul" (2,21).

---

[33] See *Spiritual Friendship*, p. 61, note 43.
[34] *Mirror of Charity*, part 1, chap. 31, p. 141.

His identification of the essence of monastic charity with that of *amicitia spiritualis* is significant, since the latter develops and is refined only within the community. His model of spiritual friendship necessarily involves mutual confidences and private benefits not shared in practice by other brothers, not wholly part of the monastery's single heart and soul. Nevertheless, spiritual friendship has a positive effect on the community of monastic friends: Aelred expresses his joy as he walks around the cloister and sees no one whom he does not love, no one who does not love him (3,82). He claims here that spiritual friendship plays its part in the realization of monastic charity's ideal of a heart and soul shared by all.

Further, he presents spiritual friendship as preparation for *amicitia Dei*: "Friendship is a stage bordering upon that perfection which consists in the love and knowledge of God, so that man from being a friend of his fellowman becomes the friend of God" (2,14). The perfection of loving and knowing God pertains to the afterlife, and the joy of spiritual friendship is a foretaste of the bliss that will follow in heaven. It is possible to understand Aelred's claims of the supreme benefits of spiritual friendship in the monastery not only as evidence in support of the concept which he is elaborating but, also, as key elements in his rhetoric of recruitment: during this period of active recruitment of adults by the Cistercians and other new orders, Aelred's description of the unalloyed sweetness of spiritual friendship, a part of heaven on earth and a way to paradise, might appear very appealing to those outside the cloister. One finds in this century many examples of 'friendship' letters of conversion in which a monk addresses a former companion living in the world to whom he describes the advantages of monastic life in attempting to bring him into his community.[35]

In regard to practice, Aelred qualifies and completes some of the practical considerations on the activity and preservation of friendship in *Laelius*. For example, Cicero said that in defense of a friend one must be willing to put his own reputation at limited risk. Aelred modifies the nature, rather than the limits, of this duty in maintaining that a spiritual friend stops his support at the point where he risks harming his own soul through sin (2,69). In the third and final book, Aelred repeats *Laelius*' process of selection, probation, and admission of friends, but he relies mostly on Scripture and the Fathers and only occasionally upon *Laelius*

---

[35] Leclercq, *Monks and Love*, p. 10.

for his choice of characteristics that distinguish the good candidate for spiritual friendship from the bad. For example, he discusses attitudes and acts on the part of a candidate which will cause friendship to fail, all of which come from Ecclesiasticus: upbraiding, reproach, arrogance, disclosing secrets, and backbiting (3,22). Such traits incompatible with *amicitia* may be revealed during the probationary period, but Aelred points out that earlier, in the selection stage, one should reject out of hand those who demonstrate irascibility, fickleness, distrustfulness, belligerence, and loquacity which will eventually lead to unfriendly actions (3,55).

Near the end of the dialogue, Aelred speaks of himself and two unnamed monks to illustrate the process, delights, and success of spiritual friendship in the cloister (3,119-27). The first man died before Aelred had a chance to test him fully, but Aelred's practical dealings with the second show the four stages—selection, probation, admission, and near perfection—of their relationship, which was for the most part one between master and disciple. Aelred met the second man while the latter was a youth, and he recruited him from abroad into his community. He selected the youth because he admired his humility, obedience, gentleness, reserved speech and manner, and an absence of indignation, rancor, and murmuring—qualities which one can identify as virtues in the monastic milieu described by John Cassian. Jean Leclercq has noted that treatises on the formation of adult novices comprised a new sort of monastic writing which developed in this period when the new orders preferred the recruitment of adults over children.[36] Aelred was a novice master in the 1140s before becoming an abbot. His account of his guidance of the new monk offers a personalized, anecdotal example of this didactic genre. In the cloister the youth at first developed the virtues of temperance and fortitude, for which he won the admiration of his brothers and brought honor and joy to Aelred. The probation was distinctly monastic, as Aelred tested the candidate's strength of character by forcing upon him the burden of the subpriorship of the community. The imposition of this burden caused the younger man to reveal his doubts and fears to his senior, and Aelred responded by confiding in him to a limited degree. After a time Aelred began to reveal some of his innermost secrets to the youth, and finding him to be most discreet, loyal, and responsive over a long period of exchange and testing, Aelred admitted him as a friend to his unreserved confidence.

---

[36] Leclercq, *Monks and Love*, p. 15.

The final stage of their friendship was near perfection in mutual trust, aid, and solace. In Aelred's old age, the younger partner supported his senior. *The Mirror of Charity* 3,39 suggests the unwritten conclusion to their exemplary spiritual friendship: eternal, mutual enjoyment of their company as equals in the presence of God in paradise.

Aelred's praise of *amicitia spiritualis* is qualified, for the relative perfection of the spiritual bond between friends depends entirely upon the degrees of perfection of love between God and mortal and of charity among brothers in the monastery, the ideals towards which it tends. It should be clear that unlike its near equivalent in Aristotelian-Ciceronian *amicitia perfecta*, in Aelred's construction of *amicitia* the link between spiritual friends founded on love of goodness in one another has no value if it is considered in strict isolation.

Aelred's portrayal of *amicitia spiritualis* and his arguments for it cannot, unlike love for God or for monastic brothers as a whole, apply to all or even most brothers in the monastery. What he describes is clearly an exceptional instance reserved for very few monastics, the most virtuous, disciplined, and privileged. The required circumstances are exceptional in the monastery: spiritual friends must have a place where they can withdraw from their brothers in order to exchange confidences (Aelred was privileged to have in later life separate quarters within the community in which to receive special friends.) Even more importantly, Aelred's personal example of self-discipline and scrupulous attention to the gradual unfolding of spiritual friendship does not apply to all monastics. The shared struggles, confidences, and benefits of less disciplined and scrupulous friends than Aelred and his companions would perhaps become ends in themselves and a distraction from monastic charity and love of God. Aelred was keenly aware of these limitations. Although Aelred does not write of the problem of potential jealousy in brothers excluded from mutual confidences and favors, his follower Walter Daniel shows in his *Life of Ailred of Rievaulx* examples of brothers' jealousy towards Aelred and his intimates which hardly contributed to an atmosphere of paradise on earth. One must conclude that Aelred's *Spiritual Friendship* represents a unique case, not a general tendency in his or other religious orders of his time.

Although the scarcity of manuscripts of *Spiritual Friendship* in monastic librairies outside England would seem to indicate that the work did not enjoy widespread distribution on the Continent, there is evidence that the work was read and valued highly.[37] In his Latin prose treatise *De amicitia christiana et de dilectione Dei et proximi* (written between 1185 and 1195), Peter of Blois[38] adapted—or, rather, plagiarized—almost three-quarters of *Spiritual Friendship* without mentioning Aelred. There also exist four Latin versions of compendia of Aelred's dialogue.[39]

The pattern and stages of spiritual friendship which Aelred describes are not limited to Christian writings which have an obvious connection to Aristotelian-Ciceronian *amicitia vera*. Two texts which we shall study shortly—again, *The Life of Christina of Markyate*, and *The Quest of the Holy Grail*—show no interest in ancient philosophy or in Aelred's rational spiritual program that joins classical and Christian traditions; yet they present illustrations of spiritualized friendship which follow much the same process of development that characterizes Aelred's model. In these two texts, as with Aelred's, there is, first, a selection based upon evidence of Christian virtue or a capacity for virtue that is deserving of God's love. Then there is an extended period of probation during which both partners increase in virtue through mutual aid and prayer. Thirdly, spiritual friendship is confirmed. Aelred served as selector, tester, and approver in *Spiritual Friendship*, but in the other two cases which we shall examine, God directly performs these three functions rather than leaving them to human judgment. After confirmation, the friends grant one another total confidence in earthly and spiritual matters, and their mutual affection grows, as does their friendship with God. In their confident love for one another because God has shown signs of His love for each, they are like one in spirit on earth. The final step, foretold in *The Quest of the Holy Grail*, is the eternal reunion of the friends in God's presence in paradise—the Christian *summum bonum*. It is this process and these characteristics which some medieval writers praise as the special gift of spiritual friendship from on high.

---

[37] McGuire, *Friendship*, p. 330.

[38] See edition by M. M. Davy, *Un traité de l'amour du XIIe siècle: Pierre de Blois* (Paris: E. de Boccard, 1932). For a study of Peter of Blois's plagiarism, see E. Vansteenberghe, "Deux théoriciens de l'amitié au XIIe siècle: Pierre de Blois et Aelred de Riéval," *Revue des sciences religieuses* 12 (1932): 572-88, and Philippe Delhaye, "Deux adaptations du *De amicitia* de Cicéron au XIIe siècle," *Recherches de théologie ancienne et médiévale* 15 (1948): 304-31.

[39] Anselme Hoste, "Le traité pseudo-augustinien *De amicitia*. Un résumé d'un ouvrage authentique d'Aelred de Rievaulx," *Revue des études augustiniennes* 6 (1960): 155-60.

Aelred attributes no miracles to spiritual friendship, nor do the other illustrations which follow. *The Life of Christina of Markyate* and *The Quest of the Holy Grail* offer many examples of miracles as benefits of *amicitia Dei*, and they also depict visions, a sign of *amicitia Dei*, associated with spiritual friendship. In this respect, spiritualized friendship is represented as taking a small part in the mystical communion of *amicitia Dei* on earth.

Aelred's personal exemplum of *amicitia spiritualis* begins with disparity between the partners. When Aelred and the youth whom he befriended first met, Aelred was the closer of the two to God, and his charity towards others was proven, for he had lived long as a contemplative in the monastery where he held a position of responsibility. He served as his younger comrade's spiritual mentor and examiner. After the confirmation of their friendship, however, they were nearly equal in virtue—that is, in good conduct and spirituality. In the other two literary examples which we shall examine, spiritual friendship begins with very unequal partners who also end up more nearly equal in virtue. Along with these two texts, we shall study in the correspondence of Peter Abelard and Heloise a model of spiritual love between man and woman as distinct from friendship.

The recluse Christina of Markyate and Geoffrey, Abbot of St. Albans, are dissimilar in sex, Christian virtues, and social position. Christina plays the dominant role in their relationship of mutual affection and devotion, for her hagiographer clearly shows her to be the more humble, virtuous, and beloved of God of the two. Through her determination and, sometimes, ruses, she preserves her virginity of mind and body, which she vowed to God when she was very young, against male lust, her family's insistence that she marry, and the interior assault of lustful thoughts inspired by the devil; but the main support of her virtue is divine protection. She does not need Geoffrey to maintain her pious life: God, Who manifests His love through many favors, makes her as self-sufficient as a living saint can be. Geoffrey, her *dilectus*, *familiaris*, and *amicus*, is a sinner saved through her intercession with God. His sin of pride disturbs, or would have disturbed, the fraternal harmony of his monastery: the hagiographer says that the proud abbot, before meeting Christina, was about to embark on a major enterprise in his house without consulting his brethren (pages 138-39). Geoffrey needs Christina's spiritual assistance in order to overcome this and other faults. Because God favors her, she is able to aid the abbot through prayer and encouragement in gaining a place in paradise.

The portrayal of Christina as a female intermediary between God and Geoffrey cannot but evoke the function of the Virgin Mary as mediatrix and redemptrix. In the medieval hagiographical genre, women saints are always in some manner living images of the Virgin. Christina's media-trix-redemptrix role figures so prominently in the text as a given of the genre that one is obliged to see in her and Geoffrey's relationship primarily the Virgin's love in the person of Christina for fallen man and, secondarily, spiritual friendship.

At the moment when Christina first learns through a vision of the abbot and his sin, she is in the company of a few other religious women who want to live and meditate in reclusion. The small group which Christina heads needs material support and protection. God, her beloved and loving spouse ("dilectus et dilector sponsor"), keeps her in poverty, which lacks "those things the absence of which increases rather than lessens virtue" (132-33), so that her *spiritualis amor* may remain fervent. Nonetheless, God provides her community with necessary material support in the person of Geoffrey, and He initiates their friendship: "… it was through this man that God decided to provide for her needs and it was through His virgin that he decided to bring about this man's full conversion" (134-35). The hagiographer describes Christina and Geoffrey's bond as "mutual love in Christ" ("mutua … in Christo dileccio," 174-75). The benefits that the two mortal friends provide one another are not of the same nature: "The affection [*amor*] was mutual, but different according to their standards of holiness. He supported her in worldly matters: she commended him to God more earnestly in her prayers" (138-41).

On one hand, their relationship involves the soliciting and granting of material benefits and protection in the social sense of *amicitia* common in medieval writing: Christina benefits from the aid of her *amicus* in the establishment and maintenance of her small community. This social sense of *amicitia* is prevalent in medieval 'friendship' letters, as in many of the thirteenth-century Latin epistles of students and benefactors which Jean Leclercq has analyzed.[40] On the other hand, the hagiographer de-emphasizes this aspect of their *amicitia* and the importance of Geoffrey's material benefaction, and he emphasizes the spiritual benefits which Christina provides, benefits which Geoffrey explicitly requests. She prays for her

---

[40] Leclercq, "L'amitié dans les lettres," pp. 399 and 402-09.

friend's salvation unselfishly, fervently: "As she became aware that he was making every effort to become more spiritual, she was so zealous on his account that she prayed for him tearfully almost all the time and in God's presence considered him more than herself. And, as she admitted, there was none of those who were dear to her for whom she could plead to God with such devotion and constant prayer" (142-45). Geoffrey plays the lesser role of the object towards which his *amica* directs her benevolence and beneficence, an object which in its spiritual improvement reflects her own virtue and divine favor. Besides praying to God, she guides, aids, and, frequently, rebukes Geoffrey.

A second vision, in which Christina sees the Holy Spirit possess Geoffrey and save his soul, indicates in regard to each of them gifts associated with *amicitia Dei*. This point in the narrative marks the divine confirmation of their *amicitia spiritualis*. Thereafter they enjoy total mutual confidence and greater spiritual love for one another because of God's proven love for them. The following passage is reminiscent of St. Augustine's inspired conversations with his mother St. Monica: "Filled with joy at this [vision], she cherished him and venerated a fellow and a companion of heavenly not earthly glory, and took him to her bosom in a closer bond of holy affection. For who shall describe the longings, the sighs, the tears they shed as they sat and discussed heavenly matters? Who shall put into words how they despised the transitory, how they yearned for the everlasting? Let this be left to someone else" (156-57). They look forward to the final steps in the perfection of their spiritual bond—death and reunion in paradise.

Often in hagiography a saintly character must overcome false public accusation of impropriety, even wantonness. The author of *The Life of Christina of Markyate* and Aelred in *Spiritual Friendship* clearly intended to represent ideals of moral conduct and spirituality. Christina's hagiographer writes, however, of rumors that her love for Geoffrey was earthly (172-73). His account gainsays, of course, this accusation of impurity, just as it shows aspersions on Christina's chastity before she became a recluse to be false. As for Aelred, his biographer Walter Daniel writes that the abbot's friendships were a source of resentment in his monastery, and some recent Aelredian studies write of his supposed homosexuality.[41] Even if unfounded, old rumors and modern psychological speculation un-

---

[41] See McGuire, *Friendship*, pp. 331-32 and 493, notes 107-09.

derscore a problem of spiritualized love or friendship—possible suspicion
or accusations of worldliness—which medieval saints or their biographers
were often obliged to confront head-on, as with Christina's hagiographer,
or to deal with in other ways.

The intimacy of spiritualized friendship is especially problematic in the
case of a female-male pair. For instance, in his teachings and by his example St. Francis of Assisi (ca. 1182-1226) appears to have been extremely cautious in regard to the public image of his relationship with St.
Clare (1193 or 1194-1253). He was responsible in large part for her becoming a nun and for the foundation of the Poor Clares,[42] and they were
friends. But in thirteenth and fourteenth-century writings by or about St.
Francis, one finds not proof of their intimacy and fervent, mutual spiritual
love but, rather, a carefully guarded distance and an impersonal sort of relationship, particularly on Francis' part. The records of Francis' visits to
Clare indicate that they met less and less as time progressed, and one reads
that Francis undertook some of these visits secretly. In the rules for his
order, Francis exhorts his brothers to avoid woman, including cloistered
nuns, because of the vow of chastity and the possibility of scandal.[43] In
avoiding even the appearance of intimacy, albeit of a spiritual sort, that
might attract notice as in Christina and Geoffrey's case, Francis and his
hagiographers offered a model for emulation. Further, his few extant writings to Clare are not personal messages for her but instruction addressed
to her as abbess and the nuns in her convent. Even in writing he seems to
avoid singling her out for conversation. The written image of Francis and
Clare's irreproachable friendship in Christ—no spiritual sighs, no inspired
intimate dialogues—is consistent with Francis' teachings on the renunciation of this-worldly values. Francis follows literally Christ's exhortation
to "love your enemies and pray for those who persecute you" in Matthew
5,44. For him, the sort of human friendship most deserving of praise,
since it earns the greatest merit in God's eyes, is that of one's enemies,
whom Francis calls friends: "Therefore, our friends are those who for no
reason cause us trouble and suffering, shame or injury, pain or torture,
even martyrdom and death. It is these we must love, and love very much,

---

[42] Thomas of Celano's *First Life of St. Francis* (1228-1229), in *St. Francis
of Assisi, Writings and Early Biographies*, p. 244.

[43] *Rule of 1221*, chaps. 12 and 13, in *St. Francis of Assisi, Writings and
Early Biographies*. See, also, chap. 11 of *The Rule of 1223*.

because for all they do to us we are given eternal life."[44] There can be no doubt, however, that Francis and Clare valued their personal association, but they—and his biographers—kept it from public view. This discretion in dealing with male-female *amicitia* or *amor* of a spiritual sort almost equals in degree the chivalric lover Lancelot's exemplary discretion in not speaking about his love of Guinevere in the *Prose Lancelot* which will be discussed in the following chapter.

In reference to the beatific vision, both *amor* and *amicitia* can be used to name the Trinity's self-contemplation, the angels' and souls' contemplation of and communion with the Trinity, and a soul's relationship to other souls and angels. On earth, too, *amor* and *amicitia* share many of the same characteristics and they overlap,[45] but they are different manifestations of affection with different sources. Whereas *amicitia* derives principally from mutual admiration of goodness and its essence, according to Aristotle, is more in loving than in being loved, *amor* is above all motivated by the subject's desire to possess the beloved object.

The Latin correspondence of Peter Abelard (1079-1142) and Heloise (ca. 1100-1163) loudly proclaims their worldly love's scandal, which it uses to arrive at an ideal of chaste spiritualized love.[46] A detailed examination of this complex and problematic literary work would take us far from the subject of spiritual preferential affection on earth. But it seems appropriate to point out that the letters' gender-specific illustrations of erotic and of spiritualized love, unlike the preceding examples of *amicitia spiritualis*, can only be imagined to apply in their time to a male-female relationship. The following discussion of the source and nature of spiritualized male-female love, rather than friendship, in the letters will be limited to some general observations and a few of many possible interpretations. The correspondence dates from the second quarter of the twelfth century, although it took its present form in manuscript in the thirteenth. The question of authorship is a subject of scholarly debate today, as are many other important particulars of the correspondence, including the questions of why it was written and for what audience. A radical position in this debate claims

---

[44] *Rule of 1221*, chap. 22, "An Exhortation to the Friars."

[45] "The fountain and source of friendship is love. There can be love without friendship, but friendship without love is impossible"—Aelred of Rievaulx, *Spiritual Friendship* 3,2.

[46] See *The Letters of Abelard and Heloise*, trans. Betty Radice (Harmondsworth, Eng.: Penguin, 1974).

that Abelard is the sole author.[47] The correspondents' autobiographical account of erotic love and of spiritualized love can be read in large part as a personalized representation of two Catholic archetypes: the fall of man and woman through Eve and their redemption through Mary's love. The history of Abelard and Heloise's worldly love and his career as a theologian recounted in the document that precedes the letters, Abelard's *History of Misfortunes (Historia calamitatum)*, is scandalous in all respects. His opponents condemn his theological positions time after time as heretical, and in regard to the scandal of their carnal love, Abelard repeatedly insists on his former uncontrollable desire to possess Heloise. Because of his lust, their marriage offends God: Abelard commits sacrilege by copulating with her in the convent at Argenteuil. Such is the condition of their fall. Finally, his castration and their withdrawal to separate monasteries curtail their lustful love and unchaste marriage. In itself, however, the curtailing of their sinful activities—according to Abelard, God put an end to them— is not enough to save their souls. Overall in the exchange of letters, sexual scandal and redemption are rhetorical complementary opposites: the more damnable are their crimes against divine law, the more glorious will be their conversion and God's gift of salvation.

The first two letters of the abbess Heloise are an adoring woman's passionate and, at the same time, brilliantly argued pleas, full of biblical and other authoritative textual support, for a husband's and lover's consolation and guidance. Abelard's two letters of response propose for their mutual consolation and salvation a spiritual program with gender-specific roles that builds upon and purifies their former worldly relationship as lovers and their present status as spouses. He exhorts her to pray for his salvation and to encourage her nuns to pray for him as well. He cites Scripture and the Fathers extensively to demonstrate that God responds most gener-

---

[47] Other possibilities are an anonymous thirteenth-century editor, Heloise as the editor of the collection, and, of course, Abelard and Heloise. John F. Benton, who in 1972 argued in favor of an anonymous editor, more recently maintained that the correspondence is Abelard's creation written as an introduction to two of his works intended for Heloise's convent, the Paraclete—"A Reconsideration of the Authenticity of the Correspondence of Abelard and Heloise," in *Petrus Abaelardus (1079-1142): Person, Werk und Wirkung*, ed. Rudolf Thomas, Trierer Theologische Studien, 38 (Trier: Paulinus Verlag, 1980), pp. 41-52. Writing against both of Benton's positions, Peter Dronke argues that Heloise composed the three letters attributed to her in the collection—*Women Writers of the Middle Ages* (Cambridge: Cambridge University Press, 1984), pp. 107-43.

ously to the prayers of a holy woman, especially a wife, and a body of holy women, the brides of Christ. Through her devoted prayers for him, she will also win heaven for herself. In this model of spiritualized love, Abelard's role is that of a suppliant to the chaste bride Heloise, whose spiritual favors he seeks. Heloise's role, prescribed by Abelard, imitates the Mary-redemptrix prototype. Joined in spirit with the convent community conceived as the single entity of the bride of Christ, she becomes like Mary, the New Eve and mystical bride of Christ: because of her great love for fallen man, she asks the New Adam, her heavenly husband Christ, to show His mercy to man so that he may overcome his sinful nature and become like the New Adam. This complex model extends through time from the Fall, reembodied in Abelard and Heloise's carnal love, to the end of time, with their chaste spiritual love in heaven.

One might also interpret Abelard's program to be partly one of spiritualized marriage on earth. As Jo Ann McNamara has noted, chaste clerical marriage—that is, without copulation—was practiced from the early Christian period.[48] In several of his writings St. Augustine praised chaste marriage on the model of Mary and Joseph as the highest perfection of Christianity.[49] Even though the Roman Church officially condemned clerical marriages in the late eleventh century, the practice continued to a limited extent for some time. Abelard emphatically rejects Heloise's repeated pleas to offer her sweet consolation as her legal husband and to recall the past and their marriage in future letters. She argues eloquently that, by all rights, he owes this to her. For him, however, what she requests amounts to mental or spiritual unchastity. Although he claims that her present spiritual bond with Christ is her only valid marriage, he nonetheless offers her spiritual support and guidance in her holy life that seem to define his role in relation to her—and to the others in her convent—as a sort of Joseph, an earthly husband and guardian of Mary's chastity. His self-designed role of spiritual caretaker is consistent with his claim that the 'weaker sex,' more than males, needs constant supervision. As her husband before his castration, he led her to unchastity and sacrilege. Now in the spiritual role of guide and protector which he writes for himself, he insists on the perfect chastity of her heavenly marriage and

---

[48] Jo Ann McNamara, "Chaste Marriage and Clerical Celibacy," in *Sexual Practices and the Medieval Church*, ed. Vern L. Bullough and James Brundage (Buffalo: Prometheus Books, 1982), pp. 22-26.

[49] Ibid., p. 28 and p. 234, note 69.

promises to aid her in maintaining it on earth. If one recognizes the component of spiritualized marriage in Abelard's conception of spiritual love on earth, then the gender-specific role that he prescribes for Heloise, along with the other brides in her convent, serves as a necessary complement to his own.

In regard to Christian rhetoric, Abelard's first two epistles to Heloise may be understood as letters of conversion in which he would turn her through persuasion to salvation. It is apparent there that he has already undergone a complete conversion, and his letters prescribe the role that the converted Heloise is to play. He praises her for the difficult, crucial part that she as woman has in his and their salvation, and he insistently belittles himself, an impotent sinner dependent upon God and her loving prayers to turn him heavenward. In considering the exalted, Mary-like role that Abelard proposes for Heloise, one should not lose sight of the alternative, that of woman as the source of sin because she is, or was, the object of *his* lustful desire. Heloise's first two letters, in which she declares her profane love and devotion for her only husband Abelard, whom she values more than Christ, fully represent her as the carnal Eve for whose love Abelard formerly composed erotic poems and sinned. In her first two letters the image of woman who would trammel man with earthly love conforms for the most part, in spite of Heloise's extraordinary eloquence and erudition, to conventional male literary projections of Old Eve. Comparisons of vocabulary, ideas, arguments, and quotations in Heloise's letters and Abelard's writings have not proven conclusively that Heloise wrote the epistles attributed to her or that Abelard or someone else wrote or edited them. One may assume, however, that the two contradictory roles that Heloise plays in her first letters and, then, in his correspond to Abelard's contradictory views of her at two distinct stages in his life—the passionate, intelligent woman whose earthly love he won before his conversion and, after, the Mary-like bride whose pure spiritual love he wants to win.

In comparing the spiritual *amor* in Abelard's letters with Christina and Geoffrey's spiritualized love mixed with friendship, one finds a similar structure in both. The male party solicits divine favor through the intermediary of a pious woman, an *amica Dei*. Both models have the same hierarchical distribution, with God at the top, the chaste, suppliant woman at the middle step, and at the bottom sinful man who gains some merit as her protector. Nonetheless, Christina and Geoffrey's relationship contains a strong strain of friendship, as with Aelred's *amicitia spiritualis*, in their privately shared affection for God Who loves them, their mutual confidences, and their love of one another's goodness. Abelard's program with its spiritualized gender roles is one of love and not friendship because of its history, its memory of lust and frustration, and marriage which serve as its this-worldly base. With Abelard this base is a constant point of reference for his expression of repentance and *contemptus mundi*. On the other hand, spiritual friendship, even though it too despises the world, does not repent of its beginnings. Different, too, are the imagined heavenly ends of spiritual love and friendship. The mutual confidence and communion of *amicitia spiritualis* on earth are perfected in paradise, where the friendly souls continue to admire one another's goodness and share the joy of their coming together into God's presence. With spiritual love between woman and man, their chaste, or chastened, love on earth is rewarded in paradise with infinitely loving joy while they contemplate in one another the redeemed Adam and Eve, the fully restored beauty, innocence, and inseparable bond between woman and man that were lost through original sin. The poet Dante portrays the spiritual lover's reward in his *Paradiso* in the rapturous vision and ardent love of the character Dante who he looks upon the loving Beatrice, his spiritual and hierarchical superior.

The anonymous French prose *Quest of the Holy Grail* (around 1225), the next-to-the-last romance in the Lancelot-Grail cycle, offers illustrations of *amicitia Dei*, fraternal charity limited to a fellowship, spiritual friendship, and spiritualized love of a chivalric stamp.[50] The author of *The Quest* interprets traditional Arthurian fictions and his own rewriting of them in relation to biblical and other texts. The author as interpreter or exegete of his fictions is often present in the text in the personas of male and female hermits, white monks—that is, Cistercians—and heavenly and diabolical messengers who most usually reveal events in the romance to be the fulfillment of prophecies found in the Bible or the romance cycle itself—for example, Merlin's prophecies. Arthurian myth is rewritten here as a Christian parable of redemption stretching from the Fall to the end of time.

The three Arthurian knights Galahad, Perceval, and Bors are friends of

---

[50] *The Quest of the Holy Grail*, trans. P. M. Matarasso (Harmondsworth, Eng.: Penguin, 1969). Hereinafter page references are included within parentheses.

God, fraternal friends, and spiritual friends in a tale of spiritual knight-errantry. The three are virtuous to different degrees. The only virgin or chaste Round Table knights, they alone possess the quality prerequisite for each of the seven principal Christian virtues and, hence, for the full enjoyment of divine love.[51] God loves Galahad the most of the three. One of the many interpreter-monks reveals to Galahad, a descendant of King David, who was thought to be Christ's ancestor through Joseph (Luke 3,23-31), that his actions represent a second Christ's coming "in semblance only, not in sublimity" (page 64). In his many adventures Galahad performs marvelous feats that are revealed as fulfillment of prophecy. The ease with which he performs them is indicative of the great love of God, Who seconds Galahad in realizing what they both will. A representation of the ideal of Christian chivalry, Galahad is a romance construct of Christ-like perfection beyond mortal attainment. In comparison to idealized Galahad, Perceval and Bors function at lower, practical levels that the Christian knight might hope to attain if he keeps the image of Christ-Galahad before his eyes. Among Arthur's knights only Galahad enjoys supernatural gifts associated with saintliness, an absolute standard of goodness. God gives him the power to perform various miracles such as healing a cripple and putting demons to flight, makes him ruler of the spiritual city of Sarras, grants his prayer to leave this life, and permits only him to gaze into the Grail, after which the enraptured Galahad dies, and angels carry his soul to heaven (270-84). These signs of God's love correspond fictionally to those associated with Christ in the New Testament.

In regard to the *amicitia Dei* of the two companions Perceval and Bors, God's love, while great, is limited in proportion to their respective abilities to 'read' His will—that is, their *intellectus* or discernment of divine volition—and to respond. Along with Galahad, only these two from among all the Round Table companions pass their spiritual tests in face of worldly and diabolical temptation, but Perceval's and Bors's scores, as it were, are adequate but hardly brilliant. Perceval almost fails to qualify, for he does not see through the trickery of the devil in the shape of a woman, and he wounds himself in the thigh in penance for sinning

---

[51] Pauline Matarasso discusses the seven theological and cardinal virtues as demonstrated in different degrees in these three knights in *The Redemption of Chivalry. A Study of the "Queste del Saint Graal,"* Histoire des Idées et Critique Littéraire, 180 (Geneva: Droz, 1979), pp. 154-65.

against the flesh in his thoughts (129). God shows His love for these two in many favors. He directs them to join Galahad in the completion of the Grail quest, and the three set off in a divinely guided boat. In Galahad's company as prisoners in Sarras, Bors and Perceval are fed by the Grail for a year in their dungeon (282), and after Galahad's death, they witness the ascension of the Grail and the Lance to heaven (284). The virgin Perceval seems to be more deserving of divine favor than chaste Bors, who because of a sorceress' spell lost his virginity in the preceding romance. In the end, Perceval, who became a religious hermit after Galahad's death, receives the great favor of being buried alongside his virgin sister and Galahad, but Bors returns to Arthur's court to bear witness to all that he has seen and heard.

In the larger context of Christian fraternal charity within a fellowship of knights of one heart and spirit, Christ receives these three companions and nine other virtue-proven knights from foreign lands in order to establish a spiritual cohort of disciples and vassals who will later serve as knights in heaven to replace Satan and his followers cast down by God. After serving His twelve vassals from the Grail, Christ orders the three to transfer the holy object to His spiritual palace in Sarras: "My sons, in name and nature both, my friends, no foes to me, depart from here" (278). In the Old French text, which reads "Mi fil et ne mie mi fillastre, mi ami et ne mie mi guerrier, issiez de ceenz," the words *mi ami* could also be rendered "my vassals," since the context clearly indicates a suzerain-liege man relation, where the lord addresses his vassal as *ami*.[52] The Old French *ami* translates *amici* which Christ used to address his disciples at the last supper in John 15,14-15. This dinner scene in *The Quest* with Christ and twelve chivalric disciples represents fraternal love within a fellowship through a temporal series of tables—the table of the last supper, then the Grail table at which Christ's follower Joseph of Arimathea and his warrior son Josephus presided, Arthur's Round Table, and finally the present one, the Grail table again, at which Josephus and Christ appear. The narrator indicated earlier that Merlin designed the Round Table to signify the universe and brotherly love (99). Because of the sins of Arthur's other knights, of

---

[52] *La queste del Saint Graal, roman du XIIIe siècle*, ed. Albert Pauphilet, Classiques Français du Moyen Age, 33 (Paris: Champion, 1923), p. 272. For *ami* as the form of address of lord to vassal, see Huguette Legros, "Le vocabulaire de l'amitié, son évolution sémantique au cours du XIIe siècle," *Cahiers de civilisation médiévale* 23 (1980): 131.

which not the least is their violence towards one another during the Grail quest, the Round Table no longer holds this meaning. The present dinner, which takes place at the end of the quest, restores the Round Table's lost fraternal love of fellow knights and transfers it to a spiritual plane.

The friendship of Galahad, Perceval, and Bors is a spiritual development of chivalric companionship. The ideal of a Christian mission for knights typical of the *chansons de geste* was not new at the time of *The Quest*'s composition. Around 1132 St. Bernard, the son of a noble knight, expressed his ideal of chivalry in praising the the newly founded religious order of the Knights Templar, soldiers of Christ whom he contrasted to secular knights, vassals of the devil,[53] and as Jean Leclercq notes, at the beginning of his exposition of the Song of Songs Bernard insists upon the comparison, which had a long literary tradition before his time, of the monastic community to an army fighting for its just king.[54] The sublime relationship of these three comrades is clearly different from the common or futile sorts of companionship illustrated by the other Arthurian knights in *The Quest*, but in what sense is it spiritual friendship? The fiction's deity plays an active, predominant part as tester, initiator, director, and confirmer in their spiritual friendship similar to God's role in Christina and Geoffrey's association. *The Quest*'s deity, in the three persons of the Trinity, tests the virtues of the three knights, brings them together, directs their joint activities—their voyage in the mysterious boat, their adventures in combating evil, the transfer of the Grail—and confirms their spiritual relationship in which they love one another for reason of God's love. As for the affective part of their preferential friendship, Perceval expresses to Galahad the delight that he experiences in his company: "I commend you to Our Lord: may He grant that our separation be a short one, for I never met a man in whose company I took such pleasure and delight as yours" (253). Never one to waste words on this-worldly matters, godlike Galahad declares to Bors, who is reunited with him and Perceval after many years of separation: "As for your arrival, as God is my help, nothing could make me happier: I longed for your presence, now I joy in it" (272). Such a declaration by a character usually exceedingly

---

[53] St. Bernard, *De laude novae militiae ad milites templi liber*, in *Treatises III: On Grace and Free Choice. In Praise of the New Knighthood*, trans. Conrad Greenia, Cistercian Fathers Series, 19 (Kalamazoo: Cistercian Publications, 1977).

[54] Leclercq, *Monks and Love*, p. 91.

reserved in speech and manner in his dealings with other knights indicates the partiality and affection, *affectus*, necessarily a part of friendship. Yet on the whole, the restraint that the narrator usually portrays in their relationship and what would appear to be a lower evaluation than with Aelred of spiritual friendship as means to higher love are typical of cautious mainstream monastic attitudes in Aelred's time and later regarding particular friendships.

The bond between the virgins Galahad and Perceval is stronger than those between each of them and Bors. Galahad behaves towards Perceval in an unmistakably friendly manner: he rescues him from mortal danger (109). He spends much more time with Perceval than with Bors or his father Lancelot, and in respect to the spiritual side of their relationship, he confides in Perceval alone what he saw in his rapture before the Grail and the divine announcement of his coming death (279-80). Such confidence is the essence of spiritual friendship, as Aelred claimed. Galahad, like his ancestor David, is greatly loved by God, and his and Perceval's mutual devotion, like that of the warriors David and Jonathan, is in accordance with divine will. Nonetheless, Galahad does not neglect to show favor to Bors: after declaring his joy at being reunited with Bors, Galahad mends the Broken Sword that wounded Joseph of Arimathea, and Bors receives the precious arm before the ceremony at which Josephus and Christ confirm the twelve knights' united spirit (273). In the association of the three knights, a spiritualized version of chivalric comradeship or *compagnonnage*, there is a strong strain of spiritual friendship. Living together in confidence, they have been brought together by God, Who has separated them from other knights; their mutual admiration and love is rational, based on observation of virtue, and they share the "similarity of life, morals, and pursuits" characteristic of Aelred's spiritual friendship.

Included within the bounds of spiritual knighthood, the friendship of Galahad and his companions is gender-specific. Women are expressly excluded from the quest (47). However, one female character, Perceval's virgin sister, joins the three chosen knights at the mysterious boat and accompanies them in life, death, and, if one chooses to speculate about her career beyond the romance's temporal limits, in the afterlife, where she would perhaps be Galahad's celestial bride.[55] She is Galahad's female

---

[55] Myrrha Lot-Borodine, "L'Eve pécheresse et la rédemption de la femme dans la *Quête du Graal*," in Ferdinand Lot, *Etude sur le "Lancelot en prose,"* Bibliothèque de l'Ecole des Hautes Etudes, Sciences Historiques et Philo-

theoretical counterpart, a martyr who willingly gives her life for the sake of a stranger who demands her death, and she provides Galahad with part of his spiritual armor, a sword-belt make of her hair which, one might guess, helps preserve his chastity. As Galahad's ladylove in spirit, to whom he pledges his fealty (237) and alongside whom he is buried, she and Galahad complete the romance's series of earthly couples—Adam and Eve, King Solomon and his wife, Lancelot and Guinevere—and perfect it in spirit as chivalric fictions of the New Adam and Eve. Thus, male-female spiritualized love is inscribed, too, in the bounds of spiritual chivalry. It might be noted that this romance's simultaneous development of female-male chivalrous Christian love of the highest order and ideal male chivalric companionship has a parallel on a this-worldly level in the *Prose Lancelot*, which precedes *The Quest of the Holy Grail* in the Lancelot-Grail cycle: there Lancelot and Guinevere's love develops in intimate conjunction with the chivalric friendship of Lancelot and Galehout.

In the examples in this chapter, spiritual friendship is praised only inasmuch as it reflects and serves the ideals of *amicitia Dei* and fraternal charity. Each example shows spiritual friendship's human-to-human interaction contained within one of a number of profession-specific spheres of activity devoted to serving those ideals. With Aelred *amicitia spiritualis* is contained within the sphere of monastic charity conducive to contemplation. Christina of Markyate's friendship with Geoffrey begins at the intersection of two very different religious bodies devoted to the same contemplative end. In *The Quest of the Holy Grail*, the Round Table, constructed to represent fraternal love, loses its intended meaning because Arthur's worldly vassals love neither God nor one another; but through three knights' love of God, their friendship, and their divinely confirmed fraternity with nine other knights, the table's spiritual significance is restored in the passage from earthly to celestial chivalry. Thus spiritual friendship and male-female spiritual love, illustrated, for example, in Abelard and Heloise's letters, begin and unfold on earth within a specific field of Christian profession as human occupation and declaration of faith; they continue perfectly, eternally in paradise, where in spiritual form they retain the mark of their earthly profession.

Medieval religious writers' praise of friendship or love within a profes-

logiques, fasc. 226, rev. ed. (Paris: Librairie Ancienne Honoré Champion, 1954), pp. 418-42.

sion contains an element of praise of the writer's vocation which is capable of incorporating meritorious *amor* or *amicitia*. One might ask what authors imagined to be the relationships between the different aspects of ideal Christian friendship or love and the act of writing. In the example of Dante's profession of Christian poetry and faith in his *Divine Comedy* from the early fourteenth century, the fictional association of Dante's persona and the spirits of Virgil and Statius is ordained in heaven. The poets' expression of mutual affection and their gradual spiritual ascent together towards paradise demonstrate *amicitia* within the profession of poetry and, in the particular relationship between Dante and Statius, that of Christian poetry. On a higher spiritual plane, Dante and Beatrice's *amor* is a prerequisite for the poets' friendship, since her spirit orders Virgil to guide Dante's persona. It is the spiritual love of Dante and Beatrice, and not the companionship of poets, that permits Dante to enter paradise, where "the New and Old Testaments / Set the goal ... / For the souls which God has made His friends" (*Paradiso* 25, verses 88-90). In Dante's ranking, love has higher spiritual value than *amicitia*; and spiritual love has greater value for Christian poetry, too, since it is Beatrice who commands her lover to record all that he has seen and heard when he returns to the living. Their *amor* is also a prerequisite for the highest-ranking loves: Beatrice's gaze prepares the poet's sight for seeing and understanding, first, the blessed company, then, after Beatrice's replacement by Saint Bernard, the Virgin, and, finally, the Trinity. In this the poet shows a fiction of himself as the humble beneficiary of divine gifts and enlightenment for the purpose of poetry. A modest claim to a part of divine love in writing about spiritual love or friendship can be noted in other Christian texts examined in this chapter—for example, Abelard's claim that God participated directly in his conversion, and his authoritative appeal to the higher laws of marriage to Christ. In his first-person account of spiritual friendship within the monastery, Aelred assumes no less Christ's presence with the writer than among spiritual friends. In this sense, the act of writing about love or friendship is a profession-specific response to divine love. In the Latin works in praise of *amicitia perfecta* discussed in the preceding chapter, each author makes a more or less transparent attempt to win the reader's praise for himself as an excellent friend because he is a writer capable of expressing the ideal. With Valerius Maximus, the writer's profession is both the experiential context and the medium for expressing his *amicitia vera* with his patron. Seneca's letters on good and wise friendship

are not merely the sage's thoughts on the topic; they form the very sub-
stance of his activity as Lucilius' true friend. And Cicero's encomium of
Scipio and the preeminent orator Laelius contains an element of self-
praise for the writer's and Atticus' friendship and for Cicero's rhetoric itself.

The preceding chapter mentioned some of the model friends from Greek
tradition, such as Orestes and Pylades and Alexander and Hephaistion,
whom classical Latin authors used and, also, replaced with native Roman
amici veri of the past and present. To conclude, we will resume the repertoire of textual prototypes used by religious writers in this chapter as
standards of *amicitia christiana*. Although ancient Greek and Roman textual models occasionally figure in medieval religious writings, the works
which we have examined employ a separate and extensive repertoire of
ideal friends exemplifying the major aspects of Christian *amicitia* and
amor. The Romans considered their native *amici veri* from the past to be
superior to those furnished by Greek tradition, and they presented these legendary and historical Roman models as measures for evaluating contemporary Roman *amicitia*, including their own. In a similar manner twelfth
and thirteenth-century religious writers replaced the stock Roman *amici
veri* who were well-known among the literate in their time with what they
held to be absolutely superior spiritual prototypes from the Bible and
Christian tradition; they presented these latter—or, sometimes, they assumed them to be so well established that they did not need explicit reference—as the authoritative standards against which the reader might measure their contemporary illustrations or fictions of the best Christian love
and friendship on earth.

Amicitia Dei and fraternal charity within a single community have celestial archetypes in the beatific vision and the community of the blessed.
In respect to their terrestrial counterparts, Paul's rapture and conversion,
miracles described in the Bible, and God's speaking with Moses in Exodus
serve as some of the principal authoritative textual standards which writers
in this chapter use for evaluation of their contemporary examples of *amicitia Dei*; for fraternal charity limited to the fellowship of those like in
conduct and spirit, the ideal standards are the first Christian community
described in Acts, Christ and the twelve disciples, and Christ and His
bride, the monastery's single body, mind, and spirit. John Cassian refers
to Christ's love for John the Evangelist and Aelred of Rievaulx, to Paul
and Philemon's friendship and Jonathan and David as biblical ideals of

monastic charity. These last three biblical prototypes might also provide measures for contemporary illustrations of spiritual friendship, as would many other friends in the Bible or pairs of saints, according to Aelred, who were willing to lay down their lives for one another because of their faith in Christ. The overlapping of prototypes and, in some cases, the applicability of a single type to different aspects of *amicitia christiana* indicate their status as archetypal Ideas roughly analogous in theoretical function to the limited number of ratios, the Pythagorean proportions, which medieval philosophers often imagined to operate throughout the cosmos. In *The Quest of the Holy Grail*, some of the biblical prototypes—e.g., Christ and the disciples, Christ's special love for John, Paul's rapture, David and Jonathan—are doubled on a level of Christian legend or romance with Christ and Joseph of Arimathea, Josephus, and their followers to form twofold models for comparison of fictional Arthurian friendships. Finally, the Virgin's relationships to the three persons of the Trinity offer the principal archetypes of female-male spiritual *amor*, but a large number of Old and New Testament women and female saints can also provide different models for the special love between God and woman, her beneficial compassion for fallen man, and, as exemplified in the legend of Solomon's wife's gifts for Galahad in *The Quest of the Holy Grail*, her love for the redeemed Adam. The concept of male-female spiritual love may include spiritualized marriage, with the celestial archetype in the mystical marriage of Christ and the Virgin and Mary and Joseph's chaste marriage as a terrestrial one.

Among the three Old French fictions to be examined in the next chapter, the epic poem *Ami and Amile* includes certain authoritative biblical standards for evaluation of its representation of two chivalric friends who become friends of God. For instance, Christ's self-sacrifice and power to raise the dead and Abraham's willingness to sacrifice his son are absolute measures of devotion and the power of God's friendship which Amile recalls when he contemplates sacrificing his sons for his friend's sake. In attempting to provide his tale of love in this world with an other-worldly dimension of *amicitia Dei*, the epic poet uses biblical types to portray perfect knightly friendship which, even if not spiritual in itself, at least possesses a spiritual system of signs. In the other two French fictions, Thomas' *Tristan* and the *Prose Lancelot*, models and standards of spiritualized *amor* or *amicitia* from the Bible and Christian tradition figure only indirectly if at all in the evaluation of worldly chivalric companionship.

An exception is the friendship of David and Jonathan, which could serve as an implicit gauge for the illustrations of the companionship of Tristan and Kaherdin and of Prince Galehout and Lancelot, David's descendant. Nonetheless, neither romance mentions David and Jonathan's friendship, nor do they include any positive spiritual features in their chivalric models. Types of Christian spiritual *amor* and *amicitia* are almost entirely absent from the three late-medieval and early-Renaissance humanistic works in Italian and French which will be studied in the concluding chapter. As literary standards for measuring their representations of contemporary, perfect *amicitia* in this world, the three humanistic writers restore the authority of well-known classical exemplars, they propose other examples from newly recovered ancient texts, or they invent their own fictional Greek and Roman *amici veri* for that purpose.

CHAPTER THREE

SWEETER THAN WOMAN'S LOVE
PRAISE OF CHIVALRIC FRIENDSHIP IN THREE TWELFTH
AND THIRTEENTH-CENTURY FRENCH FICTIONS: THOMAS'
TRISTAN, THE *PROSE LANCELOT*, AND *AMI AND AMILE*

In medieval romance, a genre that abounds in superlatives, the greatest knights and lovers are also sometimes the best of friends. Romance examples of chivalric companions in this chapter show their profound affection, solicitude, humility, service, self-sacrifice, and combat for friendship's sake similar in many respects to literary representations of chivalric love of woman, and the epic poem offers a model of affection and devotion in knightly friendship far superior to love of knight and woman.

In the first two texts studied in this chapter Thomas' *Tristan* and the *Prose Lancelot*—the chivalric friends' great mutual benevolence, beneficence, and aspirations are wholly contained within this-worldly limits. The romance writers do not suggest that their exemplary friendships possess any spiritual value. The ideal of superhuman love that guides Christian friendships is not simply absent. It is in fact impossible in these romance fictions—impossible because the knightly friends act foolishly, sin, and hold nothing dearer than their earthly love. Relying entirely on mutual aid and confidence, the chivalric friends, Christians, pursue a profane ideal. Tristan, Lancelot, and their bosom companions subordinate their friendships to passionate male-female love, to a life of intermittent joy, prolonged sorrow, and even madness that could not be further from Christian conceptions of *amicitia* as a haven of peace and security.

In Thomas' *Tristan* and the *Prose Lancelot*, the writers' high praise of chivalric friendship runs counter to Christian standards, by which the knights' troubled lives and failure to realize their ambitions can only serve to demonstrate the futility of even the best *amistié* or *compagnonnage* that is not in agreement with divine will. In fact, the *Prose Lancelot* applies these standards in one instance but, then, silences the Christian moral censure of the knights' friendship in such a way as to make the silencing itself appear to be a duty consistent with the best this-worldly *amistié*. The chivalric virtues that the friends embody are many and, in this genre, superlative—prowess, great compassion, boundless generosity, extreme prudence, constancy, love of honor, and more, all of which in the end cannot save the companions from sorrowful separation and death in the absence of Christian virtues and divine favor. The third and final text, the epic poem *Ami and Amile*, provides a divine extension to the secular friendship of two knights, and it portrays through the action of divine grace the 'redemption' of chivalric friendship in this world, where love of woman drags man down.

The two worldly fictions about Tristan and Lancelot disregard, with very rare exceptions, standards of Christian *amicitia*, and the fatal moral or spiritual defects of the knightly friendships are de-emphasized or, when revealed, are denied or suppressed. In sentimental romance, chivalric friendship acquires great relative value as it is measured against the secular literary standards of refined chivalric love, *fine amor*, exemplified in the romance's central female-male couple or couples. In this relative context, knightly friendship, with its superior moral qualities of faithfulness, courage, and generosity and its great mutual affection, confidence, and solace, complements male-female love as a giver of value to literary chivalry, and in the case of Lancelot, it demands no less right to the best knight's companionship than does Guinevere's love. The chivalric friends' affective states and emotional outpourings described by the writers are no less intense than those of the romances' lovers. The 'true romance,' one might say, of these medieval fictions resides not only in the female-male love narratives to which literary criticism has devoted its attention almost exclusively, but also in the male bonding there, a feature of epic literature to which romance authors sometimes attach new sentimental and ethical values.

Louise Horner Reiss has argued that in Beroul's French verse romance *Tristan* (late twelfth century), David and Jonathan's friendship serves as the measure for Tristan and Iseut's *fine amor*, which comes up wanting.[1] However, this position is not supported in the incomplete manuscript version by an illustration of male friendship which suggests comparison with the David-Jonathan model. But Thomas' fragmentary French verse romance *Tristan* (second half of the twelfth century) illustrates a worldly ideal of male friendship comparable to that biblical exemplum in the char-

---

[1] Reiss, "Tristan and Isolt and the Medieval Ideal of Friendship," *Romance Quarterly* 33 (1986): 131-37.

acters of Tristan, a musician and giant-slayer like David, and his in-law and comrade in arms and love Kaherdin. At the tearful parting of Kaherdin and Tristan on his deathbed, Thomas refers to their friendship in terms of loyal *fine amor*: "[Tristan and Kaherdin] weep [and] show great sorrow, / Since so their *amur* must be sundered: / It has been most excellent [*fine*] and loyal" ("Plurent, demeinent grant dolur, / Quant si deit partir lur amur: / Mut ad esté fine e leele.")[2] Although in the late twelfth century and after, French writers use both *amor* and *amistié* to name love between a woman and a man, and male-to-male *amistié* is frequently called *amor*, Thomas' ideal of loyal *fine amor* between male characters is a literary innovation by which he accommodates to a large extent chivalric friendship to male-female love. In the Thomas fragments and the *Saga of Tristram and Isönd* (1226), Friar Robert's Old Norse prose translation-abridgment of Thomas' romance, Tristan and Kaherdin's loyal *fine amor* resembles David and Jonathan's friendship in their initial attraction because of love of one another's virtue as warriors, mutual devotion, complete confidence, great affection, and kinship by marriage. Their friendship is characterized by the same loyalty and stability which are essential to the erotic ideal of *fine amor* but which, as Thomas notes (Sneyd[1] fragment, verses 292-96), almost always fall short in love of man and woman. In consideration of its steadfast, mutual loyalty, Tristan and Kaherdin's friendship, developed on a level of narrative interest secondary to Tristan and Iseut's love, functions as a romance measure of perfection along with erotic love, which they serve.

The anonymous *Prose Lancelot* (around 1220), which precedes *The Quest of the Holy Grail* in the Lancelot-Grail cycle, offers an example unique in medieval romance of chivalric friendship wholly assimilated to *fine amor*. Here, too, the greatest knights Lancelot and Prince Galehout serve *fine amor*, but their friendship equals and even surpasses at times on Galehout's side the literary measure of Lancelot and Guinevere's *fine amor*

---

[2] *Les fragments du "Roman de Tristan," poème du XIIe siècle*, ed. Bartina H. Wind, Textes Littéraires Français, 92 (Geneva: Droz, 1960), Douce fragment, vss. 1119-21. English translations of passages from Thomas' romance are my own. Constance B. Bouchard argues that Thomas is not the author in "The Possible Nonexistence of Thomas, Author of *Tristan and Isolde*," *Modern Philology* 79 (1981): 66-72. In response to Bouchard, Merritt R. Blakeslee maintains that Thomas, whose name appears in the fragments, is the author of the romance—"The Authorship of Thomas's *Tristan*," *Philological Quarterly* 64 (1985): 555-72.

in regard to adoration, self-sacrifice, humility, the confusion of extreme joy and sorrow, and, finally, fatal lovesickness. The *Prose Lancelot* provides the title character with a complement to Queen Guinevere's love in the perfect, this-worldly devotion of Galehout's *amistié/amor*, chivalric friendship or *compagnonnage* which shares many extreme affective characteristics with romance representations of erotic love. The narrator recodes male friendship as *fine amor*: the chivalric *amis* typically behave towards one another in much the same manner as the romance's *fin amant* Lancelot and his ladylove. The partial assimilation of male friendship to *fine amor* that one can observe in Thomas' *Tristan* is perfected in the *Prose Lancelot*, where the knights' *amistié/amor* developed on the primary narrative level is no less important than Lancelot and Guinevere's love.

In these two romances, perfectly faithful chivalric friendship serves as a complementary and, in many regards, comparative standard for erotic *fine amor*. But is erotic love a positive or a negative measure there? As for Tristan and Iseut, the poet Thomas, who both criticizes and sympathizes with their love, is ambiguous in his evaluation, and modern scholars disagree on whether theirs is a positive example of love and courtliness or a negative one.[3] For instance, Thomas' Tristan's reproach of Iseut for faithlessness and his attempt to put her out of his life and mind by marrying hardly illustrate right conduct and perfect faithfulness in love. Aside from considerations of courtliness, it is obvious that their exemplum cannot be positive in Christian moral terms because of its sinfulness and ends or in respect to classical philosophy because of its immoderate passion. As for the *Prose Lancelot*, the perfect fidelity and courtliness of Lancelot as *fin amant* are never in doubt. And although in one instance a character judges Lancelot and Guinevere's *fine amor* to be moral and spiritual error which will prevent Lancelot from succeeding in the Grail quest, another character argues according to the standards of sentimental romance that great honor and wisdom reside in the error and *folie* of their love. The opposing meanings or interpretations of their *fine amor* represent two distinct systems of evaluation, the confrontation of which in a single work is problematic for readers, but it is not unique in medieval amatory literature—for example, Andreas Capellanus' *De amore* teaches and praises 'honorable' erotic love

---

[3] Tony Hunt, who argues that Thomas presents Tristan and Iseut's love as a negative example, resumes the scholarly debate on the meaning of their *fine amor* in "The Significance of Thomas's *Tristan*," *Reading Medieval Studies* 7 (1981): 41-61.

in its first two books and, then, condemns it as sin in the third.[4] As will be discussed later, this *duplex sententia* or double reading according to Christian standards and those of sentimental romance applies as well to Lancelot and Galehout's *amistié/amor*.

The chapter concludes with the praise of chivalric friendship in the anonymous French epic poem *Ami and Amile* (ca. 1200), which illustrates the myth of the double with its comrades alike in appearance and mind. The two knights enjoy a three-way relationship among themselves and God, but unlike the examples of *amicitia christiana* in the preceding chapter, here the bond between the two fictional characters is stronger than those between each of them and God. Ami goes against divine will in doing what he believes to be in his friend's best interest—yet in the end God, having tested their mutual love in ordeals of self-sacrifice, sanctions their *amistié* in spite of this rebellion. As an epic poem, *Ami and Amile* is somewhat unconventional in that it pays a great deal of attention to the heroes' love of woman and their marriages. Although it presents one example of a model marriage, it portrays love of woman largely as a bitter experience for the two knights. The epic exemplum of chivalric friendship's mutual sacrifices, suffering, joy, tearful embraces of separation and reunion, and its final triumph serves as a standard of conduct and affection against which to measure the other sorts of human love illustrated in the poem. The poet's praise of the heroes' friendship calls up King David's estimation of his love of the warrior-prince Jonathan: "Very pleasant have you been to me; your love to me was wonderful, passing the love of women" (2 Samuel 1,26). The antagonism between knightly *amistié* and love of woman is a central topic in the epic narrative. Both romances also deal with the problem of conflicting interests between the two, but they offer quite different and complex solutions.

Only a part of Thomas' representation of Tristan and Kaherdin's loyal *fine amor* survives in the numerous extant manuscript fragments. In the following analysis, references within parentheses identify verse numbers in

---

[4] See the discussion of reader response and the twofold meaning of erotic love in *De amore* in Peter L. Allen, *The Art of Love. Amatory Fiction from Ovid to the "Romance of the Rose,"* Middle Ages Series (Philadelphia: University of Pennsylvania Press, 1992), pp. 59-78.

the Douce and Turin[1] fragments in Old French. References to the *Saga of Tristram and Isönd*, which supplies a good deal of information on the knights' complex relationship that is absent from the Thomas fragments, indicate page numbers in the modern English translation.[5]

Tristan and Kaherdin's friendship is a mixture of the common and the extraordinary. Their loyal *fine amor*, near the peak of perfection by romance standards, rests upon a broad base of ordinary friendship, of mutual usefulness and pleasure that the partners enjoy in their company. The superior aspect of their *amistié* comprises two interactive parts. In one part each character loves in his comrade excellent qualities similar to his own; in the other, the friends are joined through the medium of love of woman. In this second part, each friend serves as go-between in the secret love affair or affairs of his companion, and in doing so he renders faithful service to both friendship and *fine amor*. The knightly comrades perform beneficent acts towards one another for the sake of love, with which their friendship is coextensive.

On the other hand, their mutual aid in serving love could be seen as a base utilitarian aspect of their association or, worse, as pandering. This ambiguity is a problem in the Tristan-Kaherdin episodes which Thomas attempts to resolve by erasing a traditional account of the friends' faithless love and pandering and by linking their cooperation in love to the noblest of motives and solemn oaths.

The poet's correction of what he sees as faults in the Tristan-Kaherdin episodes which he received from tradition corresponds in part to Tristan's attempt to correct his own faithlessness—his marriage to Iseut Aux Blanches Mains—by devoting himself to the idea of the absent Iseut. Thomas idealizes his primary subject, Tristan and Iseut's adulterous and politically subversive love, in insisting upon the lovers' faithfulness, suffering, and fixed idea of one another during their separation in the last parts of his romance. In the Thomas fragments, which begin with Tristan and Iseut's parting, Tristan's love for Iseut is ideal for the most part because during their prolonged separation, love is an idea: Tristan's yearning, doubt, madness, adoration, and joyful and sorrowful reminiscences are his love experienced in the realm of ideas. Tristan and Kaherdin's loyal and virtuous friendship, according to Thomas' account, serves from a dis-

---

[5] The Old French text is cited according to Wind's edition given above. The translation of the *Saga* is by Paul Schach (Lincoln: University of Nebraska Press, 1973).

tance their love, physically chaste because distant, through a sort of idola-
try, and friendship partakes in this chaste love's extremes of joy and sorrow. Or on the rare occasions when the lovers meet, the friends sometimes share the rewards of their devotion. In respect to Tristan, Iseut's absence coincides for the most part in narrative time and place with Kaherdin's presence. In her absence, Kaherdin, who fixes his thoughts on the
absent Brengien, his lady, doubles for Tristan as lover of the Idea of love,
and he serves as Tristan's messenger and mirror-image other and confidant
in constant friendship. As for the absent Iseut, one might speak of her
double replacement for Tristan, first, in her statue, a passive object that he
has made for his secret cave, and, second, in Kaherdin, a responsive recipient of Tristan's love confidences.

Andreas Capellanus, in the conclusion to his Latin prose treatise *On
Love* (*De amore*) from around 1185, argues that one should shun woman's
love because, among many other reasons, it may turn friends into enemies.[6] Thomas' romance demonstrates an opposing thesis: love of woman
strengthens male friendship. In Thomas' recounting and the *Saga of Tristram and Isönd*, each of the stages of Tristan and Kaherdin's *amistié*—their
meeting and mutual admiration, their life together, the granting of total
confidence, etc.—turns immediately to one or both men's love of woman.
Woman's love is a boon of their friendship, and it serves as their common
experience, the subject of their confidences, and the medium of their reciprocal benevolence and benefaction.

Tristan and Kaherdin's initial meeting, which is absent from the
Thomas fragments, occurs after Tristan's disgrace in Marc's court and his
self-imposed exile and separation from Iseut. The *Saga* recounts that during his exile and quest of adventures as a knight errant, he meets in Brit
tany an old duke beset by enemies whom Tristan defeats with the aid of
Kaherdin, the duke's eldest son (*Saga*, page 106). From the beginning
Tristan and Kaherdin seem perfectly suited to become friends because of
their similar qualities—military valor, noble birth, courtly manners,
physical beauty, and youth. Recognizing the high value of Tristan's
prowess in service to the dukedom and also what he believes to be an
amorous attraction to his sister Iseut Aux Blanches Mains (or Isodd in the
Saga), Kaherdin encourages the courtship between the two in the hope of

---

[6] Andreas Capellanus, *On Love*, ed. and trans. P. G. Walsh (London: Duckworth, 1982), bk. 3, sections 9-12, pp. 288-91.

binding the knight to his sister, himself, his family, and his father's land. At this early stage in Kaherdin and Tristan's relationship, their feelings and hopes for one another are directed towards and, as it were, translated into love of a noble woman.

Subsequent to Tristan and Iseut Aux Blanches Mains's wedding, Kaherdin passes much time hunting with Tristan, and they lead several successful military campaigns (*Saga* 114). Here the two are companions-in-arms bound by allegiance to a common lord and by oaths or, at least, an understanding of mutual nonaggression. Somewhat like Roland and Olivier in *La chanson de Roland*, their *compagnonnage* is confirmed by and extended through marriage (in Roland's case, a promised marriage) between one *compaing* and the other's sister. Although with Roland and Olivier a difference of opinion calls the marriage into question, with Kaherdin and Tristan the marriage itself threatens to destroy their *compagnonnage*.[7] When Iseut Aux Blanches Mains confesses to her brother that Tristan has never made love to her, Kaherdin must choose between his companionship and vengeance, the latter of which would seem to be an unconditional duty to family in this case. Yet he does no more than distance himself from Tristan and speak disapprovingly of him to others. When Tristan confronts him about his change in behavior, Kaherdin replies, "If the comradeship between us were not so firm and steadfast, you would pay dearly for this dishonor" (*Saga* 125).

While comradeship stays Kaherdin's vengeful hand, the prospect of noble love draws him closer in friendship to Tristan and farther from vindication of familial honor. In response to Tristan's claim that Iseut and Brengien are superior in all ways to Iseut Aux Blanches Mains, Kaherdin promises not to seek vengeance if Tristan proves it (*Saga* 126). Though hardly morally correct, his contemplated betrayal of his sister and forsaking familial honor square with the romance's literary scale of values with loyal erotic love at the top. Even though the narrator makes no explicit value judgment regarding Kaherdin's conditional preference of woman's love to family and duty, there is an implied comparison with Tristan's betrayal of his uncle and suzerain Mark for the sake of love. It is in favoring the prospect of honorable love above or in disregard of other worldly

---

[7] For an interpretation of the *compagnonnage* of Roland and Olivier and the terminology of friendship in *La chanson de Roland*, see George Fenwick Jones, "Friendship in the *Chanson de Roland*," *Modern Language Quarterly* 24 (1963): 88-98.

honors that Kaherdin most resembles Tristan in character.

Tristan hesitates to prove his claim because in doing so, he would violate love's unconditional duty of secrecy: no one, and especially not his wife, should know of his love for Iseut. On the other hand, he must face Kaherdin's vengeance—disgrace and, possibly, death—if he does not reveal his secret. Tristan's interior deliberation poses the problem of the direct conflict between love of woman and his love of his dearest friend, whom he wants to spare from further grief (*Saga* 126-27). Here the narrator translates an obligation of *fine amor* into the duty of confiding in a friend, and he resolves the conflict on Tristan's side between love and comradeship, the latter of which is in conflict with familial duty on Kaherdin's side, by proposing honorable love as the goal, activity, and good which the two friends share. The *Saga*, which usually abridges the interior monologues in Thomas' poem, does not explain Tristan's motivation for taking Kaherdin into his confidence, but one might imagine opposing interpretations for his decision. It is possible to conjecture that Tristan reveals his secret and initiates Kaherdin's love of Brengien so that he will be blinded by love and will forget their quarrel, which Kaherdin in fact does almost immediately. An opposing explanation, according to which male friendship and *fine amor* are complementary ideals, is that he trusts that his comrade will value his love as highly as he himself does and will keep it secret. Their long acquaintance and intimacy may be interpreted to indicate that Tristan knows Kaherdin's character and has found him worthy of his unreserved confidence because of his loyalty, affection, noble spirit, generosity, and such secondary traits as congeniality and affability that Cicero mentions in regard to testing one's companion in *Laelius*. This moment marks the passage of their relationship from mere comradery in arms and kinship by marriage to a lifelong commitment and unqualified confidence. In agreeing to share love's secrets, Tristan and Kaherdin confirm their friendship, which they solemnize with oaths of mutual fidelity (*Saga* 127).

At this stage it seems that Kaherdin has no love secrets to share, but the narrative development of his love for Brengien will furnish the basis for reciprocal confidences between the friends. After Tristan leads him into the hidden cave of his love as memory and idea, Kaherdin mistakes the statues of Iseut and Brengien for living women. His error is a comical variation upon an earlier scene in the cave where Tristan, alone and mad from love, treated the statues as if they were alive (Turin[1] fragment, verses

1-70). Tristan's madness then demonstrated the intensity of his alternately bitter and sweet love. Kaherdin's delusion in the cave is a sign of his amorous madness. In asking Tristan to grant him Brengien's love, the deluded Kaherdin argues that the parallel loves—Tristan and Iseut, Kaherdin and Brengien—derive or should derive from their friendship since Tristan can thus show beneficence towards his friend. When Tristan allows him to approach Brengien's statue, Kaherdin interprets his apparent generosity thus: "This is proof of friendship and comradeship" (*Saga* 129). After realizing his error, he appeals to Tristan, as a friend, to lead him to the original. When later Tristan takes his love-struck comrade into Brengien's presence, where Iseut grants Kaherdin her confidante's company, at the same time he provides himself with a male confidant and equal other who knows the extremes of refined love's joy and pain.

The episode of Brengien's vengeance shows the interaction between erotic love and friendship in negative and positive senses: she thinks that Tristan's love service to his friend has brought her dishonor, and she forgives Tristan only when he performs another love service in acting as messenger to Kaherdin. At the point where the knights' friendship seems strongest because it results in the parallel loves, Brengien breaks the bonds of her friendship with Iseut and Tristan, and she breaks with Kaherdin. She believes the false claim of Cariado, Tristan's false friend and rival in love, that he frightened Kaherdin and Tristan into fleeing, and she vows to seek vengeance on Tristan and Iseut for having caused her dishonor in serving as panderers for the cowardly, lascivious Kaherdin (Douce fragment, verses 1-344). Her destructive wrath directed towards her sworn friends offers a female variation of Andreas Capellanus' contention that love may turn the closest friends into mortal enemies.[8] She realizes

---

[8] On the subject of female friendship, Gottfried von Strassburg's incomplete Middle High German verse romance *Tristan* (ca. 1210), inspired by Thomas' romance, praises superlatively Brangane and Isolde's mutual love and trust: "Now that the Queen Isolde had found Brangane loyal, constant, and altogether of upright character, and had smelted her in the crucible and refined her like gold, she and Brangane were so deeply devoted in mutual love and trustfulness that no difference was ever made between them in any of their affairs, so that their feelings for each other were of the happiest"—*"Tristan," Translated Entire for the First Time, With the Surviving Fragments of the "Tristran" of Thomas*, trans. A. T. Hatto (Harmondsworth, Eng.: Penguin, 1960), p. 211. Clearly, the poet intends to provide a female variation of classical male *amicitia perfecta*. He includes some of the essential Aristotelian-Ciceronian standards—Brangane's fidelity, constancy, and moral excellence—in his descrip-

her vengeful desire to separate Tristan and Iseut. She makes Tristan suffer grievously because he is Kaherdin's friend, and it is for the same reason that later she grants Tristan the joy of love that he seeks. By promising that he will go to his friend in Brittany and will have him return in order to prove Cariado's charge false, Tristan convinces Brengien to reunite him with Iseut (Douce 712-20). In this episode Brengien relates the ethical quality of the knights' friendship directly to the question of love, which cannot be honorable if the other is not.

But is Kaherdin perhaps the wanton lover that Brengien claimed (Douce 34-35) and Tristan, his companion in lust and a panderer? The question of their honorable love of woman touches directly on Thomas' superlative evaluation of their friendship. Thomas gives two versions of how Tristan received his fatal wound. The first, which he rejects as untrue, tells of Tristan's complicity in Kaherdin's womanizing and the ignoble ends to which both knights come. In this version, of which Thomas gives a very brief account, while in Brittany Tristan accompanies his comrade at a tryst with Kaherdin's other ladylove, a dwarf's wife; the dwarf discovers them, kills Kaherdin, and wounds Tristan with a poisoned weapon; the dying Tristan sends his steward Governal disguised as a merchant to England to seek Iseut (Douce 852-61). Thomas' summary corresponds to the story of Tristan's wound that Eilhart von Oberge recounts in his German verse romance *Tristrant* (around 1170).[9] Eilhart makes it clear that Tristan has

---

tion of the happy moment in *amicitia vera* when, after a successful test of virtue, two friends join as one forever. His statement on Isolde and Brangane's perfect friendship comes at a most awkward place in his telling, however, since he has just recounted Isolde's unsuccessful attempt at having Brangane assassinated—this is the smelting in the crucible to which he refers. Earlier Isolde wanted to eliminate her for fear that she might reveal the queen's secrets to Mark in order to advance her own cause and, perhaps, to eliminate Isolde. In Gottfried's recounting, the assassination attempt motivated by fearful mistrust becomes a successful test of virtues that results in firm female friendship. It is possible to interpret Gottfried's poetic transformation of Isolde's treachery into female *amicitia vera* as ironic praise. Although Gottfried's representation of Isolde and Brangane's perfect friendship fits the narrative circumstances poorly, it is consistent with the poet's tendency to idealize, with a great deal of irony, almost every aspect of Tristan and Isolde's love affair.

[9] See *Tristrant*, trans. J. W. Thomas (Lincoln: University of Nebraska Press, 1978), pp. 150-53, on the tryst and the dwarf's vengeance. One version of the Old French *Prose Tristan* gives a slightly different account of Tristan's mortal wound—see the translation of excerpts (the whole French romance according to its two main versions is as of yet unpublished) in *The Romance of Tristan and Isold*, trans. Norman B. Spector (Evanston: Northwestern University

aided in arranging the assignation as a service to his friend, whose unfulfilled love is a cause of sorrow for Tristan. Thomas rejects this version as
impossible and untrue for the reason that Governal, even in disguise,
could never serve as Tristan's messenger in Marc's realm: Governal was
so well known there that Marc's men would have seized him immediately
(Douce 865-78). The logic of the tale calls for another messenger, one un-
familiar to Marc's men—the foreigner Kaherdin—and, therefore, in the
'true' version Kaherdin cannot have died. By removing Kaherdin from the
fatal tryst, Thomas in effect erases the tryst itself and, along with it, Tristan's complicity in it. His argument is not altogether compelling, however, for the reader saw only a few hundred verses earlier the disguised
Tristan pass unrecognized, or nearly so, in Marc's city. As Douglas Kelly
has argued, the reason for Thomas' rejection of this version cannot be the
impossibility of the narrative line as he claims; it must be the version's
incompatibility with his characterization of Tristan and Kaherdin as noble-
minded, faithful lovers and virtuous friends.[10] The first version represents
Kaherdin as a philanderer unfaithful to Brengien, and Tristan is the go-between in disloyal love that the previous episode in Thomas' romance—
Brengien's wrath and reconciliation—proved him not to be. The other version that Thomas relates on the authority of his purported source is 'true'
inasmuch as Kaherdin and Tristan are upright friends and loyal lovers
there.

Thomas' true tale insists upon the pleasurable, useful, and, indeed, de-
votional activities of the two men's companionship. After their return to
Brittany, they enjoy one another's company on hunting parties, and they
participate in tournaments where they win all the prizes. Further, they
remain faithful to their respective distant ladies, whose statues they visit
secretly together in Tristan's cave: "Thus they went out to the forests / To
see the beautiful statues. / They delighted in the statues / Because of the
ladies whom they loved so dearly: / During the day they imagined there
pleasant relief / From the suffering they had at night" (Douce 895-900). In
the cave, love's sanctuary, both love and friendship enjoy relative self-sufficiency in isolation from the outside world. For their partial happiness
and solace, the friends need only themselves and the images of their loved
ladies—that is, the double replacement of the beloved by a mute statue

Press, 1973), pp. 73-77.
    [10] Kelly, "*En uni dire* (*Tristan* Douce 839) and the Composition of Thomas's
Tristan," *Modern Philology* 67 (1969-1970): 11.

and a sympathetic male 'other.' Their *amistié* for the sake of love is Thomas' original concept of loyal male *fine amor*, friendship or *compagnonnage* which acquires high value in sentimental romance because of its aspiration to and interaction with refined love of woman. This complex affective and reflective bond between friends consists at the same time of love felt for the absent woman and of affection for the friend, a confidant and kindred spirit. When later Tristan is mortally wounded while defending the faithful love of the knight Tristan the Dwarf, he calls for Kaherdin, for "he wanted to reveal [to him] the suffering, / Towards him he had loyal *amur*; / Kaherdin found him worthy of love in return" (Douce 1093-95).

The dialogue between Kaherdin and the mortally wounded Tristan converts friendship's duties into love's service, as in earlier exchanges between the two characters. In describing their grief at separation, Thomas first points to the different elements of the personal, strictly masculine relationship between the two—their companionship, mutual affection, kinship, and vows of friendship:

> Kaherdin sits next to him,
> They both weep piteously,
> They lament their good companionship
> Which will be severed very soon,
> [They lament] their love and great friendship;
> In their hearts they feel suffering and pity,
> Distress, grief, and pain;
> Each shows sadness for the other.
> They weep [and] show great sorrow,
> Since so their *amur* must be sundered:
> It has been most excellent and loyal. (Douce 1111-21)

Tristan claims that in the foreign land where he finds himself, Kaherdin is his only friend and kinsman to whom he is indebted for all the good that he enjoys there (Douce 1123-28). In his plea to Kaherdin, Tristan combines, however, the duties of friendship and those of faithful love of woman along with the obligations of vassalage. After asking Kaherdin to go as his messenger to Iseut, he adduces three reasons why Kaherdin should do this, all of which are related to solemn vows: their oath of friendship, the pledge that Kaherdin made when Iseut granted him Brengien's company, and Tristan's promise to become Kaherdin's liege man in gratitude for this service (Douce 1155-64). The vows apply to three different sorts of relationships called *amistié* in Old French—friendship, love, and vassalage—and they have in common the adjuror's fidelity and duty to serve.[11] In citing these binding oaths one after the other, Tristan appeals to Kaherdin's sense of duty.

Kaherdin phrases his positive response in terms that recall the supreme devotion of a classical *amicus verus* to his friend: he will gladly put himself in danger of death in carrying out the mission (Douce 1172-73). In Thomas' representation of male friendship directed towards love, Kaherdin's potential sacrifice of his life for his friend's love and life itself anticipates Tristan's and Iseut's successive deaths for love. The pathos and nobility of the friends' parting suggest David's lament for Jonathan and his praise of the most pleasant friendship of his in-law, prince, and comrade-in-arms. Kaherdin's and Tristan's affectionate words and gestures of farewell stand out in sharp contrast to what follows immediately: Iseut Aux Blanches Mains, having discovered that her husband betrayed her, feigns sweet words and loving embraces to conceal her wrath and vengeful design.

Thomas' portrayal of Tristan and Kaherdin's virtuous friendship characterized by loyalty, deep affection, heroism, joy, and sorrow is in some ways suggestive of the David and Jonathan model and standard of *amicitia*. In respect to the value of love of woman, however, Thomas' romance and the biblical story differ fundamentally. In both cases the young in-laws' comradery is of superior value because of their prowess and great mutual affection and devotion. Since Thomas extends friendship into refined love of woman, to which it is subjoined, he makes of Tristan and Kaherdin's *amistié* a much fuller and complex affective measure than what one finds in the biblical example, where woman's love plays a very small role. It seems clear, however, that the greater part of the high value of Tristan and Kaherdin's *amistié* must be credited not to itself but to its loyal service to love, from which it derives its exceptional measure of affection and, especially, emotional extremes. The introduction into chivalric companion-

---

[11] For the evolution of the terminology of friendship in twelfth-century French literature, see Huguette Legros, "Le vocabulaire de l'amitié, son évolution sémantique au cours du XIIe siècle," *Cahiers de civilisation médiévale* 23 (1980): 131-39. Legros notes a transfer of the terms for *amistié* from feudal relations (a bond between lord and vassal) to chivalric companionship, then to erotic love, and, in the early thirteenth century, to male friendship characterized by mutual fondness. The following study on *amor* and *amistat* in troubadour poetry is useful: Glynnis M. Cropp, *Le vocabulaire courtois des troubadours de l'époque classique*, Publications Romanes et Françaises, 135 (Geneva: Droz, 1975), especially pp. 70-74 and 379-98.

ship of love service and the extremes of joy and sorrow characteristic of romance love is the basis of Thomas' original conception of the interaction between male *amistié* and erotic *amor*, each of which augments the other's affective value. But like his representation of Tristan and Iseut's love, his literary ideal of Tristan and Kaherdin's loyal *fine amor* is ambiguous as a model of conduct in spite of its stability, faithfulness, devotion, generosity, confidence, and courtliness, and it goes against the essential values of marriage, family, and feudal rule of the fictional society from which it withdraws for the most part.

As mentioned earlier, Andreas Capellanus warned that love of the same woman may cause friends to become enemies. In Guillaume de Lorris' French verse *Romance of the Rose* (around 1230), the God of Love advises the heartsick lover to seek consolation in a friend, but only after assuring himself, through discreet inquiry, that his comrade has a ladylove of his own.[12] In light of these lessons in the art of love, one might wonder about the reason or reasons for Tristan's hesitation to prove to Kaherdin his claim about Iseut's superiority and to admit him to his confidence. Perhaps not only the dilemma concerning Kaherdin's vengeance and love's unconditional duty of secrecy made him hesitate. It would seem that Kaherdin had no ladylove of his own at that time. Did not Tristan risk finding in his friend a rival for Iseut's love? In Thomas' recounting, Kaherdin's *coup de foudre* before Brengien's statue and his loyal love of the woman prove, after the fact, that Tristan had nothing to fear. On the other hand, the *Prose Tristan*, a French romance composed from around the second quarter through the second half of the thirteenth century, plays out the alternative—rivalry in love and betrayal in friendship—to its destructive ends. There Kaherdin, a parodic character, falls in love with Iseut at first sight, and he solicits her love. When Tristan discovers Kaherdin's secret, he judges his friend's betrayal the most heinous crime possible, he tries to kill the traitor, and after wrongly accusing Iseut of disloyalty, he goes mad. In the end, Kaherdin dies pining for Iseut.[13] This version's por-

---

[12] Guillaume de Lorris and Jean de Meun, *Le roman de la rose*, ed. Ernest Langlois, Société des Anciens Textes Français, 5 vols. (Paris: Firmin Didot and Librairie Ancienne Honoré Champion, 1914 1924), vol. 2, vss. 2686-2710.

[13] See *Le roman de Tristan en prose, tome III*, ed. Renée L. Curtis, Arthurian Studies, 14 (Cambridge, Eng.: D. S. Brewer, 1985), sections 832-940, and *Le roman de Tristan en prose, tome I*, ed. Philippe Ménard, Textes Littéraires Français, 353 (Geneva: Droz, 1987), sections 85-167.

trayal of the male characters' *amistié* is antithetical to Thomas', but the
storytellers concur in subordinating the activity and fate of chivalric
friendship to the pursuit of *fine amor*, where madness and death are romance signs of excellence.

Jean Markale has commented that the friendship of Lancelot and Galehout
in the *Prose Lancelot* is modeled on the literary code of *fine amor*.[14] The
following section examines in detail the *Prose Lancelot*'s representation
of friendship as a literary variation of *fine amor* between two male characters, whose behavior towards one another mirrors the attitudes and actions
of romance's *fin amant* and, in some instances, those of the ladylove herself. This section will refer to two literary models with which to compare
Galehout and Lancelot's *amistié/amor*, an example of male bonding so intimate that it borders on the homoerotic. The first is Aristotelian-Ciceronian perfect friendship, in respect to which Galehout and Lancelot's relationship marks an extreme degree of deviation. Secondly, Tristan and
Iseut's *fine amor* in Thomas' romance and that of Lancelot and Guinevere
in the *Prose Lancelot* serve as the erotic models to which Galehout and
Lancelot's *amistié/amor* conforms in most respects.

One might identify many varieties of codes of *fine amor* in medieval
theoretical works and fictions which treat this ideal. Although Galehout
and Lancelot's *amistié/amor* shares many essential characteristics with a
number of literary representations of refined erotic love, its male-to-male
nature is an original variation which contradicts the principle that *fine
amor* can exist only between partners of different sex. While conforming
in many regards to the code or codes of love found in theoretical works
and romance—especially, the *Prose Lancelot* itself—their male-to-male
example is a radical modification of the erotic theory from which it
derives. As an extreme variation on literary *fine amor*, Galehout and
Lancelot's nonsexual *amistié/amor* lacks the very essence of its erotic
models.

The narration of Lancelot and Galehout's relationship illustrates both
cooperation and tension between refined love of woman and male friend-

---

[14] Markale, *Lancelot et la chevalerie arthurienne* (Paris: Imago, 1985), p.
80.

ship: the ladylove Guinevere and the best friend Galehout vie for
Lancelot's companionship, and they strike a deal by which each gets a
share of him. In the long Galehout section, the narrator effects a radical
revision of chivalric friendship according to romance models of *fine amor*
in his representation of Galehout: he transfers the characteristics of Tristan's and Lancelot's all-consuming passion for Iseut and Guinevere, their
suffering, sacrifice, and humiliation for love, their short-lived joy, and
their contempt for all honors but one, to Galehout as the impassioned
friend of Lancelot. Whereas the *fins amanz* Tristan and Lancelot fix their
attention and affection primarily on their ladies and secondarily on their
comrades, the refined friend Galehout reverses that order in directing nearly
all his affectionate attention to his comrade, and the remainder he gives to
his ladylove. As Lancelot's *ami*, Galehout acts towards him as the *fin
amant* Tristan does towards his lady—that is, passively, in forsaking
honor, ambition, and security and in dying of lovesickness. The transfer
of the *fin amant*'s mental attitudes and actions to Galehout makes chivalric friendship perfectly ambiguous.

Some scholars find Galehout and Lancelot's chivalric *amistié/amor* to
be unambiguously homosexual. Christiane Marchello-Nizia sees in the
young Lancelot's actions towards Galehout a kind of erotic seduction of
the older knight, and Galehout's feelings and actions towards Lancelot
indicate a strong homosexual attraction which is displaced, at least partially, in Galehout's role as mediator in the love affair of Lancelot and
Guinevere.[15] Jean Markale notes that Galehout's intermediary role is the
only means available to him for preserving with Lancelot his homosexual
relationship, and he cites as "irrefutable proof" of homosexuality a passage (which Ch. Marchello-Nizia also quoted) in which Galehout enters
the room where Lancelot is sleeping and, according to Markale's reading,
lies next to him in bed.[16] While not denying that Galehout and Lancelot's
amistié/amor must appear to modern readers as latent homosexuality, the
present writer believes that J. Markale has read into this passage a specifically sexual suggestion which the narrator took pains to obviate. The passage in question indicates that the room contains four beds, of which
Lancelot occupies one and two of Galehout's knights two others. In the
quotation which J. Markale gives, "And when Galehout knew that

---

[15] Marchello-Nizia, "Amour courtois, société masculine et figures du pouvoir," *Annales. Economies—Sociétés—Civilisations* 36 (1981): 974-81.
[16] Markale, *Lancelot*, pp. 78-82.

[Lancelot] was asleep, then he lay down alongside him as quietly as he could, and two of his knights, too" (LIIa 63),[17] "alongside" refers to the bed next to Lancelot's, not to Galehout's sleeping in the same bed as Lancelot. The passage is equivocal, as are many others that might be cited, in respect to the nature of Galehout and Lancelot's *amistié/amor*. The sexual potential of their attraction is realized or, rather, diverted through a double heterosexual displacement, as Ch. Marchello-Nizia has noted, whereby Galehout encourages the affair between Lancelot and Guinevere, and Guinevere encourages the liaison between Galehout and the Lady of Malohaut. Here the narrator circumscribes the activity of Galehout and Lancelot's *amistié/amor* within the limits that romance sets as proper for erotic love and for male friendship.

---

[17] Chapter and subsection numbers refer to *Lancelot, roman en prose du XIIIe siècle*, ed. Alexandre Micha, Textes Littéraires Français, 247, 249, 262, 278, 283, 286, 288, 307, and 315, 9 vols. (Paris—Geneva: Droz, 1978-1983). In this edition the Galehout-Lancelot narration begins in volume 8 (chapters and subsections XLIXa 1-LIIIa 7, pp. 1-132; LXIIa 1-3, pp. 323-25; LXIXa 1-LXXIa 49, pp. 417-90), and it continues and ends with Galehout's death in volume 1 (I 1-IX 52, pp. 1-175; XV 1-8, pp. 214-17; XXIX 17-XXXV 3, pp. 354-89). The death of Galehout's ladylove and Lancelot's entombment of his friend are in volume 2 (XXXVI 3-5, pp. 2-3; XLI 9, pp. 99-100; XLIX 5-25, pp. 210-19; L 57-59, pp. 252-54) and volume 4 (LXXVIII 56, p. 209). There is also a short redaction in volume 3 (principally, I* 1-22, pp. 1-22; XXIX* 8, p. 222; XXXV* 1-2, pp. 250-52). The reader will find a detailed summary in French of the portions of the romance dealing with Galehout and Lancelot in Jean Frappier's article, "Le personnage de Galehaut dans le *Lancelot en prose*," in *Amour courtois et table ronde*, Publications Romanes et Françaises, 126 (Geneva: Droz, 1973), pp. 183-87.

English translations of passages from the *Prose Lancelot* are my own. At the time that I was writing this chapter, the Garland Press edition of the *Prose Lancelot* in English translation was not yet available.

There is also an early-thirteenth-century noncyclic *Lancelot*, which according to its editor is the first stage in the development of the Lancelot-Grail prose cycle: *Lancelot do Lac: The Non-Cyclic Old French Prose Romance*, ed. Elspeth Kennedy, 2 vols. (Oxford: Clarendon Press, 1980). Partial translation into English: *Lancelot of the Lake*, trans. Corin Corley and introduced by E. Kennedy, The World's Classics (Oxford—New York: Oxford University Press, 1989). E. Kennedy has also published a thorough analysis of this self-contained version, which ends with Galehout's death, and a comparison with the Lancelot-Grail cycle in *Lancelot and the Grail: A Study of the Prose "Lancelot"* (Oxford: Clarendon Press, 1986). The Lancelot-Galehout story in the noncyclic redaction differs considerably from that in the cyclic *Prose Lancelot*—compare the plot summary of the noncyclic version in *Lancelot and the Grail*, pp. 5-8, and Kennedy's abstract of Micha's volume 1 and part of volume 3 on pp. 254-55.

On the other hand, the problem of Galehout's attraction to Lancelot is not resolved by the narrative displacement of male-to-male affection to female figures. Galehout strives not so much for Lancelot's love as his companionship. Galehout and Arthur share as rivals the goal of winning Lancelot's *compagnie*, his companionship, and both lords use a sole woman, Guinevere, as means to that goal while she manipulates each of them, and Lancelot, too, in order to achieve her own ends. These three figures of great political power—Prince Galehout, Arthur, and Guinevere—state individually what they would give to have Lancelot's company. Arthur says that he would share with Lancelot all that he has, except for Guinevere, who declares in an indirect manner that she would offer Lancelot her body,[18] and Galehout claims that he would exchange his great honor for shame in order to have Lancelot's company forever (LIIa 85). Galehout pays this inordinate price for Lancelot's companionship, and Arthur, who later directs Guinevere to draw Lancelot into service at the Round Table, exchanges for Lancelot's fidelity/infidelity precisely what he excepted. It would seem that for neither of the two male competitors is Lancelot's love in itself the primary goal, for what each admires most in him is not, as Ch. Marchello-Nizia suggests, his seductive, youthful beauty but his quality as an unbeatable warrior which makes his company and service useful politically. Although Galehout accepts ungrudgingly Lancelot's placement of his affection in Guinevere, he is most jealous of his rights to Lancelot's company, rights which he negotiates with Guinevere. It is principally in terms of winning and preserving Lancelot's companionship rather than enjoying his affection that one must understand the thoroughly possessive and jealous attitude of Galehout towards Lancelot. Indeed, at Galehout's entrance in the *Prose Lancelot*, the narrator clearly points to his primary concern as possession and power: his first intention then was to seize for himself by force of arms Arthur's kingdom and queen. The subsequent sudden displacement of his aspiration to Lancelot, recognizably the main support of Arthur's power, does not alter the political character of Galehout's ambition.

The narrator emphasizes the moral paradox in Galehout's character

---

[18] Earlier in the same passage Gauvain says that to have Lancelot's company forever, he would be the fairest maid in the world and would give him his/her love. This odd declaration made in the context of courtly badinage surely does not reflect Gauvain's desire; it serves, rather, to prelude and, also, obfuscate Guinevere's statement to the same effect in Arthur's presence.

whereby the influence of great affection and ambition causes each of his superlative virtues to become, in an Aristotelian sense, a vice, an extreme. Galehout's friendly attitudes and actions invite a comparison with *Laelius* and its Greek sources. His benevolence, beneficence, disinterestedness, sacrifices, and affection for Lancelot are extreme, and, therefore, they transgress the ethical limits of the classical code of *amicitia*. As an *ami*, Galehout excels in the sense of transgressing. The son of a giantess, he acts, thinks, and feels on a gigantic scale, excessively. In wishing well for his comrade, he disregards his own best interests, and his relatives reproach him for bringing dishonor upon himself. His apparent disinterestedness may be viewed as pure selfishness or its contrary vice, the complete absence of self-love. His magnanimity, one of the most praiseworthy virtues in the *Nicomachean Ethics*, is blameworthy. His enormous sacrifices that come from his supreme generosity towards Lancelot amount to nothing good—on the contrary, they add up to his dishonor, a debt that Lancelot could never repay, and, in his service to Lancelot and Guinevere's illicit love, the self-destruction of the Round Table recounted in *The Death of Arthur*, the conclusion to the Lancelot-Grail cycle. His affection is such that he cannot bear to be separated from Lancelot; it is the extreme of affection of which Cicero disapproves in *Laelius*. As a fictional example, Galehout poses the following problem regarding love, character, and characterization: just how greatly can the most magnanimous warrior-prince love his companion, the romance's greatest knight and lover? Galehout's perfectly possessive and, at the same time, self-forgetful sentimental attachment to Lancelot would seem to answer that such a character can love his knightly *ami* at least as strongly, devotedly, and, in the final count, futilely as romance's most refined *amanz* do their ladies.

The *Prose Lancelot* offers two distinct standards for evaluating Galehout and Lancelot's *amistié/amor* which one might consider as partially complementary measures. The negative moral judgment on Lancelot and Guinevere's *fine amor* as sinful that a sage expresses in strictest confidence to Galehout (IV 36-37 and 45) must apply to Galehout, too. For love of Lancelot, Galehout serves as go-between in his and Guinevere's affair, and the sins of that liaison, the principal of which is pride, carry over into Galehout and Lancelot's *amistié/amor*. This instance of a Christian moral censure of the romance ethos of *fine amor* and, by extension, of Galehout's love is isolated and even silenced in the narrative circumstances of secrecy. By the standards of sentimental romance, however, the recognition of sin and *folie* in *fine amor* does not mean that it is an entirely negative model: the Lady of the Lake argues that Lancelot and Guinevere's love is necessarily sinful and foolish, but nonetheless it possesses great honor and wisdom (LXXIa 13). As we shall see, Galehout presents a similar argument regarding his *amistié/amor*, which is equal to the romance measure of Lancelot and Guinevere's exemplary love. Given this problematic double standard, readers have a number of options for evaluating Galehout and Lancelot's *amistié/amor*. Among the possible choices, one is suggested by medieval Christian readings of classical ethical works such as *Laelius*—that is, to identify and appreciate moral qualities presented there which, although incomplete in themselves, might be brought to perfection by Christian virtues and divine grace. Applied to the cycle of Lancelot-Grail romances, such a reading would recognize in Galehout and Lancelot's relationship the prowess, fortitude, devotion, humility, and other qualities that prefigure in part the Christian virtues and friendship of Galahad, Perceval, and Bors in *The Quest of the Holy Grail*. Just as Guinevere and Lancelot's worldly *amor* is perfected in the spiritual love of Lancelot's son and Perceval's sister in *The Quest*, so, too, Galehout and Lancelot's faithful friendship might be seen to announce the perfect Christian knights and friends in the following romance.

Galehout's love affair with the noble Lady of Malohaut, Guinevere's confidante, serves, as does Kaherdin and Brengien's liaison, to double as backdrop for the primary love story with which its main stages—meeting, vows of fidelity, kisses, lovemaking, painful separation, reunion—coincide in time and place. In this narrative of secondary interest with no outstanding features of its own, the writer gives not a hint on Galehout's side of an emotional intensity in erotic love comparable to his strong feelings for his *ami*. Although he behaves as an impeccably courteous *amant*, he shows none of the characteristics of the romance lover—total submission, rapturous adoration, lovesickness, jealousy, the extremes of joy and pain, etc.—that are apparent in his friendship.

While the affair of Galehout and the Lady of Malohaut functions as a mostly colorless backdrop to the main love story, Galehout and Lancelot's *amistié/amor* matches and even outdoes Guinevere and Lancelot's *fine amor* in display of emotion and devotion. The following passage is one of many examples that show the great reciprocal affection of Lancelot and Galehout. After acknowledging Galehout's having sacrificed his honor and ambitions for the sake of friendship, Lancelot "bursts out sobbing since he can speak no more, he joins his hands and goes down on his knees before Galehout. And when Galehout sees him, he can stand it no longer, rather he lifts him in his arms and weeps most bitterly: thus they carry on so grievously together that they both fall on a bed in a faint and remain lying for a long time in this manner. And when they recover from their fainting, both lament very grievously" (IV 6). The portrayal of knights' embracing and swooning is not uncommon in romance, but the frequency and intensity of such scenes with Lancelot and Galehout in the *Prose Lancelot* indicate a depth of affection between the characters that goes beyond conventional representations of *compagnonnage*. Galehout's devotion far surpasses Tristan and Kaherdin's loyal *fine amor*, for example, in his determination to be with Lancelot or to die if he cannot. The *Prose Lancelot*'s portrayal of Galehout and, to a large extent, Lancelot remodels romance *compagnonnage* according to an unconventional and ambiguous literary ideal of knightly companions as highly refined romance lovers. In Galehout's case, even though he negotiates with Guinevere his rights to Lancelot's company, he, like the lovers Tristan and Lancelot, finds himself in the impossible position of the *fin amant* whose idea of joy—constant companionship—is unrealizable because of his beloved's obligation to a third party.

Although Galehout and Lancelot are more or less alike in status, prowess, generosity, love of honor, and other qualities which characterize them as equal friends, their relationship tends to be unequal on the model of romance *fine amor*. Galehout subordinates himself to Lancelot, and he seeks his permission before undertaking action. Lancelot's role is similar to those of Iseut and Guinevere in *fine amor*: as the superior party, he has absolute authority over the direction that their relationship will take, he grants or withholds permission to act, and he considers his own interests (here, Guinevere's love) above those of Galehout. Sometimes Lancelot displays, too, a certain testiness towards his companion that calls up Guinevere's and Iseut's occasional irritability (see, for example, Guinevere's testy remark when Lancelot dares to act without her permission, XVIII 7.) As Margaret Burrell has observed,[19] the heroines in Chrétien de Troyes's romances, including Guinevere in *Le chevalier de la charrete*,

---

[19] Burrell, "The Participation of Chrétien's Heroines in Love's *Covant*," *Nottingham French Studies* 30, no. 2 (1991): 24-33.

typically demonstrate less emotional involvement in *fine amor* than their lovers, and by thus distancing themselves from love's passion or *folie*, they exert rational control over their lovers' actions. In the *Prose Lancelot*, the title character maintains in regard to Galehout a similar emotional distance whereby he, like Chrétien's heroines, is able to direct—indeed, to manipulate—the impassioned Galehout. Even though Galehout and Lancelot's *amistié/amor* is mutual, the two reciprocate in degrees and manners that conform to the unequal roles of refined male-female lovers in romance.

Let us now examine some of the characteristics of excellent male friendship in the Aristotelian-Ciceronian tradition—mutual admiration, confidence, affection, proper mental attitudes such as humility and generosity, living together, and the pursuit of wisdom and honor—which the narrator refashions according to the moral and affective nature of romance *fine amor* illustrated by the Tristan-Iseut and Lancelot-Guinevere examples.

MUTUAL ADMIRATION. Galehout and Lancelot's initial meeting, at which they show great mutual admiration for moral and knightly qualities, provides a hard test of character and Galehout's declaration of vassalage, followed by his admission to and complicity in Lancelot's secret love and his performance of a love service for his *ami* (LIIa 48-91). Galehout observes Lancelot's prowess in the service of Arthur, Galehout's enemy, whose troops battle his own, and he is immediately taken with him, even before meeting him face to face. Galehout's instant admiration for Lancelot because of his military valor and great worth to the king recalls the initiation of classical *amicitia perfecta* on account of good repute. But the distance from which Galehout first observes him and the suddenness and intensity of his affection suggest, too, Lancelot's *coup de foudre* for Guinevere at first sight from a distance earlier in the romance (XLVa 1-2). Galehout sends him his own horse when Lancelot's is killed and offers him lodging. Lancelot is surprised at the generous offers from a man whose army he has just defeated, but Galehout reassures him by promising that he will grant whatever boon Lancelot desires. Lancelot responds with jesting distrust: "Certainly, sire, you are a very good promiser! I do not know how it will be with fulfilling [your promise]" (LIIa 55). Galehout swears to grant Lancelot's request, which is that as soon as Galehout's troops, with Lancelot at their head, defeat Arthur's, Galehout will surrender himself to Arthur and beg for his mercy. Lancelot's request is

'amatory' in that he protects and honors Guinevere by thus winning
supremacy for her husband. It is possible to interpret his demand as a severe test of Galehout's character, for he orders nothing less than for
mighty Galehout, the conqueror of thirty kings, to disgrace himself. In
romance this sort of dishonoring command is not unusual. In Beroul's
Tristan and some of the Lancelot romances, Iseut and Guinevere do not
hesitate to make dishonoring demands of their knightly lovers, who do
not or dare not hesitate to comply. For example, Guinevere twice orders
Lancelot to fight his worst, not to defeat his opponents (XLI 8-12). In the
present instance Lancelot, not an all-powerful ladylove, orders Galehout to
bring shame upon himself. When Galehout willingly and courteously
submits to Arthur, Lancelot is overwhelmed with admiration and compassion: "And when the good knight sees Galehout leave and do himself such
great harm because of him, so he thinks well and says that no one ever
had such a good *ami* nor true companion. And he has such great pity for
him that he sighs from the bottom of his heart and weeps copiously beneath his helmet and says under his breath: 'Fair lord God, who can compensate for this?'" (LIIa 69). Here and often later Lancelot is remorseful
for the role that he plays in bringing his mighty friend low. Romance's
adulterous ladylove often plays the same part as Lancelot here in her
lover's humiliation, but she seldom voices regret.

CONFIDENCE. In spite of his admiration for Galehout, who after sub-
mitting to Arthur claims Lancelot as his *seigneur* and companion (LIIa
80), Lancelot refuses to do what Galehout asks of him—to confess why
he spends sleepless nights weeping and sighing. It is only indirectly and
by stages that he permits Galehout to enter into his confidence. When
Galehout asks how he should answer the queen, who wants him to arrange
a secret meeting with Lancelot, he replies evasively; the perfect *fin amant*,
he keeps the secret of his love strictly to himself. While revealing
nothing, he nevertheless permits Galehout to arrange the tryst. In all this,
the fearless knight Lancelot is exceedingly discreet, as befits the fearful
romance lover about to meet in private for the first time the lady whom
he has loved from a distance. Without a doubt Galehout knew from the
beginning that Guinevere was the cause of Lancelot's suffering, for every
time that Galehout mentioned her name, Lancelot became pensive; but
Galehout, though he could guess the cause, did not ask his companion
outright if he loved her. Galehout's failure to talk openly about the trans-

parent secret mimics the extreme discretion of the romance lover, of whom Lancelot is the model. Just as Lancelot would not dare compromise Guinevere by naming her as the object of his love, so Galehout does not dare offend Lancelot by naming her in respect to love.

Lancelot's refusal to speak about his love illustrates perfect compliance with *fine amor*'s code, which forbids the lover to reveal anything that might compromise his lady and, thus, hurt or anger her. As Lancelot's *ami*, Galehout demonstrates this trait of the *fin amant* by refusing to reveal to Lancelot grave secrets that might cause him sorrow. Galehout had two dreams which, as interpreted by sages, signified his death because of Lancelot and Guinevere's love and, also, Lancelot's future failure in the Grail quest. Galehout recounts the dreams to Lancelot, who maintains on grounds of friendship that it would be wrong to conceal anything from the man who loves him above all other men in the world (II 9-10); but Galehout refuses to tell him their meaning on grounds of friendship, too, and he lies to him for the best of motives—to spare him sorrow. The moral principle that Galehout repeatedly invokes to justify his nonconfidence is that one should never tell a friend anything that might cause him grief or shame or make him angry. Cicero enjoins the *amicus* from saying or doing anything that might vex his companion (*Laelius* 27,103). In the present instance, with Galehout's silence and pious lies, it would seem that this rule of *amicitia* has been modified, if not wholly perverted, in its recoding in conformity with the romance lover's caution about offending or angering his lady.

After his secret meeting with a sage who foretold his death, Galehout lies to the grieving Lancelot: "Ah, fair sweet companion, … do not be upset, for I just heard news which has made me very happy and which will bring you great joy, for I know well that you are bothered for my sake" (V 1). When Lancelot explains that he is troubled because he thinks that the sage knows of his affair with Guinevere, Galehout lies again and says that the sage did not mention her and that he predicted that Galehout would live a long life. As the narrator notes, Galehout "said this to make Lancelot happy" (V 3). He also lies about the meaning of one of the dreams, which, he says, portended the death of a relative. To give support to this fabrication, he lies further in claiming that as he was leaving the sage, a messenger arrived to announce Galehout's mother's death (V 3). While asserting that he has never concealed anything from Lancelot, Galehout excepts news that might cause him pain or future misfortunes that cannot be averted (V 5). Paradoxically and in a spirit of extreme refinement, Galehout's nonconfidence and false confidences are proof of the best friendship in that they spare his partner anguish. Although he is Galehout's confidant in love, in friendship Lancelot, too, hides the truth. On one of their voyages together, the melancholic friends dare not speak for fear of upsetting one another (I 1-II 5). Their gloomy silence continues until a crisis forces speech—but, then, only half confidences emerge. In another instance, Lancelot, wounded in a joust, believes that Galehout will go mad if he hears about the injury. Therefore, he conceals the wound in Galehout's presence and asks Arthur to keep it secret (VI 9-11). Nonconfidence, hiding the truth, and silence are characteristic of Galehout and Lancelot's refined *amistié/amor*, in which consideration for one another's feelings makes them behave not as mutually trusting friends but as the romance lover who holds his tongue in constant check for fear of provoking anger or grief.

AFFECTION. The alternation of extreme happiness and dejection that characterizes *fine amor*'s highly unstable affective state carries over to Galehout as the refined friend. One sees him at times sorrowful, lost in his melancholic musings, when he mirrors Lancelot's sadness or he fears to lose or upset him, or at others he is exhilarated when he shares Lancelot's joy and his company.

As well as undergoing an alternation of emotive extremes, Galehout experiences a coincidence of affective opposites, a simultaneity of conflicting emotions that romance usually reserves for the confused *fin amant*, as in Lancelot's experiencing joy and fear before his first tryst with Guinevere (LIIa 92). When Galehout hears of the false Guinevere's grave accusation against Guinevere at Arthur's court, he feels sorrow and joy at the same time, "sorrow because he knew that Lancelot would be very grieved and angry for this reason ... [and] on the other hand he was joyful because he would probably have Lancelot's company longer if it happened that the king and queen were separated" (IV 1). Galehout's simultaneous joy and grief are modeled on the *fin amant*'s confusion of passions.

Among the many signs of affection characteristic of romance love that carry over to Lancelot and Galehout's *amistié/amor*, the most common is swooning as a sign of solicitude. When Lancelot sees Galehout tumble from his horse and he fears him dead, "the deep suffering that he feels in his heart because of his great fear for [Galehout's] death benumbs him, and he stretches out beside him and falls in a faint to the ground" (II 6). When Galehout hears that Lancelot has been wounded, he faints, then Guinevere faints, and he refaints (VI 7-8; Guinevere outdoes him by swooning seven times in one sentence, but not because of Lancelot, VII 8.) Later, upon hearing that Lancelot will never fight again, Galehout swoons (XXIX 7), as he also does upon learning that his friend has been imprisoned (XXX 5). Jacques Roubaud has noted that Galehout shows all the symptoms of lovesickness, *li mals d'amors*, which one finds in many medieval medical treatises and romances.[20] The principal signs are loss of sleep and appetite, melancholic imaginings, weeping and sighing, madness, and, finally, death. The romance lover's sleepless nights, such as Lancelot's nocturnal lament for unfulfilled love (LIIa 77-79), carry over to Galehout's night-long complaint for fear of losing Lancelot, who sleeps in the same room but whom Galehout does not waken with his weeping (II 4). One might compare Galehout's appetite loss due to melancholy or solicitude (LXXIa 3, XXX 2-3, XXXV 1-2) and his gloomy trance (II 5) to Lancelot's melancholy and loss of appetite because of lovesickness (LXXa 1). Both Galehout and Lancelot shed many a tear and breathe many deep sighs for love of one another (e.g., LXXIa 42). Galehout is frequently on the brink of madness when he fears for Lancelot's safety (e.g., LXXIa 3). Lancelot offers, too, an example of madness when he discovers Galehout's tomb: he grieves so over Galehout's death for his sake that twice he is on the verge of committing suicide (XLIX 11 and 22).

Galehout and Lancelot's verbal expression of affection alters the gender of the romance lover's discourse. For example, when Galehout fears that he may lose Lancelot, he asks: "And what shall I do, I who have placed in you my heart and my person?" Lancelot replies: "Surely, sire, ... I should love you above all [other] men in the world, and indeed I do" (LXXIa 42). Lancelot's expression of love here is the same as that for Guinevere except for the replacement of "above all other women" with "men." For Galehout, too, the verbal gesture of granting his body and heart typifies the romance lover's pledge to his ladylove.

MENTAL ATTITUDES. Among the attitudes proper to the romance

---

[20] Roubaud, *La fleur inverse. Essai sur l'art formel des troubadours* (Paris: Ramsay, 1986), pp. 82-99.

lover that the narrator transfers to Galehout's *amistié/amor* are humility, generosity, veneration, a 'reasonable' degree of jealousy, and the preference for death to life without love. As for the last of these, Thomas' Tristan and Iseut die because they cannot live without one another. The very life of the refined *ami* Galehout depends, in his mind, upon Lancelot. When Arthur asks him to convince Lancelot to join the Round Table, Galehout replies that this would mean his own death since he cannot live without Lancelot (LXXIa 46). He repeatedly tells Lancelot that he loves him so much that he could not survive his death or the loss of his companionship (II 20, II 21, IV 7). Galehout seems more than just resigned to his death for love, he seems to wish it. The chapter that recounts his final agony and demise is hardly plausible without his desire to suffer and die for love, since he could have avoided death by seeking Lancelot, who, mad but far from dead after his sudden departure from Galehout's castle, was wandering in the forests. A few chapters before the account of his demise, Galehout, during one of his many mental crises when he wrongly believes Lancelot hurt or dead, "shows the greatest grief of which he is capable, and he turns his thoughts to this, that he could not live after [Lancelot's death] and that he will want to subject his body to all the torments that he can endure, excepting that which might lead to the damnation of his soul" (XXX 16). He seizes every opportunity to suffer for his *amistié/amor*.

During his long agony, Galehout's melancholic, constant contemplation of the absent *ami* in the substitute form of Lancelot's shield simulates the *fin amant*'s veneration of his ladylove. The shield as object of substitution recalls Thomas' Tristan's replacement of Iseut with her statue in his cave and the comfort that he seeks in contemplating the icon. When earlier Galehout, in search of Lancelot, found only his shield, he thought that "since he cannot have the knight, he would like to carry away his shield" (XXX 9), and he defeats some twenty knights to win it. In coming into possession of Lancelot's shield, Galehout possesses his identity, as the shield painting is the emblem by which knights are identified. Further, the shield as an emblem of *amistié/amor* doubles for another shield that the Lady of the Lake sent earlier to Guinevere as proof of Lancelot and Guinevere's complete love (LXXa 35-36). In his uninterrupted contemplation of this relic-fetish of his friend and his love, Galehout pines and dies.

In twelfth and thirteenth-century amatory theory, moderate jealousy is essential to the *fin amant*'s psychological makeup. Too much jealousy works against love—it may cause the lover to offend or harm his beloved—while too little indicates indifference antithetical to love.[21] Galehout's attempts to have Lancelot all to himself, preferably in his isolated realm of Sorelois, confirm Gauvain's claim that Galehout is more jealous of Lancelot than any knight is of a young woman (LXXIa 41). Although Guinevere acknowledges his rights to Lancelot's company, Galehout expresses hard feelings about her influencing Lancelot to join the Round Table. He considers this action on her part to constitute a breach of their contract (II 20), and he constantly fears losing Lancelot to the queen, the king, or both. Nonetheless, his jealousy is tempered by the knowledge that Lancelot belongs first and foremost to Guinevere. As the main character responsible for the realization and perpetuation of Lancelot and Guinevere's affair, he knowingly promotes the conditions of his own jealousy.

Mimicking the perfect lover, Galehout humbles himself before his comrade without a moment's hesitation and with no second thoughts. He shows his humility by declaring publicly that he is Lancelot's vassal and by his persistent efforts to accord Lancelot a standing, physical and hierarchical, above himself. On the first night that Galehout gives lodging to Lancelot, he has a chamber equipped with four beds, the first of which is large and high, the second is less high and big, and the remaining two, much smaller and lower (LIIa 62). He says that he will sleep in another room, but as soon as he believes Lancelot to be asleep in the first bed, he enters the chamber quietly, lies in the second bed, and in the morning slips out before Lancelot can observe his act of humility. Shortly afterwards, he proclaims Lancelot as his *seigneur*, although there is no ceremony of vassalage. On another occasion he proposes that Lancelot accept half his realm and that at their double coronation Lancelot be crowned first. He claims that Lancelot, the son of a king, should by rights be above himself, the son of a poor prince, and that Lancelot should have superiority (but not too much) over him (V 5-6).

Galehout's humility typically passes to the extreme of humiliation. For the sake of remaining with Lancelot, he willingly abases himself by yielding, without hesitation, to his enemy Arthur, and when without

---

[21] See, for example, Andreas Capellanus, *On Love*, bk. 1, pp. 146-51, and bk. 2, pp. 228-29 and 282-83. Gottfried von Strassburg discusses the necessity of a certain amount of doubt and suspicion in love—*Tristan*, trans. Hatto, pp. 223-24.

warning Lancelot joins the Round Table, Galehout, one of the world's greatest princes, the conqueror of thirty kings, immediately seeks to join, too (LXXIa 47). Galehout's willingness to suffer shame for Lancelot is a leitmotiv in his friendly discourse. His self-dishonoring humility is antithetical to the ancients' *amicitia perfecta*, but in all respects it mirrors the mind-set appropriate to romance's *fin amant*. His willing acceptance of shame as the price for his *amistié/amor* corresponds to Tristan's and Lancelot's abandoning honor for the sake of adulterous *fine amor*.

In medieval love doctrine, generous giving is not only a sign of the *fin amant*'s noble-mindedness. His gifts may also serve the lady as collateral to insure that he will remain true to his oaths of fidelity. An example of the lover's generous donation as security is found in an anonymous Anglo-Norman love treatise in the form of a fictive letter addressed to Dame Desyree and dated 1299. The writer advises the lady to test her prospective lover for seven years, and if he proves to be discreet, highminded, courteous in manner and speech, true to his word, valiant, genuinely lovesick, and wholly devoted to her, then in the seventh year she should give him her love after he pledges before a witness to turn over himself and all his goods to her keeping.[22] Galehout's liberality is one of his outstanding traits, and Jean Frappier rightly called him a paragon of

---

[22] "Anglonormannische Texte im MS. Arundel 220 des Britischen Museums," ed. John Koch, *Zeitschrift für romanische Philologie* 54 (1934): 20-56. The text is on pp. 50-54. This prose treatise is one of several shorter Anglo-Norman and French works of the thirteenth century on courtship and love. "Un art d'aimer du XIIIe siècle: [*L'amistiés de vraie amour*]," ed. Jacques Thomas, *Revue belge de philologie et d'histoire* 36 (1958): 786-811, a prose treatise by Richard de Fournival (1201-1260) or a Picard clerk of the same period, defines love as "concordance de diverses volentés, de .ii. esperites accordans en toutes coses humainnes sans departies" (p. 798), and as an elevating experience by which the poor become rich and the foolish, virtuous (p. 803). *L'amistiés de vraie amour* was reworked by Richard de Fournival in his prose *Puissanche d'amours*, and it was adapted by an anonymous writer in the second half of the thirteenth century in "Une définition d'amour en prose anglo-normande," ed. Paul Studer, in *Mélanges de philologie et d'histoire offerts à M. Antoine Thomas* (Paris: H. Champion, 1927), pp. 433-36. The *Remedes d'amours*, an anonymous late-thirteenth-century poem erroneously attributed to Jacques d'Amiens, refashions erotic love in the tradition of Andreas Capellanus' *On Love* as chaste Christian love, and the poet assures sexually abstinent lovers that their desires will be satisfied in heaven—see *"L'art d'amours" van Jakes d'Amiens*, ed. Deeuwes Talsma (diss. Leiden, 1925), pp. 141-58, especially verses 597-610.

generosity.[23] His proposal that Lancelot accept half his realm along with a crown recalls the ancient idea of the joint property of *amici perfecti* as well as Jonathan's promise to share the throne of Israel with David (1 Samuel 23,16-18). However, in consideration of the Anglo-Norman love treatise mentioned above, Galehout's generous offer of lands and titles includes not only a ceremonial confirmation of their bond of friendship in the double coronation but, also, an apparent amatory motive. The letter's lover gives his person and goods so that he may possess the lady now and forever. Likewise, Galehout's offer is clearly an attempt to tie Lancelot to himself and to a part of his isolated realm of Sorelois in order to have him forever near—and away from Guinevere, for as a ruler, Lancelot would be obliged to spend much time in his own kingdom. Galehout's superlative generosity towards Lancelot is hardly disinterested.

LIVING TOGETHER. The description of Galehout and Lancelot's life together bears several stamps of romance love. Galehout's desire to have Lancelot all to himself—the romance lover's greatest good—is realized when they reside together for some time in isolated Sorelois. For Galehout, this intimacy outside Arthur's domain is a source of joy because of his exclusive possession—Lancelot's company. Lancelot, however, suffers from longing for Guinevere (LIIIa 5), and he feels imprisoned and complains that he and Galehout are wasting their time and youth there, away from jousts and knightly adventures. Galehout responds to his complaint by taking him to an even more remote place, the nearly inaccessible Lost Isle, for he wants to keep him from combat and possible injury (LXIXa 1-2). Here the narrator converts the bonds of friendship to love's bondage. This episode involving Galehout as the loving jailer and Lancelot as his suffering, immobilized prisoner would seem to be a variation on the imprisonment of Lancelot earlier in the romance by the Lady of Malohaut, who fell in love with her captive.

The friends' life together in another instance combines *amistié* and chaste *fine amor*: Guinevere, having been repudiated by Arthur after the false Guinevere's accusation, lives with the two friends and the Lady of Malohaut for two years in Sorelois (IX 1-36). Galehout negotiates with Arthur Guinevere's retirement to Sorelois ostensibly to honor her and to protect her from her enemies, but his hidden motives are to relieve

---

[23] "Le personnage de Galehaut," p. 206.

Lancelot's ennui and to keep him near. As soon as she arrives in Sorelois, she orders Lancelot not to make love to her. The narrator's curious invention of the cohabitation of chaste love and firm friendship in Sorelois is not, however, one of perfect bliss, for Guinevere, like the banished Iseut, regrets having lost the honor she enjoyed in the court of her husband the king. The cohabitation ends when, as with Tristan and Iseut's sojourn in the forest, the queen returns to her husband.

WISDOM AND HONOR. The author praises Galehout as a valiant prince second only to Arthur and as the wisest man in his time (I 2, XXXV 3; in the short redaction, he is the valiant Solomon of his age, XXXV* 2), and he lauds his Christian works (XXXV 3). Before meeting Lancelot, he strove to win the greatest honors and possessions by military conquest. His *folie* is that he follows the dishonoring and passive course that Lancelot's will charts for him—submission to Arthur and the submission of his *amistié/amor* to Guinevere and Lancelot's love. For Lancelot's sake he contemplates foolish enterprises, such as kidnapping Guinevere so that she can be with Lancelot in Sorelois, but he gives up the idea when he realizes that Guinevere would be angry and that as a consequence of her anger, Lancelot would go mad and perhaps die (IV 9). His dreams of power, too, must go unrealized because he assumes the passive position of the *fin amant* who picks up arms only at the will and command of his beloved. No longer interested in military conquest for his own sake and honor, he tries to convince Lancelot that together they should set out to win back Lancelot's realm of Benoïc; but Lancelot rejects this honorable proposition because Guinevere has not authorized it.[24] Lancelot, for his part, regrets that his company has changed the world's most vigorous knight into the most idle.

The essentially contradictory elements of the narrator's portrayal of Galehout—once mighty, now fallen, a wise man become foolish—would seem to call for the judgment that his *amistié/amor* is blameworthy. The contradictions are resolved, however, in a manner that makes sense only in terms of romance logic and values—that is, through the conversion of loss into gain, folly to wisdom, and dishonor to honor. Galehout replies to his relatives who reproach him for having dishonored himself in order

---

[24] Galehout's plans to kidnap Guinevere and to conquer Benoïc show another of the mental attitudes proper to the *fin amant*: the lover's anticipation of his beloved's wishes. Cf. *Laelius* 13,44.

to win Lancelot's company:

> Then he answered that he had never gained so much nor won such great honor, "for it is not," said he, "wealth of land or goods, but of a good and noble man [*preudome*]; nor do lands ever make men worthy, rather worthy men make lands so, and a rich man should always aspire to possess what no other man has." In this way Galehout counted as wisdom and gain that which others considered loss and folly, nor might anyone dare to have the courage to love good knights as much as he did. (I 3)

What others (and the reader) must see as dishonor—that is, loss of esteem, power, and high standing—and folly Galehout sees as gain, wisdom, and honor because of the worthy end, the possession of something so singularly valuable that no lesser man than the son of a giantess might aspire to it. In spite of his enormous loss, he boasts of possessing what no other man has.

Galehout's peculiar accounting for his losses as the greatest gain is suggestive of the Christian reversal of worldly values in regard to the *amicus* or *amica Dei*'s otherworldly love. Within the *Prose Lancelot*, however, Galehout's paradoxical argument—folly is wisdom, loss is gain—echoes the Lady of the Lake's exhortation to Guinevere concerning her love of Lancelot:

> And so I ask you to retain and take care of and love above all else him who loves you above all things; and put aside all pride towards him, for he wishes nothing nor values anything more than you; nor can one commit worldly sin without folly, but he is very much right who finds wisdom and honor in his folly; and if you happen to find folly in your love, this folly is to be honored above all other things, for you love the master and the flower of the whole world. Therefore you can boast that never has a lady been able to do what you can, for you are the companion [*compaigne*] of the most worthy man and the lady of the best knight in the world, and you have gained no small thing in the new dominion which you have, for you have won him henceforth who is the flower of all knights. (LXXIa 13)

Had the Lady of the Lake addressed Galehout and her protégé Lancelot about their *amistié/amor* instead of Guinevere, she might have used the same terms, with necessary gender modifications and a shift to Galehout as the wise fool of love. Galehout does, indeed, find his folly to be the most honorable and reasonable thing in this world because he achieves through it his goal of the companionship of the finest knight, and he puts aside all pride to reach that proud end. Yet just as his earlier ambition to conquer ever more kingdoms was prideful, so, too, is his desire to win and maintain Lancelot's companionship. His ambition spurs him to what he sees as the greatest good, the greatest knight's friendship, and to Christian sin, for it values man too highly.

If one accepts that Galehout's death for love of his *ami* is as noble, pathetic, and, still, futile as the demise of Thomas' Tristan for Iseut and of Iseut for him, then it is difficult to agree entirely with Jean Frappier's view that for Galehout friendship serves as an instrument of divine punishment for hubris in an Oedipus-like tragedy.[25] Galehout repeatedly claims that he cannot live without Lancelot, and his death proves his claim and the perfect fidelity of his *amistié/amor*.[26] Divine punishment would seem to have no part here, at least from Galehout's point of view. It is apparent, however, in another incident in the Galehout-Lancelot narration—namely, the miraculous destruction of Galehout's castles and, with it, the end of his prideful ambition for conquest. Divine chastisement of Galehout for his inordinate pride probably indicates the narrator's disapproval of the chivalric romance ethos—in this instance, conquest for personal glory—as he also censures other features of that ethos, such as Lancelot and Guinevere's illicit love. But Galehout, after recovering from the initial shock of seeing his castles and ambitions destroyed, weighs his personal loss against his *amistié/amor* and declares the loss small in comparison to all that he has gained with Lancelot (II 19). Unrepentant, he boasts of having won a uniquely worthy prize in Lancelot. If Galehout learns anything from his tragedy, it is certainly not, as Frappier suggests, that the greatest friendship is a heaven-sent curse. His *amistié/amor* is hubris itself, not an instrument.

As a romance exemplum, Galehout and Lancelot's *amistié/amor* offers a paradoxical measure of affective and moral extremes. Its very essence is

---

[25] "Le personnage de Galehout," pp. 189-90 and 201.

[26] The *Prose Tristan* resurrects Galehout and recasts him as Tristan's friend and a supporter of Tristan and Iseut's affair. On the wedding voyage from Ireland, Tristan and Iseut, driven ashore by a storm, find their first refuge of love in Sorelois, where Tristan defeats Galehout's father, the ruler, and beheads his giantess mother. Galehout returns to Sorelois to avenge his parents, but after capturing Tristan, he befriends him and plans to share his lands with him and, of course, with Lancelot. See *Le roman de Tristan en prose, tome II*, ed. Renée L. Curtis, Arthurian Studies, 13 (Cambridge: D. S. Brewer, 1985), sections 449-81. Galehout survives in Thomas Malory's *Le Morte Darthur*, in which book 8 recounts much the same story as above and names him Galahad. In other books he is Prince Galahalt or Galahault, little more than a name in Malory's catalogues of knightly notables.

self-contradiction. First, it takes its model from romance erotic love, to which it serves as a complement; but at the same time, it works at cross-purposes with the romance's central *fine amor* narrative. Lancelot, for instance, sets his love against his friendship when he rejects Galehout's offers of a crown and the conquest of Benoïc because of the interests of his love; and Galehout, while aiding Lancelot and Guinevere in their love, is also Guinevere's amicable rival for Lancelot's company. Second, the contradiction of affective extremes which characterizes the knights' *amistié/amor* equals in measure that of the model romance lover, Lancelot. The application of this conventional affective measure of *fine amor*—the confusion of emotional extremes—to male friendship is an original feature in the *Prose Lancelot* by which the narrator radically modifies another convention—*compagnonnage*. The consolidation of extremes in Galehout and Lancelot's *amistié/amor* results in its inherent ambiguity which has positive meaning only when interpreted according to the contradictory standards of romance valuation, as illustrated in the Lady of the Lake's lesson on *fine amor*. Finally, the example is morally ambiguous, since the narrator sets up what would seem to be mutually exclusive ethical contradictions within it. Its excellent qualities of perfect loyalty, devotion, generosity, benevolence, beneficence, magnanimity, and love of chivalric virtues are in conflict with the sage's Christian evaluation of Lancelot and Guinevere's affair, towards the maintenance of which Lancelot and Galehout's friendship operates. The narrator's praise of Galehout as the wisest prince second only to Arthur in power and honor is contradicted by Galehout's own romance-style rationalization of his folly and fall from might as the greatest wisdom and honor. And within Galehout's character itself, the very virtues which make of him a praiseworthy prince cause his downfall when through a paradoxical excess of goodness, they become vices, extremes. The crux of essential contradictions in Lancelot and Galehout's chivalric friendship makes of it a moral paradox in the sense of "an unorthodox object of wonderment," as Cicero renders the Greek *paradoxon*.[27]

In Thomas' *Tristan* and the *Prose Lancelot*, the refinements of literary *fine*

---

[27] Cicero defines *paradoxa* as "admirabilia contraque opinionem omnium," *Paradoxa Stoicorum* 4.

amor and its passion permeate chivalric friendship. The anonymous *Ami and Amile*, composed perhaps around 1200, presents the same basic cast of characters as in these romances—two knightly friends and their women—but without a hint of refined love. One of more than thirty known medieval versions in several European languages of the tale of the two perfect friends and doppelganger, the text is a *chanson de geste*, or epic poem. Nevertheless, it contains features of hagiography, such as Christian miracles and angels, which also appear sometimes in *chansons de geste*, and its focus upon the heroes' personal lives and loves is more typical of romance than of epic.[28] Here the two knights' dealings with women serve to prove their perfect love for one another, not for their women. One of the main female characters, Ami's wife Lubias, is among French literature's most maleficent villainesses. She does her utmost to destroy the heroes' friendship and the bonds between her husband and son, and the poet condemns her faithlessness for rejecting her lawful spouse. The other lead female, Belissant, Charlemagne's daughter, behaves early in the work in a manner that, by the standards of 1200, is sexually wanton, and although later she becomes a perfect wife and mother, her husband Amile leaves her in the end to embark on a pilgrimage with his friend. In the absence of refined love, *Ami and Amile* develops three main fields of relationships: those of the two male characters to God, to one another, and to their women. In the following, we will examine, first, the poem's elaboration of a spiritual dimension—God's love for the two—and the ways in which this literary construction functions in giving positive value to the exemplum of knightly friendship. Then, in regard to the dichotomization of chivalric *amistié* and love of woman, we will consider the representation of woman's love as a mostly negative moral and affective measure—in this negative manner, the poet highlights the virtues and self-sufficient affection of male friendship.

God participates in almost every phase of Ami and Amile's interaction, and the friends demonstrate free will in choosing to respond or not to divine will, which angels and dreams make known to them. The many ex-

---

[28] See the discussion of hagiographical and romance elements in *Ami and Amile, Translated from the Old French*, trans. Samuel Danon and Samuel N. Rosenberg (York, South Carolina: French Literature Publications Company, 1981), pp. 6-9 and 16-18. Old French edition: *Ami et Amile, chanson de geste*, ed. Peter F. Dembowski, Classiques Français du Moyen Age, 97 (Paris: Honoré Champion, 1969). English translations into unrhymed verse are my own.

tant versions of the Ami and Amile tale, of which the oldest dates from around 1090, are often quite different from one another in respect to the relative importance of religious elements. In light of these differences, twentieth-century scholars have divided the versions into two groups, of which one, the romantic, emphasizes the secular side of Ami and Amile's friendship, and the other, the hagiographic, portrays the two as saintly or nearly so.[29] There has been a good deal of scholarly debate over the importance of the many Christian features in the circa-1200 version. Thomas E. Vesce considers the religious elements so important that he interprets the version as a tale of martyrs and saints,[30] and William Calin writes of the transformation of the knights' friendship and love of chivalry and family into *caritas*, love of God, in an epic struggle between good and evil.[31] Others consider the religious elements of secondary importance in this version, especially since many of the heroes' actions are in conflict with accepted Christian values. Samuel N. Rosenberg sees there above all the poet's concern for ideal secular friendship, where "everything, even obedience to God's laws, must yield to the advancement of that good," but he admits that the poem "is more than passingly expressive of a Christian spirit."[32] Yet given the abundance of Christian elements in the poem which Geneviève Makida has noted in detail,[33] it seems impossible to attribute to religion a minor role here. The present study proposes a reevaluation of the religious and secular elements in the poem, and it gives nearly equal weight to the divine and secular sides as they interrelate. The fiction's God foreordains and tests the pair's friendship, which develops as a loyal secular relationship and only in its final stage takes on what might be considered a religious character *per se*. Ami and Amile respond to divine will by faithfully preserving and reaffirming their friendship during

---

[29] See the introduction to *Amis and Amiloun*, ed. MacEdward Leach, Early English Text Society, Original Series, 203 (London: Oxford University Press, 1937), and Kathryn Hume, "Structure and Perspective: Romance and Hagiographic Features in the Amicus and Amelius Story," *Journal of English and Germanic Philology* 69 (1970): 89-107.

[30] Vesce, "Reflections on the Epic Quality of *Ami et Amile: Chanson de geste*," *Mediaeval Studies* 35 (1973): 129-45.

[31] Calin, *The Epic Quest: Studies in Four Old French Chansons de geste* (Baltimore: The Johns Hopkins University Press, 1966), p. 98.

[32] Rosenberg, *Ami and Amile*, pp. 7 and 3, respectively.

[33] Makida, "La religion dans *Ami et Amile*," in *"Ami et Amile," une chanson de geste de l'amitié. Etudes recueillies par Jean Dufournet*, Collection Unichamp, 16 (Paris: Honoré Champion, 1987), pp. 39-50.

the severe tests to which God puts them. In response to what God has willed from the beginning—nothing less than their indissoluble oneness—Ami and Amile place their friendship above human and even divine laws, which each disobeys for the sake of his friend's good. Each act of disobedience is accompanied, however, by the characters' strong affirmation of belief in divine justice, and God forgives their misdeeds. God's favor and the heroes' confidence in divine love are important elements in the poet's idealization of Ami and Amile's *amistié*.

Unlike the Christian friends in the preceding chapter, Ami and Amile do not appear to love one another for the sake of God, except, perhaps, in the concluding stanzas. The poet illustrates the constant strength of their *amistié* in the face of difficult trials, but he does not question at any point their devotion to God, not even when they sin—indeed, in the scenes in which they sin deliberately, their unshakable belief in God's justice and omnipotence is most apparent. Even though there is nothing specifically spiritual or religious about Ami and Amile's *amistié* in itself except for their final pilgrimage, the poet goes to great lengths to elaborate an extension to their personal relationship wherein their mutual love and God's love correlate. In the narrative this extension, with God and His representatives as forces friendly to Ami and Amile, counteracts the unrelenting evil of Lubias and her family who would destroy their friendship. In the poem's multilayered construction, the triumph of good over evil coincides with the repeated confirmation of chivalric *amistié*. Most important in respect to ethical evaluation is the apologetic function that the poet's elaboration of a spiritual dimension—God's friendship—performs regarding the base tale received from tradition. In the traditional tale the friends commit great sins—bigamy, false oath, and infanticide—in order to aid one another. In the epic poet's elaboration, these sins committed for the sake of friendship provide the occasion for God to dispense justice and mercy and, in the end, not only to absolve the penitent sinners but to impart to them something of an odor of sanctity. While on a worldly level the friends' enormous sacrifices for one another's good in disregard of personal welfare and Christian laws are proof of their perfectly faithful *amistié*, on a spiritual level God's intervention and favor serve to validate the agreement between their willing sacrifices and divine will.

The fiction's deity and its representatives act in the creation, preservation, and sanctioning of Ami and Amile's perfect oneness. First, before their birth an angel announced "their companionship of very great loyalty" (stanzas 1 and 2—all references are to numbers of epic stanzas, or *laisses*, in the edition and translation.) One assumes that the poet means two an-nunciations, as with those of John the Baptist and Christ in Luke, but with the difference that here the messenger appears to both families at the same or nearly the same time. Ami and Amile are conceived the same night, are born the same day, and are baptized on the same, and their common godfather Ysoré, the Roman pope, gives them goblets made from a single mold. Because God worked a miracle in forming them (2), Ami and Amile so resemble one another that, later, not even their wives can tell them apart. Beyond their miraculously perfect resemblance, the narration emphasizes their natural affinity as each young knight under-takes a seven-year quest of the other, after which they exchange vows of friendship (3-13).

Divine will which made the two identical later makes them physically dissimilar by disfiguring Ami with leprosy. When for Amile's sake Ami knowingly violates the sacraments of matrimony and oath (*sarment* in Old French, from *sacramentum*), an angel, whom he alone can see and hear, tells him that God will punish him with leprosy and that only Amile and the pope will aid him (90). Thus, the angelic intermediary, even though he announces divine punishment for sin, reaffirms God's will that Ami and Amile be friends and, also, that the sinner find refuge in the Church. After his disfigurement, Ami, rejected by his wife Lubias and his own brothers, receives his godfather's protection, and then he seeks refuge with his friend. At this point, when Ami is so disfigured that even Amile can-not recognize his alter ego, the pope's gift, the twin goblet, serves to establish his identity. One should recall the spiritual and sacramental as-sociation of the goblets with baptism, which washes away original sin and initiates one's life as a Christian. A leper and penitent sinner, Ami uses his goblet to beg, but his wife and brothers turn him away. Amile, however, recognizes the goblet, and he responds as a good Christian in embracing the leper, his Christian friend. The heavenly messenger appears for the third and last time and informs Ami that he will be cured if Amile beheads his two sons and bathes Ami in their blood.

One might ask if the fiction's God, in putting the knights to hard tests suggestive of the trials of Job in the Old Testament, is trying their devo-tion to Himself or the strength of their friendship, and whether the friends' actions are responses to God's or to one another's love. One might derive reasonable, though not perfectly orthodox, answers from Ami's judicial combat, false oath, and bigamy. At Charlemagne's court in Paris, the evil Hardré, Ami's relative by marriage, accuses the unmarried Amile and Belissant of fornication (43-44). When later Ami proposes to Amile in secret that he fight Hardré in judicial combat in Amile's stead, it is apparent that God has predetermined the outcome—Ami's victory and Amile's acquittal—for Ami had a dream in which he beheaded Hardré (49). The dream is both a divine portent and a sort of telepathy whereby Ami sees Amile's distress at a great distance. Thus, Ami responds both to divine will, manifested in his dream, and to his friend's love in choosing to act as the instrument of Hardré's destruction and as a true friend. In slaying Hardré, Ami strikes down the archfiend's supporter, for Hardré claims to fight in the devil's name (84). In Ami's mind, however, the combat is personal, for he prays that God permit him to kill his opponent so that he may see his friend again (84). The fiction's deity, for its part, defends its own interests through Ami and confirms the right of Ami and Amile's friendship in granting victory; further, as in the case of Iseut's ambiguous oath, God favors Ami's legal trickery and his oath of innocence which is false in spirit (73). To answer the questions posed earlier, one could say that the activities of knightly friendship and divine love and will are concurrent here since they work towards the same ends—the triumph of good over evil and the confirmation of the knights' *amistié*.

Immediately after slaying Hardré, Ami plights his troth to Belissant and, thus, is guilty of false oath and bigamy. He makes every effort, but in vain, to defer the betrothal until he and Amile can change places again. Obviously, Ami does not wish to marry Belissant, since she is Amile's lady and Ami already has a wife. Nor is it God's will that Ami promise to marry her—an angel warns him of divine punishment. Circumstances—Charlemagne's insistence and the likelihood of immediate execution for falsification if Ami reveals his true identity—make clear why Ami takes the oath, but neither they nor Ami's good intentions excuse his misdeed in God's eyes. Ami prays for divine guidance, and he recognizes his sin:

> Advise me, Father of all creation.
> With the consent of my barons I already have a wife,
> And no knight in the world has one so beautiful.
> If I take another, God, what will become of me then?
> So I will swear in my companion's name,
> I will do penance for it through to the end;
> My wife will never know it. (88)

His humble acceptance of God's punishment shows his penitence, and it

is understood that God pardons the truly repentant. The association between Ami and God here is that of sinner to punisher, which later the
poem converts into a relationship between the double penitents Ami and
Amile and the divine pardoner. Even in committing the sin and acting
against his own interests, Ami responds and submits to divine will. His
role as sinner and penitent is determined no less by his love of his friend,
in whose best interest he sins, than by his confidence in the loving God's
pardon.

Near the end of the poem, Amile's immolation of his two sons,[34] an
act which suggests Abraham's willingness to sacrifice Isaac mentioned in
stanza 69, shows the concordant interrelation of redemptive love above
and here below. In order to cure Ami's leprosy, Amile claims that he
would offer anything, including his wife and children, as proof of his
friendship, for "in need one can prove / Who is a friend and who wishes to
love him" (147). He trusts in God Who can work miracles; he thinks: "It
is a very great thing to restore a dead man to life, / And yet it is evil to
kill the two children: / No one could pardon the sin / Except for the God
of glory Who permitted Himself to suffer" (150). Here, as with Ami earlier, Amile's prudence yields to Providence. He transgresses the bounds of
Christian morality and puts his soul in jeopardy for the sake of friendship
in part because of his faith in God's power to forgive even the greatest
misdeed, provided that the sinner is truly penitent.

Emanuel Mickel has argued that Amile sacrifices his sons in order to
expiate his and Belissant's sin of fornication.[35] According to this interpretation, Amile and Belissant are forced to pay through their sons' lives for
their part in Ami's misfortune. Nonetheless, one must note that the poet
does not invoke Amile's earlier sin at this critical moment in his narration. If Amile is penitent for his and Belissant's sexual transgression
which is the indirect source of Ami's sin and punishment, he remains silent on the point. In his deliberation he weighs Ami's cure against the
crime of infanticide and the consequences for himself:

    ...He begins to weep,

---

[34] For ancient and medieval literary references to healing leprosy with the
blood of innocents, see Saul N. Brody, *The Disease of the Soul. Leprosy in
Medieval Literature* (Ithaca and London: Cornell University Press, 1974), pp.
147-97, especially p. 152.

[35] Mickel, "The Question of Guilt in *Ami et Amile*," *Romania* 106 (1985):
35.

He does not know what to do, nor can he utter a word.
It is very painful for him and it saddens his heart much
Regarding his two sons whom he engendered—
How can he slaughter them, slay them?
If people knew it, no one could protect him
From being both hanged and shamed.
But, on the other hand, he begins to think
About Count Ami whom he loved so much
That he would let himself be slain for him—
Not for anything in this world could he refuse him aid
At a time when his friend can regain his health. (150)

Faced with what seems to be the choice between mutually exclusive love of friendship and paternal love, Amile does not view his sacrificing his children as expiation for sin but as sin itself and a crime for which he will suffer disgrace and death. His confidence in God's pardon and power to work miracles also enters into his deliberation. As with Ami earlier, the commission of sin in sacrificing for friendship is justified in part by the sinner's belief in divine justice and mercy. The test of friendship's fidelity is also a test of faith in God, and it is surprising to find here miracles— the curing of the sick and raising of the dead—associated with male friendship that one would expect to serve as illustrations of *amicitia Dei*. After discovering her resurrected sons, Belissant enthusiastically approves of her husband's action and, in retrospect, wishes that she had shared in it: "Lord Amile, good baron, / Had I thought that this morning at dawn / You intended to decapitate my children, / I would have remained, I swear to you, / On one side to collect their bright blood" (166). In the poet's apology for Amile's sacrifice, Belissant's support of his friendship above parental love functions, as do the miraculous cure and resurrection, to vindicate the infanticide, to make it a virtue worthy of public admiration.

It would be wrong, however, to overvalue the human-divine relationship in the poem. Huguette Legros is right to contend that Ami and Amile's friendship goes far beyond the bonds and duties of conventional epic *compagnonnage*, but her claim that from early on in the poem the two are represented as spiritual friends on the model of Aelred of Rievaulx's *Spiritual Friendship* does not agree with what the epic version in fact recounts: the two are not friends for the sake of Christ as she argues, nor is it at all certain that God puts them through their ordeals in order to bring them to salvation.[36] The friends' placing their souls in

---

[36] Legros, "*Ami et Amile*: Compagnonnage épique et/ou amitié spirituelle," *Bien dire et bien aprandre* 6 (1988): 120-29. Very often she mixes up the title

jeopardy for one another's sake goes against Aelred's principle, and need-
less to say, the account of their worldly lives and loves suggests nothing
of the spiritual virtues essential to Aelredian *amicitia*. The poet's elaboration of a spiritual dimension to Ami and Amile's friendship serves mainly
to second their decisions and actions regarding one another, and in respect
to outside forces working on the friends, it provides a positive counter
which offsets the negative, evil influence of Lubias and his family. The
two knights, faithful Christian sinners, are not primarily interested in religion or spirituality, and their friendship takes a spiritual direction as a
combined quest for God's love only in the last three stanzas, where they
take up the cross and go to the Holy Land.

The two central narrative crises—Ami's leprosy and Amile's sacrifice—
have a double import as they relate not only to the heroes' similarity but,
also, to their social identity. As for the latter consideration, Ami through
his bigamy and Amile through his infanticide lose or expect to sacrifice
their social identity as family members and lords. Lubias' rejection of her
leprous husband, her separation of father and son, and Ami's brothers' rejection of him indicate that the family no longer recognizes him as its
own, and he loses his status as lord and citizen when he is removed from
his city. Amile expects to suffer dishonor and death at the hands of his
countrymen for his infanticide. With Ami's cure, the physical and moral
identity of the pair is restored, and their social identity—society's and
their own recognition of themselves as lords, fathers, and husbands—is
reaffirmed. But the poem's ending marks a definitive break between what
one might call 'friendship as identity' and the characters' social roles. In
the end, the characters' casting off these roles as they take up the cross and
depart may seem anticlimactic and contradictory, since their renunciation
and abandonment destroy the dénouement's reaffirmed social order and the
characters' reintegration into society. Yet this closure, whereby the same
renunciation which confirms their identity as friends nullifies the reestablished social order and their authority in it, does perhaps illustrate a certain
consistency and an ethical lesson. The personal sacrifices by which each
friend proves his faithful *amistié* are also conscious violations of fundamental social obligations and laws. As with Galehout's *amistié/amor*,
Ami and Amile value their love and company above any honor or good
that society can offer. The proof of their *amistié* is, therefore, also a sign

---

characters' names.

of their contempt for society and its values. Their pursuit of absolute friendship, not subject to social duties and laws, is incompatible with the social roles proper to their station. The lesson here is perhaps that friendship such as Ami and Amile's does not have a place in the social order of family and feudal state.

The poet presents love and marriage as the principal causes for the separation of the friends, who are together in only 77 of the poem's 177 stanzas. Once they eliminate the causes, they are reunited forever. Love and marriage are portrayed as snares that a woman or a traitor lays for each of the heroes. From the beginning, the wife Lubias tries to set Ami and Amile against one another, and Ami considers the maid Belissant no less a threat to their friendship than the villain Hardré. The friends consistently react to offers of love and marriage with resistance. When Hardré offers Amile Lubias' hand, Amile protests that the honor is too great, and straightway he asks Charlemagne to grant her to Ami, his better (28). Hardré's present is a poisoned gift much like Saul's bestowal on David of his daughter Michal's hand in marriage in order to snare and destroy him (1 Samuel 18,21). Later, Amile resists Belissant's amorous advances. He does not respond to her repeated solicitation or to her appearing scantily clad before him (37-38), and he refuses most emphatically to sleep with his suzerain's daughter. The poet makes it clear that Amile is more interested in obtaining a fief from Charlemagne than in possessing his daughter (32 and 38). The seemingly innocent victim of woman's wiles, he makes love to her only because she tricks him, under the cover of darkness, into thinking that she is not Belissant (39-40). When after the judicial combat Charlemagne insists that Ami accept Belissant's hand, Ami resists until he obtains a domain for Amile in a package deal (85 and 87).

Besides the acquisition of lands and honors, one of the few things that seem to give positive value to marriage for the protagonists is male progeny, as Ami's dutiful and valiant son Girart offsets Lubias, who embodies man's worst nightmares of marriage. And Belissant, who becomes the perfect wife and mother in the end, in the beginning as the unexpected answer to a lonely knight's dreams[37] hardly demonstrates the maidenly modesty that would reassure a bachelor about his future wife's fidelity. As with Ami's harsh correction of Lubias near the poem's end (175), it is

---

[37] Michel Zink discusses similar male sexual fantasies in medieval poetry in "Lubias et Belissant dans la chanson d'*Ami et Amile*," *Littératures* 17 (1987): 15-18.

only within male-dominated marriage that Belissant comes into possession of goodness as a female, as wife and mother. The poet's contradictory
representations of Belissant parallel in obvious respects the mutually exclusive projections in Abelard and Heloise's correspondence of the two
Heloises—one sensual, the other selflessly supportive—who differ according to Abelard's varying needs, circumstances, and desires.

The poet's view of chivalric *amistié* puts it at odds with love of woman
and marriage. On one hand, woman's love separates the friends, and on the
other, Ami and Amile wholly exclude their wives from their confidences
and decisions—and especially those regarding marriage itself.[38] They confide all to one another but reveal none of their secrets to their wives (see,
for example, Amile's declaration that a man would be mad to confide in a
woman, 67.) They switch mates without consulting or informing them,
although Ami finally tells the confused Belissant which of the two will
be her husband right before her wedding (97). Earlier, when in order to be
with his wife Ami left Amile in Paris, the two wept, embraced, and asked
one another not to forget their friendship. Ami warned him to beware of
Hardré and the virgin Belissant (the pairing can only mean that she is a
she-devil): "Don't give a thought to loving Charles's daughter / Nor to
embracing her waist, / For once a woman enslaves a man, / She makes
him forget father and mother, / Cousins and brothers and his relatives
[*amis charnéz*]" (34). Ami's statement, perhaps a misconstruction of St.
Paul's teaching on marriage in Ephesians 5,31, is at least half true. Lubias, who does her utmost to turn her husband against his friend (see 29-
30 and 66-67), is that bitter half-truth. On the other hand, Belissant does
not wholly belie his statement. One might trace the source of the friends'
dissimilarity because of Ami's leprosy to Belissant's seduction, and the
poet situates in the background, as a narrative afterthought, her support of
Ami and Amile's friendship through her hypothetical, after-the-fact sec-

---

[38] Sarah Kay gives a feminist interpretation of the male characters' exclusion of Lubias and Belissant in "Seduction and Suppression in *Ami et Amile*,"
French Studies 44 (1990): 129-42. According to Kay, the pattern of female seduction which challenges paternal authority and male bonding (homo-
sociality) puts the two female characters in a negative relation to the male
language of the epic, and as a consequence, the heroes do not heed or believe
their words: Amile does not respond to Belissant's repeated declarations of
love because they go against Charlemagne's paternal authority, nor do he and
Ami pay attention to Lubias' repeated accusations against Amile since she is a
treacherous character who would use seduction to destroy their bond.

onding of her husband's double infanticide. In the end, Amile chooses
definitively between friendship and marriage: from afar, he sends word to
his wife that he will embark with his friend on a pilgrimage from which
he knows he will not return (175). While the poet draws attention to the
friends' sacrifices as they relate to one another and to God, he consistently
omits noting the import of their actions in respect to their wives.

As husbands, fathers, and knights, Ami and Amile are representatives of
the active life, but their friendship finds its perfection in opposition to
and, finally, outside the spheres of activity of family and chivalry.
Through their mutual sacrifices and quests, they confirm their exclusive
trust in one another and God. Such is the nature of their *amistié* as an absolute that they can only go against the world and withdraw from it, for
their relationship has no place there. On the other hand, in spite of the
poet's construction of a supernatural extension to Ami and Amile's personal interaction, the two cannot be said to have a well-defined place in
the spiritual domain. With the poem's rapid close, Ami and Amile's turning their backs on the world and their pilgrimage indicate perhaps not so
much the spirit of Christian penitence and renunciation as they suggest
escapist fantasies that one finds in erotic fictions of the period. One might
mention by way of comparison Marie de France's *lai* "Lanval," which
closes with the chivalric lover Lanval's departure with his fairy mistress
from the court of an ungrateful Arthur and lascivious Guinevere and their
journey to his lady's otherworldly realm. In a similar manner, Ami and
Amile's pilgrimage might be read as an escape to another, distant world
conceived ideally for self-sufficient, uninterrupted togetherness.

To close this chapter, we will note two features which the representations of chivalric friendship share in the three French fictions discussed
here. First, the knightly companions are marginalized. Part of the activity
of their friendship is the dissociation of the relationship from the fiction's
society at large: the *amis* gain prominence and honor for prowess at the
center of an important political sphere—the court of an emperor, a king,
or a duke—from which they eventually isolate themselves. In the secrecy
and security of their mutual confidences and trust, the knightly companions develop their relationship outside or on the fringes of society—in
Tristan's cave, Sorelois and the Lost Isle, and on the pilgrims' route. The
three examples are characterized by the exclusion of other knights and
even the interests of the friends' suzerain or titular chieftain from their
private deliberations. In the cases of Tristan and Ami and Amile, the

heroes take great care that their wives not learn their secrets. While the friends shut out all others, it should be noted that in each instance one of the pair is himself an outsider, an outcast: Lancelot, Tristan, and Ami are exiles, strangers in a foreign land who share a companion's home. In the three examples, the friend who provides a refuge works towards the social integration or reintegration of his excluded other; he is also responsible in part for the continued alienation of his companion and for the marginalization of their friendship. Galehout's plans for Lancelot to have a crown and lands in Sorelois or Benoïc might seem to offer social and political integration, but all that they could provide the dispossessed Lancelot is another sort of alienation as Galehout attempts to isolate their *amistié/amor* beyond the confines of Arthur's realm. Kaherdin affords Tristan the opportunity to become integrated into his family while, on the other hand, he participates in and encourages Tristan's love and thus estranges both himself and his friend from his family. The withdrawal of the two to Tristan's cave is, in effect, their shared exile as they define their common activity outside or in opposition to interests of the family and the dukedom.[39] And Amile, who takes the banished Ami into his home and, then, returns with him to reclaim Ami's domain from Lubias, is in part responsible both for Ami's earlier exile and for their abandoning home and family to embark on a pilgrimage of no return. Each of these fanciful constructions of perfectly faithful friendship seeks, through the dynamic of its internal contradictions, the margins of the fiction's society as its proper place.

Second, the twofold structure which the three examples share is a formal means whereby each writer idealizes chivalric friendship. In the texts in the preceding chapter, explicit or implicit biblical and traditional Christian archetypes served as ideal measures for contemporary or fictional representatives of Christian *amicitia*. Unlike those illustrations, the present models combine chivalric friendship with a fully developed in-text ideal measure wholly different in nature. By this process, conventional chivalric friendship both acquires added value and is radically modified in nature. In Thomas' *Tristan* and the *Prose Lancelot*, *compagnonnage* is assimilated to *fine amor*, from which it gains value as an exceptional measure of the heroes' mutual affection—for example, in regard to the confusion of emotional extremes. There conventional characteristics of literary *compagnon-*

---

[39] Joan Tasker Grimbert discusses Tristan's feelings of social alienation in "Love, Honor, and Alienation in Thomas's *Roman de Tristan*," *The Arthurian Yearbook* 2 (1992): 85-89.

nage or *amistié*, such as the companions' nearly equal prowess, fidelity to
a common lord, and an exchange of oaths of mutual aid and nonaggression, persist. But as George Fenwick Jones has noted, in traditional epic
friendship, affection between knights is of secondary importance at best.[40]
In *Tristan* and the *Prose Lancelot*, however, the heroes' mutual affection
becomes one of the most important narrative elements along with faithful
service not to a lord but to a companion as *fin amant*. The romance narratives of knightly friendship and erotic *fine amor* are thoroughly inter-
twined, and they develop simultaneously. But in neither romance does it
seem that the exemplum of chivalric *amistié* could stand alone, since it
derives its narrative interest and affective value largely from the erotic love
which it serves. In *Ami and Amile*, the knights' *amistié* acquires Christian value through the poet's elaboration of a spiritual dimension in God's
love. Unlike refined love of woman in the two romances, Ami and
Amile's relationship to God does not function, however, as an absolutely
necessary element for explaining or giving value to the two knights'
friendship in itself. Only in the epic's closing stanzas does God's love appear to alter the nature of chivalric *amistié*, since the friends relinquish
worldly knighthood and honors. In the three twofold constructions, the
combination of chivalric friendship and an essentially different but highly
valued sort of *amistié* or *amor* serves to lend support to the praise of the
former as a model of perfection.

The late-medieval and Renaissance humanistic representations of perfect
friendship in the following chapter are also twofold, and the two components differ in nature, but they are not synchronous. In emphasizing ethical matters, the humanistic writers link an ancient philosophical or
antique-style illustration or theory of *amicitia perfecta* between men to a
contemporary, self-contained group of friends rather than a pair. Relying
in large part on the virtues of rhetoric to establish the authority of their
new collective ideals and standards, the early humanists compare most fa-
vorably their exempla of contemporary goodness and wisdom, the guaran-
tors of excellent friendship, with ancient authorities. Disregarding courts
of legendary rulers and havens of Christian friendship, these humanists re-
fit in the vernacular classical ideals and old-time virtues to new contexts—
princely and papal courts of power, wealth, and learning, the extended
mercantile family, and literary circles of honorable friends. Their double

---

[40] Jones, "Friendship," p. 89.

representations in time omit for the most part the intervening literary traditions of Christian *amicitia* and chivalric *amistié* with their value-giving
agents of love of woman and God's love. By bringing together ancient and
modern textual models of excellent friendship, the humanistic constructions point to the continuity and fulfillment of classical tradition in the
present.

CHAPTER FOUR

MODELS OF AUTHORITY IN THE NEW AGE: BOCCACCIO, LAURENT DE PREMIERFAIT, AND LEON BATTISTA ALBERTI

The late-medieval and Renaissance humanistic texts which are the subject of this chapter—novella 10,8 of Giovanni Boccaccio's *Decameron*, Laurent de Premierfait's two prefaces to his French translation of *Laelius*, and Leon Battista Alberti's dialogue *Dell'amicizia*—exhibit a reverence for ancient Greek and Roman virtues that they translate into high ethical aspirations for their own times. Each writing contains those aspirations within a specific context that gives new meaning and direction to old-time *amicitia*. Novella 10,8 is the only one of the *Decameron*'s hundred tales set in ancient Rome and Athens. Its unique setting at the end of the Roman Republic, in the distant and prestigious locus of *amicitia perfecta*, provokes by way of contrast the fictive storyteller's lament about contemporary vices and an exhortation to emulate the virtues of a brighter, fictional past. In light of the depiction in the *Decameron*'s introduction of Florence at the end of the Middle Ages, with its pestilence, social disorder, and generally horror-inspiring features, novella 10,8 inspires hope for the noble band or *brigata* of storytellers that virtuous friendship will overcome the foul strokes of Fortune. The *Decameron*'s narrative frame of a harmonious community of aristocratic female and male storytellers illustrates in its own way and time the virtues praised in the antique-style novella.

Ethical and political aspirations go hand in-hand in the other texts in this chapter. In his two prologues Laurent de Premierfait situates his translation of *Laelius* in the context of the intellectual activity of the court of Louis II, duke of Bourbon, brother-in-law to King Charles V and uncle to Charles VI, and the program of *studia humanitatis* to which his translation contributes gives a prominent place to Aristotle's conception in books 8 and 9 of the *Nicomachean Ethics* of ideal concord between a beneficent ruler and his subjects. The Aristotelian model of citizens who cultivate virtuous *philia* under a benevolent prince supports the political ideals of the French feudal lords while, at the same time, it belies the monarchical crisis during the reign of a mentally unstable king and a long period of intense civil and international strife. In contrast to the second

part of Leon Battista Alberti's dialogue which examines philosophical
aspects of ideal friendship, ancient and contemporary, the first part gives a
practical account of an Alberti elder's successful career as courtier and confidant to princes of church and state. In this first part, a guide to winning
the friendship of rulers, moral and political aspirations are realized in the
court, where the arts of *amicizia* and statecraft conjoin. The writer presents
the dialogue as an example of political and ethical discussion among
males in his own prosperous, middle-class family who offer an ideal of
family-centered friendship to their younger relatives. The dialogue is not,
however, simply a lesson in individual success. The author envisions his
work on virtuous friendship as a political and moral guide for raising his
city and family to a level of authority and eminence comparable to that of
the Roman Republic and its illustrious families.

Each of the texts studied in this chapter associates a contemporary ideal
of friendship with major ancient and medieval literary and philosophical
traditions. In novella 10,8 of the *Decameron* Boccaccio effects a merging
of the classical *amicus perfectus* with Cicero's ideal orator. There the two
antique-style protagonists, one Athenian and the other Roman, and the fictive late-medieval female storyteller as well prove their strength of character and worth as virtuous friends through oratorical excellence. Boccaccio
sets this double Ciceronian ideal in the literary context of the medieval
novella collection, a genre which he perfected. In the prologues to his
translation of *Laelius*, Laurent de Premierfait summarizes books 8 and 9
of the *Nicomachean Ethics*, and he discusses for his princely patron and
circle of friends and courtiers the literary and philosophical links between
the Greek and Latin treatises. His prologues take the form of the medieval
accessus ad auctores genre, which he modifies to serve in part as a defense
of his translation itself. *Dell'amicizia,* which takes its form from the Ciceronian dialogue, juxtaposes moral observations drawn from Alberti family tradition and a great variety of ancient philosophical sources, especially Plutarch and Diogenes Laertius. Further, the dialogue's account and
defense of an early-fifteenth-century Italian courtier's friendships with
rulers are part of the medieval literary tradition that extends well beyond
the Renaissance of writings pro and contra the courtier's vocation.

The three writings' different genres bear directly on their great differences in style and the sorts of information which they provide. Novella
10,8 of the *Decameron* is a narrative fiction which illustrates the *amicitia
perfecta* topos. It adapts a medieval tale of two friends' reciprocal generos-

ity to a classical setting. Consistent with the ancient setting are the commonplace elements of classical *amicitia perfecta* which the narrative adds to the received tale. For example, the narration of each friend's attempt to die in the place of his comrade recasts the Orestes-Pylades exemplum that Cicero mentions in *Laelius* 7,24, and their education together, shared possessions, and life under one roof are commonplaces of the classical topos. A feature of the novella not characteristic of the narrative genre is the large part of the text given over to speeches in a distinctly declamatory mode. Since the two protagonists are not only perfect friends but are also highly skilled orators, the novella moves between storytelling and speech-making. The several speeches on conventional rhetorical and, especially, declamatory topics—e.g., the praise of *amicizia*, friendship's duties, love versus friendship, Fortune's power, and Rome's greatness versus that of Athens—determine to a large extent the text's content as rhetorical matter and its style as rhetorical performance. In this regard, the novella, which offers a fictional, antique-style exemplum of *amicitia perfecta*, is itself an exemplum of classical rhetoric. Recently Virginia Kirkham published a detailed analysis of elements mainly in the narrative sections which derive from the classical commonplaces of *amicitia perfecta* and which the two protagonists illustrate.[1] In the following, we will study in particular the speeches, or nonnarrative segments, as examples of rhetorical performance in a classical style and their relationship to virtuous *amicizia* among the *Decameron*'s storytellers.

Laurent de Premierfait's two prefaces to his translation of *Laelius* are representative of the medieval academic genre of *accessus ad auctores*, or introduction to authoritative classical and medieval Latin texts and translations. In conformity with this genre, the prologues limit their content for the most part to providing answers to a number of specific questions about the ancient text which conventional *accessus* address. The prologues' academic, highly refined literary style in treating philosophical subjects is characteristic, too, of the *accessus* genre, while their direct appeals to Laurent de Premierfait's princely patron demonstrate another style—the high-flown rhetoric of adulation typical of dedications to im-

---

[1] Kirkham, "The Classic Bond of Friendship in Boccaccio's Tito and Gisippo (*Decameron* 10.8)," in *The Classics in the Middle Ages*, ed. Aldo S. Bernardo and Saul Levin, Medieval and Renaissance Texts and Studies, 69 (Binghamton: Center for Medieval and Early Renaissance Texts and Studies, 1990), pp. 223-35.

portant personages in medieval writings. The prologues are unrepresenta-
tive of the academic *accessus*, however, in their accommodation to a
nonacademic audience which did not necessarily possess a firm knowledge
of Latin or of classical philosophy. Laurent de Premierfait adapts the
genre of introduction to authoritative texts to serve as an introduction in
the vernacular to ancient philosophy and letters in the ducal court.

Leon Battista Alberti's *Dell'amicizia* is a philosophical dialogue modeled on *Laelius*. As with its model, the Italian dialogue aims principally
to provide moral instruction and examples of rhetorical excellence. The interlocutors, elders of the Alberti family, address speeches to two young
relatives on a novel variation of the *amicizia* topos—the Alberti family's
true friendship. Here the family as a whole is the basic unit of friendship
which the individual Alberti males serve as faithful, affectionate *amici*. In
regard to the dialogue's content, the elder Alberti speakers themselves ex-
emplify 'true friends of the family,' men of virtue and wisdom who have
brought honor and wealth to the family through their love and service.
Furthermore, their speeches illustrate different oratorical styles, such as
courtly and erudite delivery, as models of rhetorical excellence for their
young listeners to admire and imitate. One of the objectives of
Dell'amicizia is to promote the study of classical letters, and, consequently, the dialogue includes in Italian a considerable amount of quotations, anecdotes, and exempla adapted from ancient works.

The three works restrict their scope to worldly friendship as a good in
itself and, with rare exceptions, to secular authorities and models. The
Christian writers Boccaccio, Laurent de Premierfait, and Leon Battista Alberti show here no contempt for the world, and they praise most highly
virtuous friendship's beneficial action in the community. Their humanistic ideals of friendship include as some of the chief elements the study of
classical letters and philosophy, urbanity in language and manners, the
rule of reason, and Aristotelian-Ciceronian virtues associated with reciprocal affection and beneficence among males, but there is no specific mention of Christian faith, hope, or charity. The noninclusion of Christian
virtues and spiritual objectives distinguishes these works from another
major sort of writing on *amicitia* in the later Middle Ages and early Renaissance—that is, the Christian humanistic approach to the topos.
Although this chapter does not deal with Christian humanism, brief mention of one Latin text from the mid fifteenth century which illustrates a
humanistic program of Christian *amicitia* and rhetoric seems appropriate

here. In his prose treatise *De contemplacione amicicie* from 1454, Jean Serra (ca. 1400-ca. 1470) presents a systematic, allegorical interpretation of true friendship from its inception to the death of one of the friends.[2] In a long series of paired chapters, he develops in a first chapter the idea of cooperation and mutual assistance among different parts of the body and the soul as an example of *amicitia*. For this part of his exposition, Serra relies on Christian authorities such as St. Jerome, Augustine, and, especially, the pseudo-Augustinian *De spiritu et anima*. Then, in the second chapter of the pair, he interprets this specific aspect of body-soul *amicitia* as an figure for commonplaces of Aristotelian-Ciceronian *amicitia perfecta* which serve to demonstrate the truth of Christian teachings. For example, in chapter 23 he notes, on the authority of Augustine, that man is drawn between the desire to know God and the attraction of worldly things and that man's free will, situated between these two attractive forces, is corrupted if it yields to the worldly. In the following chapter he treats the Ciceronian ideas of two friends' complete agreement of wills and the necessity of correcting a friend who abandons the pursuit of virtue for the inferior goals of pleasure or utility—if such correction fails, then the friendship should be dissolved. As a rhetorical exercise, Serra's treatise operates through somewhat the same system of the orator's 'discovery' of similarities between apparently dissimilar entities or categories that we will discuss later in regard to Leon Battista Alberti's dialogue. Serra's *De contemplacione amicicie* reconciles spiritual principles of Christian *amicitia* with moral principles of classical *amicitia perfecta*: the Christian virtues of faith, hope, and charity and ancient philosophical moral virtues complement one another, but the latter are 'true' only inasmuch as they derive from the former. The work is typical of Christian humanistic writings on *amicitia* in that its main objective is to praise the reciprocal love of God and mortals. The treatise may be seen to continue the long tradition of Latin writings on Christian friendship beginning with John Cassian's "On Friendship," Ambrose's *De officiis ministrorum*, and, most important, Augustine. It is noteworthy, however, that Serra's treatise does not specify a context or contexts, such as the monastic community, in which its abstract principles might be realized or observed. Audience is a factor

---

[2] *De contemplacione amicicie*, in *Humanistes français du milieu du XVe siècle. Textes inédits de P. de la Hazardière, Jean Serra, Guillaume Fichet*, ed. Evencio Beltran, Travaux d'Humanisme et Renaissance, 235 (Geneva: Droz, 1989), pp. 27-55.

which contributes to the Christian spiritual orientation of Serra's work: he dedicates his treatise to the Archbishop of Toulouse. On the other hand, Boccaccio, Laurent de Premierfait, and Leon Battista Alberti address their works on secular friendship to specific groups of lay readers—lovers, the court, the family—whose interests, one assumes, are primarily worldly, not spiritual.

In this chapter's texts, writing in the vernacular is at issue. Can the Italian language or French impart the same majesty and gravity to philosophical thought and rhetorical discourse that Latin, the privileged and prestigious conveyor of elevated expression, had done for well over a millennium? The attitudes of Boccaccio and Laurent de Premierfait towards their works in the vernacular are not without ambiguity. The opinion of the intellectual elite that thought worthy of serious consideration is necessarily conveyed and, at the same time, concealed in Latin was prevalent at the time of these writings. Composed in the mid fourteenth century, Boccaccio's *Decameron* in Italian prose, though very popular from the beginning, was ignored or disparaged by scholars and even Boccaccio's biographers until the late fifteenth century. The eighth novella of the tenth day is one of the more serious of the hundred tales that make up the *Decameron*. In it Boccaccio imitates Latin oratory; thus he translates, as it were, Latin eloquence to the vernacular. Throughout his long literary career Boccaccio was a staunch defender and promoter of Dante's writings in Italian, yet after completing the *Decameron*, he devoted himself almost entirely to composing works in Latin. Boccaccio's friend Francesco Petrarch, who admired the *Decameron* but claimed to have read it in haste and rather carelessly, showed his approval of the concluding novella about Griselda by adapting it in his Latin version, *De oboedientia ac fide uxoria mythologia.*

Although in the later Middle Ages Latin continued to hold sway as the voice of the intellectual elite, translators and adapters of philosophical works from Latin sought to reform the vernacular so that it might approach the level of authority accorded the Latin language. In the early fifteenth century Laurent de Premierfait defended his French translation of *Laelius* against those who might accuse him of profaning the Latin work in making it accessible to the ignorant and unworthy and of abasing in the vulgar tongue the majesty of the original. He did not conceive of his translation as independent from the original, for he proposed a collateral reading in which the French text plays an ancillary role to the Latin. Linguistically and stylistically, his translation and two prologues to it are remarkable because of their Latinate vocabulary, syntax, and rhetorical postures. There Laurent de Premierfait attempted to elevate and convert the French idiom by assimilating it to Latin, the prestige language. Leon Battista Alberti's *Dell'amicizia* from 1441, which is included in the collection of four Italian dialogues titled *I libri della famiglia*, has two main sections, of which the second is erudite and theoretical in its reflections upon classical texts on *amicitia* which the author adapts in Italian. Leon Battista, who wrote many treatises in both Italian and Latin, composed the first Tuscan grammar, and argues the superior utility of Italian over Latin for the vast majority of his "not extremely lettered" ("non litteratissimi") fellow citizens in book 3 of *Della famiglia*, had no reservations at this stage in his literary career about the Italian language as a worthy vehicle of philosophical expression.

These humanists' assimilation of ancient textual models and measures of *amicitia perfecta* is accompanied by a counteraction of dissimilation and differentiation. Even though they honor old-time *amicitia*, they regard as no less authoritative the contemporary models that their texts propose. This chapter addresses itself in part to the double process by which the present writers, like earlier Christian adapters, derive authority from classical tradition and, in perfecting and updating it, deliberately differentiate their own measures of virtuous friendship from it. The chapter considers, on one hand, the adaptation of ancient references to contemporary literary genres and the refitting of old-time standards to the new conditions of the princely court, the merchant-class household, and woman's authoritative voice which the writers offer as new conveyors of worthy friendship. On the other hand, it examines the writers' strategies for establishing the self-sufficient authority of their texts, along with their new models and moral measures.

The *Decameron* which Giovanni Boccaccio (1313-1375) composed around 1348-1351 is subtitled "Prince Galeotto," that is, Galehout. The subtitle, which calls up Galehout's role in two earlier medieval vernacular fictions, the *Prose Lancelot* and Dante's *Divine Comedy*, perhaps suggests both a warning about the *Decameron*'s moral content and a beneficent intention on the author's part.[3] Francesca, Paolo's mistress in canto 5 of the *Inferno*, points to their reading of the romance about Lancelot, Guinevere, and the go-between Galehout as the inspiration for their first kiss and the cause of their damnation. The subtitle's reference to Galehout serves to warn readers about the contents of the book, for not a few of the hundred novellas lead to the consummation of illicit love. In the novella studied here, the eighth of the tenth day, the Athenian protagonist Gisippus is no less a pander than Galehout: not only does he give his fiancée, without her knowledge or consent, to his lovesick Roman friend Titus, he even drives into his own nuptial bedchamber his hesitant comrade. On the other hand, just as the magnanimous Galehout of romance served and comforted his lovelorn *ami* Lancelot, so, too, the *Decameron*'s stories offer, as Boccaccio claims in his preface, friendly consolation to his noble, high-minded female readers for the secret pains of love that they suffer in their idle, solitary hours. Novella 10,8 presents an example of friendship's aid to the lovesick in Gisippus' consolation and conversion of his friend's amorous melancholy and longing for death to joy.

The *Decameron*'s youthful, amorous, and noble-born storytellers, having fled plague-stricken Florence, recount their tales to drive away sadness caused by the plague and by their own secret love with narrative that in most cases provokes smiles, laughter, or applause. Each of the seven fictional female and three male storytellers becomes the queen or king of one of the ten days of tales, and the ruler dictates the theme of the stories during the session over which he or she presides, although the rulers of the first and ninth days give the tellers leave to treat whatever subject they wish. Panfilo, the king of the tenth day, commands them to tell "of those who have performed liberal or munificent deeds, whether in the cause of love or otherwise" (p. 731; "di chi liberalment o vero magnificamente al-

---

[3] For summaries of modern critical interpretations of the subtitle, see Robert Hollander, *Boccaccio's Two Venuses* (New York: Columbia University Press, 1977), pp. 102-06, and Janet Levarie Smarr, *Boccaccio and Fiammetta: The Narrator as Lover* (Urbana and Chicago: University of Illinois Press, 1986), pp. 275-76, note 78. According to Giuseppe Mazzotta, the subtitle suggests that "[a]ware of literature as an erotic snare—a commonplace of medieval romances—Boccaccio seems intent on assigning to this text the role of erotic mediator, and thus unmasking the threats and seductions of his own artifact"—*The World at Play in Boccaccio's "Decameron"* (Princeton: Princeton University Press, 1986), pp. 56-57.

cuna cosa operasse intorno a' fatti d'amore o d'altra cosa").[4] He offers this topic in the hope that all by telling and, furthermore, imitating such deeds will be encouraged to undertake noble endeavors. The lofty topic and high moral intentions of the tenth day's novellas set it above the concerns of the preceding days. But in spite of the tenth day's serious theme and aspirations, it cannot be said to rise above a level of gravity that one might expect from romance. The theme itself, *magnificenzia*, would seem to call for romance's characteristically superlative treatment: magnificence, that is, doing great good, is a degree or more above doing good, beneficence. As Giorgio Cavallini has pointed out, the opening pages of novella 10,8 abound with the Italian superlative suffix -*issimo*.[5] Here one enters into the domain of romance idealization.

Novella 10,8 is related thematically to the French fictions in the preceding chapter in that one of its main problems is the conflict or cooperation between love of woman and male friendship. The novella presents near its beginning an interior monologue which illustrates the contention of Andreas Capellanus, whose *On Love* Boccaccio admired, that love of the same woman poses a great threat to male friendship, and the tale works through this problem to arrive at a harmonious combination of *amistà* and matrimony. Even though the male protagonists behave wrongfully towards an innocent maid and her and Gisippus' families, they put the blame for any wrong on love itself and the victims of their fraud, especially the girl, and they and the female storyteller Filomena voice the highest praise for friendship's innocence, generosity, and noble-mindedness. The novella's representation of and apology for loyal male friendship are in some ways similar to those in the French fictions examined in the preceding chapter: Boccaccio's male protagonists place by their words and actions the interests of their personal relationship above the norms, codes, and ends of society. And as in *Ami and Amile*, novella 10,8 contains an instance of the chaste exchange of a wife which serves to demonstrate the moral excellence of male friendship. Here, too, the female character, the 'swapped bride' as it were, pays the price for the friends' mutual

---

[4] Page references within parentheses are to *The Decameron*, trans. G. H. McWilliam (Baltimore: Penguin, 1972). The Italian original is cited from *Tutte le opere di Giovanni Boccaccio*, vol. 4: *Decameron*, ed. Vittore Branca, I Classici Mondadori (Milan: A. Mondadori, 1976).

[5] Cavallini, *La decima giornata del "Decameron,"* Biblioteca di Cultura, 172 (Rome: Bulzoni, 1980), p. 130.

generosity. Unlike the earlier French fictions, however, Boccaccio's novella situates male friendship not on the margins of society but at its center: the protagonists demand in private and public hearing that society and woman in particular accommodate themselves to the uncompromising requirements of their faithful friendship, and they offer *amistà*'s benevolence and powerful protection to the social group, the family, which opposed them.

Among the problems to which critics have pointed in novella 10,8 are its unique, distant setting, the male protagonists' seemingly less than honorable behavior in a tale illustrating virtuous *amistà*, and the prominent role that rhetoric plays. As for the setting, Salvatore Battaglia has argued that in placing this tale in the distant past, Boccaccio intended to indicate that in his own time and with his contemporaries, the story and the protagonists' dubious morality would not be plausible; Boccaccio used this "strategic historico-social distance (and, consequently, a human and psychological one) to make acceptable a case that he felt anachronistic and abnormal."[6] In consideration of the protagonists' deceitful behavior and what might appear to be their cynical justification for it, one could find Filomena's unqualified praise for the virtues of their *amistà* and her listeners' enthusiastic approval to be misplaced or even incomprehensible; or one might find Boccaccio's example of virtuous, philosophical friends of old to be parodic. As we shall argue later, in spite of the great differences that seem to set the protagonists' actions apart from the mores of Boccaccio's time, the novella's exemplum illustrates some of the chief virtues that the fictive *brigata* praises in itself.

The exceptionally large part that the novella gives to oratory is problematic in that it is difficult to evaluate the importance of rhetorical performance there in respect to the narrative elements—that is, to characterization and the protagonists' actions. Mario Baratto, for example, finds rhetoric itself to be the novella's true protagonist since it, more than the friends' acts, consoles and aids human weakness,[7] and Barbara L. Blackbourn asks if the novella is a rhetorical exemplum of the *amicizia* topos or an example of rhetoric itself.[8] Some scholars have interpreted the

---

[6] Battaglia, *La coscienza letteraria del medioevo*, Collana di Testi e di Critica, 2 (Naples: Liguori, 1965), p. 521—my translation.

[7] Baratto, *Realtà e stile nel "Decameron"* (Vicenza: Neri Pozza, 1970), p. 65.

[8] Blackbourn, "The Eighth Story of the Tenth Day of Boccaccio's *De-*

novella's discourses mainly as stylistic exercises: Thomas G. Bergin judges Titus' long speech of defense in imitation of classical rhetoric to be "a masterpiece of its tedious kind,"[9] and Vittore Branca considers Filomena's closing address as an example of medieval Latin prose style, particularly that recommended by Isidore of Seville.[10] The following study addresses the problem of the relationship between the novella's speeches and its characterization: what role does rhetoric play in the novella's representation of perfect friendship? One might note, first, that it is likely that Boccaccio adapted a medieval tale to two ancient settings because of their relationship to rhetoric: Athens is "where the supreme power of oratory was both invented and perfected" according to Cicero's dialogue *De oratore* (*On the Orator*) 1,4,13, and Rome is rhetoric's second home.[11] The novella's action takes place during Octavian's triumvirate, which began in 43 B.C., the year of Cicero's death. The situation in time, as well as in place, hints at a relationship to Cicero's oratory and philosophy.[12] The present study proposes to compare the characterization and discourses in the novella with the attributes of the ideal orator in Cicero's *De oratore*, and in doing so it will suggest that one essential virtue, or *virtù*, which Boccaccio associates with excellent friendship is the orator's virtue, *vis* or *virtus* in Latin, which Cicero defines in his treatise. In other words, a good part of the originality of Boccaccio's representation of perfect friends in the antique mold is his revision of classical *amicitia vera* according to

---

cameron: An Example of Rhetoric or a Rhetorical Example?" *Italian Quarterly* 27 (1986): 6.

[9] Bergin, *Boccaccio* (New York: Viking, 1981), p. 323.

[10] Branca, *Boccaccio: The Man and His Works*, trans. Richard Monges and Dennis J. McAuliffe (New York: New York University Press, 1976), pp. 229-31.

[11] Two other novellas with ancient settings are 7,9, which takes place in Achaia, and 9,9, set in Solomon's Jerusalem. As Vittore Branca has noted, novellas 5,10 and 7,2 are adaptations of tales by the Latin author Apuleius—*Boccaccio: The Man and His Works*, p. 203. Boccaccio gives these last two medieval settings. One of the probable sources for novella 10,8 is the Latin tale (derived from an Arabic story) "The Perfect Friend" from the early-twelfth-century collection of moral fables *The "Disciplina clericalis" of Petrus Alfonsi*, translated into English by P. R. Quarrie from the edition and German translation of Eberhard Hermes, The Islamic World Series (Berkeley: University of California Press, 1977), pp. 107-09.

[12] Victoria Kirkham believes that the allusion to Octavian's triumvirate points to the beginning of the Christian era: Octavian, Gisippus' sentencing to crucifixion, and Titus' rescue prefigure Christ's coming, the Crucifixion, and the Emperor Titus' vindication—"The Classic Bond," pp. 230-31.

the standards of the orator's virtue and his identification of ethically superior friendship with the ideal orator's ethos, or character.

The main subject of discussion at the beginning of *De oratore* is whether oratorical excellence depends "upon the trained skill of highly educated men," as Cicero argues, or "on a sort of natural talent and on practice," as Cicero's brother Quintus maintains (1,2,5). The ensuing discussion pro and contra establishes that both are absolutely essential in the ideal orator, even though in individual great speakers the proportion of one to the other—the refinement of learning to talent and practice—varies. In the opening passage of the novella Filomena points out many elements that identify for the hearer or reader Titus and Gisippus as typical *amici perfecti* of antiquity: their upbringing and life under one roof, aristocratic rank, equal intellectual abilities, their feeling of ease and complete happiness only in one another's company, the sharing of joy and grief, etc. But most important in respect to the *De oratore*'s discussion of the sources of oratorical excellence is Filomena's sketch of their training, native skill, and practice. According to her description, the two youths measure up to what both Cicero and his brother require. In Athens, where they live together in the house of Gisippus' father Chremes, the long-standing friend of Titus' father, they study for three years under the philosopher Aristippus.[13] They are noted for their equally great *ingegno*, natural talent or genius. Her statement that "they scaled the glorious heights of philosophy side by side, amid a hail of marvelous tributes" (p. 777), can only be understood to refer to their practice of oratory. It is clear from the novella's opening passage that these *amici perfecti* are *oratores perfecti* as well. The rest of the novella demonstrates how the virtues of the latter make up for circumstantial deficiencies of the former.

Boccaccio effects a merging and identification of the virtues of oratory with those of *amicizia* in three segments of the novella which deal principally with reasoned argument and discourse rather than storytelling. The three discourses which we will examine are Titus' love soliloquy and Gisippus' consolation, Titus' plea before the families of his wife Sophronia and of Gisippus, and Filomena's concluding argument. Each of the segments demonstrates different qualities of the ideal orator or oratory itself as Cicero defines them. The first example, Titus' love soliloquy and

---

[13] For ancient and medieval references to the ethical hedonism of Aristippus (ca. 435-366 B.C.), founder of the Cyrenaic school, see Mazzotta, *The World at Play*, pp. 255-57.

Gisippus' consolation (pp. 778-83), poses the problem of *virtù* in the sense of oratory's persuasive power as it relates to dialectic and to the orator's upright character, and it gives negative and positive illustrations of rhetorical virtue. After her opening portrayal of two typical *amici perfecti*, the narrator depicts romance's conventionally lovesick hero in Titus, who is enamored of Sophronia, Gisippus' promised bride: he broods and sighs, he is assailed by conflicting thoughts and feelings, he neither eats nor sleeps, and, finally, in a state of exhaustion, he lies ill in bed. When later he confesses to Gisippus his love for Sophronia, Titus explains that not only does he expect to die from lovesickness, he hopes for death because of his shame for having betrayed friendship: "If only the gods had so willed it, Gisippus, I would rather have died than continued to live, when I think how Fortune has driven me to the point where my virtue [*virtù*] had to be put to the test, and where, to my very great shame, you have found it wanting" (p. 779). Clearly, the claim of deficient virtue refers to Titus' violation of the duties of friendship in that he persists in loving his friend's fiancée—his *virtù* is doubly wanting as a friend and as a philosopher who aims to overcome or, at least, not to bend under the fell blows of Fortune. Less obviously but just as importantly, the deficiency also refers to the *virtù* of his soliloquy which precedes this explanation. Cicero claims that the true virtue of the orator is either in rousing hearts to passions or in recalling them from passion to mildness (*De oratore* 1,12,53). In his soliloquy Titus is unable to recall his heart from passionate love to equanimity. His inability to persuade himself through dialectic and rhetoric to abandon love proves his deficient *virtù* as orator. As G. Cavallini notes, Titus' interior debate is a conventional rhetorical exercise in contrasting the duties of friendship with love's power.[14] Titus' mental rhetoric, which does not resolve the question, fails to compel him to do what he knows is right and reasonable, and so it fails friendship, too. The weakness in Titus' character—his inability to dominate his passion—corresponds to the weakness of his rhetoric, which Gisippus will show to be faulty.

Titus claims that he does not love Sophronia for the reason that she belongs to Gisippus, but Giuseppe Mazzotta suspects that his disclaimer betrays a rivalry between the friends of which Sophronia is the prize.[15] Nev-

---

[14] Cavallini, *La decima giornata*, p. 131.
[15] Mazzotta, *The World at Play*, p. 258.

ertheless, rivalry between the protagonists is obvious in the domain of
oratory as they strive to outdo one another in their speeches: first, in his
response Gisippus forcefully defeats his friend's arguments, and, later, Titus argues before the families that he is a more worthy man than Gisippus.

After Titus repeats to his friend in confidence his opposing arguments,
Gisippus responds in an elaborate speech which refers to the main
premises in the soliloquy and uses them as the basis for a reconciliation
of *amistà* and love of woman. His response shows both his virtue as a
friendly consoler in love and as a persuasive orator. One might note that
in both Titus' soliloquy and Gisippus' response, the speakers follow Cicero's advice not to separate rhetorical commonplaces from specific instances, which, as Cicero claims, is a common error among professors of
oratory (*De oratore* 2,31,133). In his monologue Titus does not separate
the duties of *la vera amistà* from his specific duties to his friend, nor does
he separate abstract considerations on all-powerful Love and Fortune from
his particular case. Gisippus in his response relates the commonplaces of
amicizia and its duties directly to his friendship with Titus.

Gisippus begins by responding to three of the main points in Titus' soliloquy. First, Titus contended that he would violate friendship's code if
he continued to love Sophronia. But Gisippus maintains that Titus violated the code in not confiding in him from the beginning (Gisippus will
fail in his duty later in the tale, when, destitute in Rome, he does not confide immediately in his friend.) As for Titus' second point, that he was
right to fall in love with Sophronia because of her great beauty, Gisippus
agrees entirely, and he commends his friend's loftiness of spirit. Thirdly,
Titus put the blame on Fortune for having given the woman he loves to
his friend rather than to some other. Gisippus contends, on the contrary,
that this is good fortune, since as a friend he will share with Titus what
other men would keep. Gisippus makes his introductory critique not with
the intention of reproving Titus but of converting him to his own position: "I should be a poor sort of friend if I were unable to convert you to
my own way of thinking when the thing"—Titus' marriage to Sophronia—"can be so decorously arranged" (p. 780). Gisippus' declaration of intention is most noteworthy in that he relates the persuasive power of
rhetoric directly to the virtue of his *amistà*. He emphasizes the force of his
intention when, faced with Titus' reluctance, he declares: "If ... our friendship is such as to enable me to force your acquiescence in any single of

my decisions [*che io a seguire un mio piacere ti sforzi*], or if I can induce you to consent of your own accord, now is the time when I intend to exploit it to the full" (p. 781). These strong statements of intent place the orator's *vis* at the center of true friendship in that Gisippus will save Titus' life by compelling him to yield to arguments that are specious at best, since what he proposes as an honorable solution to the present problem is a deceitful scheme to be practiced on an unwitting and trusting girl, her family, and his own. In itself, Gisippus' offer to prove his friendship by giving his promised bride to Titus is not enough to save his comrade's life. Titus wavers between delight at the prospect of marrying Sophronia and shame at taking advantage of an offer so generous that acceptance would be unseemly, but he is inclined to accept death rather than the offer. In the verbal contest of wills between the two *amici*, Gisippus' powerful rhetoric is more of an aid to *la vera amistà* in that it saves Titus' life by converting his will than is the extremely liberal offer itself.

Gisippus' speech contains some exaggerated arguments that derive as much from romance as from rhetorical theory. When Titus objects that he will try to conquer his grievous love, Gisippus responds: "If you were to go on like this you would perish, in which event there is no doubt that I should speedily follow you. So even if I had no other cause for loving you, your life is precious to me because my own life depends upon it" (pp. 781-82). Gisippus' exaggerated claim recalls Galehout's vital dependency upon his *ami*, and it also conforms in its own extravagant way to Cicero's description of the extremes which ideal oratory aims to portray: "The orator ... by his words greatly magnifies and exaggerates the grievousness of such things as in everyday life are thought evils and troubles to be shunned, while he enlarges upon and beautifies by his eloquence whatever is commonly deemed delectable and worthy to be desired" (*De oratore* 1,51,221). As Gisippus continues his reasoning, his use of "with the greatest ease" recalls the low evaluation of marriage and the high value of male friendship in *Ami and Amile*: "I should not perhaps be so generous, if wives were so scarce and difficult to find as friends, but ... I can find another wife, but not another friend, with the greatest ease" (p. 782). One might note that in Petrus Alfonsi's tale about Muslim merchants which is a probable source for this novella, the Egyptian who gives away the maid he planned to marry already has several wives.[16]

---

[16] For the harem subject in this tale, see Louis Sorieri, *Boccaccio's Story of*

Gisippus' claim that his very life depends upon Titus' conforms to Cicero's principle that in pleading a case the orator should argue necessity, duty, or agreement with codes of permissible conduct: "Now all acts may be defended as justifiable which are such that the doing thereof was a duty, or permissible, or necessary" (*De oratore* 2,25,106). Gisippus justifies his proposed course of action as a duty in that it will preserve their *amistà* and as necessary in that it will save both their lives. His defense on grounds of duty, necessity, or what is permissible seems most questionable, however, when he invokes the code of friendship to support his claim that, were he already married to Sophronia, he would still share her with Titus: "Ever since our friendship began, I cannot recall possessing anything that was not as much yours as it was mine. Just as I shared my other possessions with you, so I would share Sophronia, if I were already married to her and no other solution were possible" (p. 780). Boccaccio may have had in mind historical precedents—for instance, Cato the Younger divorced his wife so that his friend Quintus Hortensius could marry her[17] — but sharing one's wife with a friend without her consent was neither ancient Greek and Roman custom nor a duty of *amicitia*'s code under its joint-property clauses. In fiction, however, such an action may serve to prove male friendship's fidelity, as in the case of Ami and Amile's chaste wife-swapping. Since Gisippus is not married, he does not need to defend his contrary-to-fact hypothesis. Here his speech, rather than action, proves his dutifulness. In her concluding argument Filomena will point to Gisippus' constant chastity in regard to the desirable Sophronia as evidence of his perfect faithfulness to his friend.

Cicero identifies three elements which are necessary in successful oratory. In *De oratore* the speaker Antonius claims:

> Under my whole oratorical system and that very readiness in speaking which Crassus just now lauded to the skies, lie three principles, as I said before, first the winning of men's favor, secondly their enlightenment, thirdly their excitement [*una conciliandorum hominum, altera docendorum, tertia concitandorum*]. Of these three the first calls for gentleness of style, the second for acuteness, the third for energy. (2,29,128-29)

Each of the two main parts of Gisippus' speech before he gains Titus'

Tito e Gisippo in European Literature, Comparative Literature Studies (New York: Institute of French Studies, 1937), p. 35.

[17] See Branca's note 1, p. 1531, in his Italian edition. Cf. the near-contemporary example of friends who share their wives at the end of novella 8,8.

consent demonstrates these three elements. In the first part (pp. 780-81), he begins with a most gentle reproach of Titus' lack of confidence and an appeal to true friendship; then he demonstrates that it was proper for Titus to fall in love with Sophronia and that it is good fortune that Gisippus is her fiancé; he concludes this part with the happy prospect of Titus' marriage and a rousing appeal to leave melancholy and to rejoice: "Fret no more then, cast aside your gloom, retrieve your health, your spirits, and your gaiety; and from this time forth, look forward cheerfully to the reward of your love" (p. 781). The second part (pp. 781-82) follows the same order, but the appeal to friendship in an attempt to gain Titus' favor is even more strongly stated than in the previous part. Secondly, he shows the necessity of Titus' marriage in order to preserve both friends' lives and their *amistà*. Finally, he makes an energetic emotional appeal which, as in the previous part, moves from melancholy to joy: "I entreat you here and now to cast aside your sorrows and bring solace to us both. Take heart, and prepare to enjoy the bliss for which your ardent love is yearning" (p. 782) This repeated threefold movement from a gentle appeal to the hearer as friend, through a logical demonstration, to a call to rejoice overcomes Titus' reluctance. As an exemplum of rhetoric that conforms to the principles and objectives of ideal oratory in the Ciceronian mode, Gisippus' response is a positive counterpart to Titus' soliloquy, a failure as persuasive argument with its harsh opening, "Ah, Titus, what a beggarly way to behave!" (p. 778), its demonstrations which Gisippus shows to be false for the most part, and its concluding appeals to shame or passionate love, neither of which wholly overcomes the other.

The friends' circle of arguments is very much closed upon themselves, and it is only at the end of their discussion that Gisippus takes into consideration the interests of Sophronia, her family, and his own kin in respect to his sham marriage and the swap: he maintains that they will have to accept the exchange whether or not they like it (p. 783). In this novella rich in speech and dialogue, there is no direct discourse by Sophronia and the two families. As a narrative strategy, silencing the parties who object to the friends' ruse—that is, the victims of their deceit—aims at making the 'virtue' of Gisippus' gift of friendship as well as the *virtù* of his rhetoric convincing for the storyteller's audience. After carrying out their scheme, the friends are eventually forced to reveal the truth to Sophronia, and she denounces them to her relatives, who want Gisippus punished. In his long public speech of defense which follows, Titus alleges Sophro-

nia's silence as rightful grounds for blaming her: if she married the wrong
man, then it was her fault because she failed to ask his name in the dark
nuptial chamber when she agreed to be his wife (p. 788).[18] At the end of
Titus' defense, the silence of his Athenian opponents and accusers signifies their defeat and that of their case.

The storyteller comments disparagingly on the nature of the Greeks and
their general manner of speaking: "Knowing the Greeks had the habit of
raising an enormous clamor and intensifying their threats until such time
as they found someone to answer them back, when they would suddenly
become not only humble but positively servile, [Titus] decided that their
prattle could no longer be allowed to pass without a rejoinder" (p. 784).
The storyteller's scorn for the Greeks as speakers might be given as a reason, if one were needed, for her omission of their spoken words. Yet her
disdain mirrors Cicero's attitude towards the Greek orators of his day in
general, to whom he refers as "Greeklings," "Graeculi," in *De oratore*
1,9,47, 1,22,102, and 1,51,221. In the novella an attitude of Italian superiority comes into play which finds support in the authority of Cicero and
promises to win the favor of the Italian audience to whom Filomena addresses her story.[19]

In the first segment which we examined, the perfect friend merges with
the consummate orator in Gisippus' speech, where rhetoric serves and preserves *amistà*. In the second segment, Titus' tirade (pp. 784-89), Titus in
turn proves his *virtù* in oratory and friendship by persuading the Athenians to reestablish amicable relations with Gisippus, whom they wished to
punish, and by winning for himself as a Roman patron the friendship of
the client Athenians. In Titus' response to the two families' accusations,
it must appear odd to present-day readers that Titus speaks principally
about himself and his great worth while he has relatively little to say
about Gisippus—he even argues that Gisippus is less worthy than him-

---

[18] Stavros Deligiorgis sees Sophronia, whose name is related to the Greek
word for 'wisdom,' as a representative of the Stoic virtue of prudence—*Narrative Intellection in the "Decameron"* (Iowa City: University of Iowa Press,
1975), p. 223. Nevertheless, in spite of the meaning which her name suggests, the very young character Sophronia, duped by the friends for a long
time, in no way demonstrates prudence.

[19] For Giovanni Giustiniano di Candia's response in Italian to Titus' defense
from a fictive Athenian's point of view, see a synopsis and excerpts from the
mid-sixteenth-century publication in Sorieri, *Boccaccio's Story of Tito e
Gisippo*, pp. 80-86.

self. Titus' apparent immodesty in talking about his own nobility, wealth, and influence illustrates in an exaggerated manner an important feature of Cicero's oratory, that of the speaker's ethos or moral character as a persuasive force. As James M. May has noted, Aristotelian rhetoric was based on three sources of demonstration and persuasion: ethos, or the speaker's moral character; pathos, or putting the hearer in a certain frame of mind; and logos, or proof of argument offered by the speech itself. The Romans were of the general opinion that ethos was bestowed by nature or inherited, and a Roman who had many good ancestors was likely to be considered good, too; further, in regard to *auctoritas*—i.e., authority, reputation, trustworthiness, and influence—a Roman needed to prove by his acts or ancestry that his moral character deserved to be held in respect.[20] As for the relationship between ethos and pathos in persuasive speaking, Cicero states in *De oratore* 2,43,182: "Now feelings are won over by a man's merit [*dignitas*], achievements [*res gestae*], and reputable life [*existimatio*]." According to George A. Kennedy, the lack of modesty characteristic of Cicero's speeches is a constant feature in Roman oratory: unlike Greek orators, the Romans commonly emphasized the speaker's ethos in their pleading, and they frequently argued that because the speaker is of such distinguished character, the hearers should do or believe what he says.[21] This does not mean, however, that Roman or Ciceronian oratory promoted the advocate's or the client's ethos above the facts of the case or skilful pleading. Titus' tirade strays from the Ciceronian model in that it relies to such a great extent on ethos as a persuasive force while it treats the protagonists' wrongdoing in a casual manner. Titus puts the issue of his character and, specifically, his Roman *auctoritas* at the center of his pleading, so that its pathos and logos depend for the most part on the demonstration of ethos. Let us now examine the features of his oration that argue ethos as he attempts to prove the advantages of a friendly alliance with himself and, at the same time, to intimidate the 'Greeklings' into submissive silence.

After maintaining that Gisippus is worthy of the highest praise rather than censure because he acted according to the sacred laws of friendship (p. 785; "le sante leggi della amicizia"), Titus argues his second point, that

---

[20] May, *Trials of Character. The Eloquence of Ciceronian Ethos* (Chapel Hill and London: North Carolina Press, 1988), pp. 1-7.

[21] Kennedy, *The Art of Rhetoric in the Roman World, 300 B.C.-A.D. 300* (Princeton: Princeton University Press, 1972), pp. 100-01.

Gisippus, in choosing Titus as Sophronia's husband, was wiser than the families which chose Gisippus. In proof of his point he attempts to show himself to be a worthier man and match than Gisippus. In the five-part comparison between Gisippus and himself which he undertakes, three parts dealing with their status as natives of Athens and Rome, as nobles, and as men of wealth and influence argue Titus' personal authority and the superiority of Rome and Romans. In respect to their status as citizens of Athens and Rome, Titus compares the merits of the two cities in an imaginary debate between himself and Gisippus, who loses (p. 786), but he does not state the obvious conclusion regarding character: just as Rome is superior to Athens, so the Roman is superior to the Athenian. The argument of Rome's authority and, particularly, her power over Athens as a reason for the Athenian hearers to submit to this Roman's judgment is only implied here, but at the end of his tirade he invokes the *auctoritas* of Rome to strike fear into their hearts.

Secondly, Titus describes his distinguished ancestry, but he does not compare it with Gisippus' family (p. 786). His mention of the antiquity of his lineage, its past renown, and its even greater present glory is meant to prove his *dignitas* and excellent reputation as well as the achievements of his family, all of which contribute to his personal *auctoritas*. In this part of his demonstration he attempts to convince his hearers that what he says deserves to be believed because he is of reputable character.

The third part regarding the great riches that he possesses in Rome (p. 787) would seem on the face of it not to lend itself to a proof of character, but Titus treats the subject so as to demonstrate his virtuous ethos in a Ciceronian manner and his *virtù* or influence as a Roman *patronus*. As for his riches, Titus says, "Of these I have abundant store, not out of avarice but out of the kindness of Fortune," and he offers to use his wealth to benefit his Athenian hearers, who "will discover me to be an excellent host to you [in Rome], as well as a valuable, solicitous, and excellent patron [*padrone*], who will be only too ready to assist you, whether in your public or your personal concerns" (p. 787). Titus' wealth shows his good character negatively in that he did not amass it through avarice, and in a positive manner his offer of benefaction demonstrates his goodness in the sense that Cicero advises the orator to call to mind in a panegyric:

> A panegyric must also treat of those goods of nature and fortune in which the highest praise is not to have been puffed up in office or insolent in wealth, or to have put oneself in front of others because of fortune's

> bounty—so that wealth and riches may seem to have provided opportunity and occasion not for pride and license but for beneficence and temperance. (*De oratore* 2,84,342)

Titus uses his wealth here as an opportunity to be or appear beneficent and, hence, worthy of praise. The particular relationship between himself and his hearers which he suggests, one between *patronus* and clients, is a form of *amicitia* as a social and political alliance which was mentioned in the first chapter of this book. As George Kennedy notes, in *De oratore* the ideal orator is thought of as a Roman *patronus* upon whom clients could call to defend them in all sorts of suits,[22] and even though Titus does not specifically offer to defend his Athenian hearers in Roman courts in the future, the circumstances—his present defense of Gisippus—imply just such a possibility. Titus makes a comparison of equality between Gisippus and himself in stating that just as his hearers have found Gisippus to be valuable to them in Athens, so, too, will they find Titus to be an asset in Rome. In this instance oratory and *amicitia* of the patron-client sort are joined.

Pathos plays an important role here as it supports the demonstration of ethos and *auctoritas* and calls up the pleasant or unpleasant consequences of the proof for the audience. The gentle nature of Titus' offer of patronage contrasts with the rest of his address to the families, for he begins his oration with the hostile declaration that they are senselessly arrogant, he continues to treat them as fools, and he concludes by promising to visit them with the destructive wrath of a Roman enemy should they decide to oppose him. Most of his address to the Athenians is marked by somewhat the same virulent attack on their character that one finds in Cicero's orations against Catiline and Mark Antony. Titus' offer and its amiable quality along with his arguments about Gisippus' disinterestedness in acting as he did conform to Cicero's observations about the ideal orator's successful appeal to emotions:

> We observe that love is won if you are thought to be upholding the interests of your audience, or to be working for good men, or at any rate for such as that audience deems good and useful. For this last impression more readily wins love, and the protection of righteous esteem; and the holding-out of hope of advantage to come is more effective than the recital of past benefit. You must struggle to reveal the presence, in the cause you are upholding, of some merit or usefulness, and to make it plain that the man, for whom you are to win this love, in no respect con-

---

[22] Ibid., p. 215.

sulted his own interests and did nothing at all from private motives. (*De oratore* 2,51,206-07)

Titus' offer of *amicitia* as a Roman patron is a gentle appeal to love and to gain which his hearers can accept or refuse. His concluding appeal to fear as he evokes his Roman *auctoritas* and threatens to ruin his hearers should they refuse him leaves little room for choice. He does not sway his hearers in the end by his words alone. After he stops speaking, he leaves the gathering, his face twisted with anger, and he looks menacingly at his audience. This posturing imitates the much praised skill of Crassus, a model of the ideal speaker in *De oratore*, in his dramatic gestures, and it follows Cicero's advice that the advocate must show stamped on himself all the emotions that he wants his hearers to feel (2,44,188-89). As Filomena remarks, after Titus' departure the Athenians renew their friendship with Gisippus and accept Titus as their relative and friend partly because of the force of Titus' arguments and partly from their alarm at his conclusion (p. 789). As an orator Titus is persuasive largely because of his contradictory appeals to gentle emotions in the friendship which he offers and to fear as he shows the face of enmity.[23]

In the first segment *amistà* and oratory were limited to the interaction between Titus and Gisippus, and in the second they extended to the wide range of sociopolitical relationships involving a powerful Roman patron and his Athenian kin and clients. The third segment, Filomena's concluding argument (pp. 793-94), is an appeal to her listeners to embrace and cherish friendship above family, wealth, and rank. In speaking in praise of the virtues of Titus and Gisippus, Filomena may be seen to demonstrate another of the effects of ideal oratory which Cicero describes, that is, its power to make the speaker appear virtuous:

> To paint [the speaker's clients'] characters in words, as being upright, stainless, conscientious, modest, and long-suffering under injustice, has a really wonderful effect; and this topic, whether in opening, or in stating the case, or in winding-up, is so compelling, when agreeably and feelingly handled, as often to be worth more than the merits of the case. Moreover so much is done by good taste and style in speaking, that the speech seems to depict the speaker's character. For by means of particular types of thought and diction, and the employment besides of a deliv-

---

[23] For an analysis of the structure of Titus' speech, which consists of an introduction, a statement of case, affirmative arguments, refutations, and a conclusion, see Branca's note 6, p. 1538, in his Italian edition. Cf. *De oratore* 1,31,143.

ery that is unruffled and eloquent of good nature, the speakers are made to appear upright, well-bred, and virtuous men. (*De oratore* 2,43,184)

If one accepts in principle this function of speech as a demonstration of ethos, then it can be argued that Filomena's display of her *virtù* as an orator through her eloquent discourse on her protagonists' superlative qualities shows, too, her upright, well-bred, and virtuous character. As an encomium of *amistà* and a persuasive argument, her speech aims at gaining her listeners' favor for her tale of virtuous friendship because she and they, unlike most of their contemporaries, are virtuous. At the beginning of her tale, she announced that she would speak of noble citizens like the members of her audience. In the manner of the interlocutor Laelius in Cicero's *De amicitia*, Filomena addresses her listeners confidentially and sets herself and them apart from the common herd. Laelius is not only a model *amicus*; he is also given as a model of rhetorical excellence in *De oratore* 1,13,58. In the context of the tenth day of the *Decameron*, Filomena's conclusion may be interpreted to refer to the friendly, virtuous activity of the fictive tellers themselves in that they share with her protagonists the specific moral qualities which she underlines in her conclusion.

The first sentence of Filomena's conclusion sets the tone for her remarks as encomiastic: "Friendship, then, is a most sacred thing, not only worthy of singular reverence, but eternally to be praised as the deeply discerning mother of munificence and probity [*discretissima madre di magnificenzia e d'onestà*], the sister of gratitude and charity, and the foe of hatred and avarice, ever ready, without waiting to be asked, to do virtuously unto others that which it would wish to be done unto itself" (p. 793). There is a strong hint of Christian moralizing in the first part's praise of charity as well as in the last words, where the Golden Rule and the first law of *amicitia* in *Laelius* 13,44 are combined. Nevertheless, the virtues of *amistà* which she describes are strictly secular, in no way spiritual, since there is no suggestion that they derive from God or love of God, and the circumstances of her delivery and of all the other novellas offered to the fictive *brigata* point to a secular sort of charity or partiality and affection within the group, whose members live harmoniously within the same walls according to the rule which they established for their conduct. Panfilo, king of the tenth day, praises the group's communal harmony and probity in his reflections on its shared activities in his concluding address: "From what I have seen and heard, it seems to me that our proceedings have been marked by a constant sense of propriety, an unfailing spirit of harmony, and a continual feeling of brotherly and sisterly amity [*continua onestà, continua concordia, continua fraternal dimestichezza*]. All of which pleases me greatly, as it surely redounds to our communal honor and credit" (p. 825). In contrast to the social disorder in plague-stricken Florence, where "all respect for the laws of God and man had virtually broken down and been extinguished" (pp. 52-53), the orderly, fraternal community at the country villas is utopian. One might compare the idealized brotherly and sisterly *dimestichezza* or familiarity of the band with Filomena's description of the harmonious life shared by Titus, Gisippus, and their wives which precedes the first sentence of her conclusion cited above: all four lived happily in the same Roman house, and Titus and Gisippus' friendship grew stronger with every day (p. 793). The friendly, fraternal cohabitation of her protagonists and their spouses and the *brigata*'s harmonious life together serve as complementary fictions of the perfect concord of love and friendship, with the notable difference that the band's unmarried females are fully equals to their male companions.

In the middle section of her conclusion Filomena argues that the two principal virtues which she noted above—probity or *onestà* and munificence or *magnificenzia*—are evidenced in Gisippus' and Titus' actions. This section consists of six rhetorical questions, three about Gisippus and three about Titus, all of which require the answer that friendship alone could cause the protagonists to give such extraordinary proof of virtue. One question concerning Gisippus' sexual self-restraint emphasizes his probity: "Except for the power of friendship, what laws, what threats, what fear of consequence, could have prevented the youthful arms of Gisippus, in darkened or deserted places, or in the privacy of his own bed, from embracing this delectable girl [Sophronia], occasionally perhaps at her own invitation?" (p. 793). This remarkable effect of friendship, continence in circumstances where one might expect unchastity, does not apply to Gisippus alone. Panfilo, before praising the members of the band for their *onestà*, notes many circumstances of their life together which normally encourage lust and shameful acts: "For as far as I have been able to observe, albeit the tales related here have been amusing, perhaps of a sort to stimulate carnal desire, and we have continually partaken of excellent food and drink, played music, and sung many songs, all of which things may encourage unseemly behavior among those who are feeble of mind, neither in word nor in deed nor in any other respect have I known either you or ourselves to be worthy of censure" (p. 825). Under these circum-

stances, the continence of the members of the band is exemplary, especially since the males are secretly in love with certain of their female
companions, who in turn love but do not name the object of their affection. Filomena's praise of Gisippus' probity may be seen, through the
optic of Panfilo's subsequent claims of the *brigata*'s constant *onestà*, to
refer, also, to the character of her companions who, like herself, maintain
chaste *amistà* in spite of the seductive circumstances of their life together.

Most of Filomena's rhetorical questions deal with an exceptionally generous gift to a friend: Gisippus gives his fiancée to Titus, who offers his
life for Gisippus',[24] gives him his sister to wed, and makes him the co-
owner of his enormous fortune. These instances illustrate the friends'
magnificenzia which Filomena cites in the first sentence of her conclusion. *Magnificenzia* in the sense of generosity applies especially to
Filomena's delivery and to the other tales of the tenth day. In her closing
sentences, Filomena argues that the common desire to rule over a large
household is futile, since no relative or servant can be counted on in a difficult or dangerous situation to subordinate his own interests and safety to
those of the head of the household (p. 794). Only friends will behave unselfishly in the event of great danger, *pericolo*. The *pericolo* to which she
refers is abstract, but one need not look far to discover a concrete illustration—the plague in Florence from which the *brigata* has fled and to which
it will return the following day. The band's storytelling which offers the
hearers entertainment gives cheerfulness, *allegrezza*, and, thus, acts as a
remedy for the malady from which Florence's survivors suffer—melancholy.[25] No less dangerous, as many of the *Decameron*'s tales show, is
the amorous melancholy from which most of the tellers themselves suffer
to varying degrees. The members of the band, of which Filomena ad-

---

[24] According to A. C. Lee, the scene before the Roman magistrate in which
each friend confesses to murder so that he may die in the other's stead has its
source in the Damon and Phintias legend of which Valerius Maximus gives an
account in his *Memorable Acts and Sayings*, book 4, chapter 7—"*The Decameron.*" *Its Sources and Analogues* (1909, reprint ed.; New York: Haskell
House, 1972), pp. 335-36. It is just as likely, however, that this scene, of
which a version appears in Petrus Alfonsi's *Disciplina clericalis* (see note 11
above), comes from the legend of Orestes and Pylades which Cicero describes
in *Laelius* 7,24.

[25] See the discussions on the hygienic function of storytelling in the *De-
cameron* in Glending Olson, *Literature as Recreation in the Later Middle Ages*
(Ithaca: Cornell University Press, 1982), pp. 164 ff., and G. Mazzotta, *The
World at Play*, pp. 30-33.

dresses the ladies as *magnifiche donne* in her introduction, are generous in offering to one another healthful entertainment, and they are even more so when their tales, as those of the tenth day and especially Filomena's, offer moral instruction and encouragement along with good cheer. By offering their tales, they fulfil Panfilo's command to speak "of those who have performed liberal or munificent deeds, whether in the cause of love or otherwise"—namely, of themselves as narrators. One of the main lessons of Filomena's tale, that *la vera amistà*, with the aid of eloquence, can convert love's difficulties and pains to joy, is reflected in the cheer produced through the *brigata*'s verbal interchange marked by mutual benevolence and beneficence and by constant, honorable amity.

In conclusion, the *Decameron*'s narrative staging recalls the literary courts of love imagined in book 2 of Andreas Capellanus' *De amore*, where female and male lovers present to noblewomen, authorities on the art of honorable love, their cases and fictions for arbitration and approval. The *Decameron*'s aristocratic *brigata* presents its tales, in good part about love, for the group's judgment, and all but nearly a dozen of the novellas are addressed specifically to the band's ladies. Two of the principal events in Filomena's final tale also take place in court or deliberative assembly, where the protagonists seek the favor of their audience—the Athenians in one case, and a Roman magistrate in the other. It is with reference to the equality of her protagonists and her fellow narrators-listeners-judges that Filomena opens her tale, when she announces that she will recount noble deeds "performed by people like ourselves" or "our equals" (p. 776; "de' nostri pari"). In her attempt to gain approval for her story, she encourages her medieval listeners to see their own semblance in the protagonists. Although her tale and her manner of telling mark a return to ancient values, they highlight no less the virtues of the present company which constitutes a fictional court of honorable love and *amistà*.

The intimate relationship between excellent friendship and rhetorical excellence in the novella suggests two major modifications of the standards of Ciceronian *amicitia vera*. Although in *Laelius* ease and skill in speech are traits of only secondary importance to be sought in an *amicus*, in the novella Gisippus and Titus could not have brought their friendship to perfection had they been less than first-rate speakers. The highest standard for a true friend's speech evident in the novella is implied, however, in *Laelius*, where the principal speaker and *amicus* is a preeminent orator and the author, the chief authority in Latin rhetoric. Secondly, the fact that the

female narrator Filomena serves as the novella's principal model of oratorical excellence suggests the possibility of an amendment to the code of
amicitia perfecta to admit woman. Did Boccaccio mean to indicate that
since Filomena has scaled the heights of rhetoric, she, like her protagonists, might qualify for the highest friendship? It is tempting to answer
affirmatively and to see here a mark of Boccaccio's originality, but it
seems likely that this tale of male generosity, mutual confidence, and eloquence in which the main female character is silent and, consequently, at
fault points to no such privileged status as *amica perfecta* for the fictive
narrator. Further, the tale is problematic in that the female narrator gives
the highest praise to male *amistà* which totally disregards the interests of
the main female character. Boccaccio's turning over the friends' defense to
a woman advocate is, perhaps, solely a strategy to hide their (and his?)
distrust of woman behind her skirts. One should probably consider the
virtues of Filomena's skilful oratory in regard to the *Decameron*'s dis-
creetly romantic narrative frame and chaste pleasure-seeking, especially
that of the tenth day's moral entertainment, where her delivery proves her
onestà, magnificenzia, and high-mindedness, essential traits of the noble
lady worthy of the finest love in the tradition of courtly literature. In the
Decameron's medieval contextualization of antique-style *amicitia vera*,
Filomena's virtues would seem to apply to the limited sphere of a fictional court of love, where here the numerically inferior males, suitors,
defer to woman's voice of authority.

For some time Laurent de Premierfait (ca. 1365 1418) has been of interest
to scholars mainly because he was the first French translator of a vernacular work, the *Decameron*, which he rendered not from the original Italian
but from a Latin version made expressly for his translation. Although a
man of letters of nowhere near the stature of Boccaccio, Laurent de
Premierfait is a noteworthy figure in late-medieval French literary history,
especially since his production, mostly translations, offers an example of
the sort of works commissioned by noble and bourgeois patrons in the
early fifteenth century. He participated in a major movement which began
in the reign of Charles V (1364-1380) and continued through that of
Charles VI (1380-1422) for the translation into French of ancient and medieval Latin texts. His work evidences a keen interest at the time in the

writings of the later Middle Ages and renewed, sustained attention to ancient literature.

Besides composing Latin poetry, letters, commentaries, and compendia
of Statius' epic poems the *Thebais* and the *Achilleis*, Laurent de Premierfait translated Boccaccio's Latin prose *On the Misfortunes of Famous
Men* (*De casibus virorum illustrium*) and *On Famous Women* (*De
mulieribus claris*) in 1400 and again in 1409, Cicero's *On Old Age* (*De
senectute*) in 1405, the *Decameron* in 1414, and *Laelius de amicitia* in
1416, and in 1418 he revised an earlier French version of the *Economics*,
a spurious Aristotelian treatise.[26] His production in Latin and from Latin
to French exemplifies the literary bilingualism favored by French court
writers of his time, and his translations of *On Old Age* and *Laelius*, the
first to be made in French, are particularly significant as part of the late-
medieval translation movement in France in that they shift the focus of
study of these Latin classics from schools and the university, where they
remained among highly literate clerics for many centuries, to the court. In
his prologues to *Laelius*, Laurent de Premierfait characterizes his intended
reader as moderately lettered, that is, one who knows both French and
Latin but may need help with the latter. In analyzing his two unpublished
French prologues (see the English translation in Appendix B), the present
study will demonstrate how Laurent de Premierfait attempts to establish
his French version for the use of the moderately lettered as an authority in
its own right.

One should note certain circumstances regarding Laurent de Premierfait's patrons for his translation of *Laelius* which are not mentioned in the
prologues. The prefaces and version were completed in 1416, and they are
dedicated to Louis II, duke of Bourbon, who died in 1410. Laurent de
Premierfait began the project for Louis II in 1406-1407, and he resumed
work on it in 1414-1416 at the request of Jean, duke of Berry, who died in
1416.[27] Bureau de Dampmartin, a merchant and moneylender who became
the French royal treasurer in 1411, commissioned the completion of the

---

[26] R. C. Famiglietti, "Laurent de Premierfait: The Career of a Humanist in
Early Fifteenth-Century Paris," *Journal of Medieval History* 9 (1983): 32-37.

[27] Jacques Monfrin, "La connaissance de l'antiquité et le problème de
l'humanisme en langue vulgaire dans la France du XVe siècle," in *The Late
Middle Ages and the Dawn of Humanism Outside Italy. The Proceedings of the
International Conference, Louvain, May 11-13, 1970*, ed. G. Verbeke and J.
Ijsewijn, Mediaevalia Lovaniensa, Series 1, 1 (Louvain: University Press,
1972), p. 142.

work.[28]

As for prior French translations of ancient and medieval works on *amicitia*, Nicole Oresme translated for Charles V in 1370 the *Nicomachean Ethics* from thirteenth-century Latin versions.[29] In his prologues to *Laelius*, Laurent de Premierfait says a great deal about the *Ethics*, but he does not mention Oresme's important text, which was first printed in 1488. Oresme's translations of Aristotelian treatises on ethics, politics, economics, and astronomy and of Ptolemy's *Tetrabiblos* on astrology are works of practical value or application, as were many of the other 'service translations' done for Charles V, a king of studious nature whom Christine de Pisan praised for his excellent knowledge of Latin.[30] Charles V also commissioned Jean Goulein's translation of John Cassian's *Conferences* (1370) and Simon de Hesdin's version of Valerius Maximus' *Memorable Acts and Sayings* (incomplete, ca. 1383; Nicolas de Gonesse finished the work for Jean de Berry in 1401.)[31]

Laurent de Premierfait's introduction to his translation of *Laelius* is typically medieval in form. His two prologues in French are elaborate examples of the *accessus ad auctores* or academic prologue genre, usually in Latin, developed as an introduction to authoritative classical and medieval Latin works, as well as the Bible, in the Middle Ages. The first prologue, which makes up almost five-sixths of the introduction (1-60; arabic numerals in parentheses refer to numbered paragraphs in Appendix B), is of the extrinsic sort, that is, it draws its explanations and arguments from outside *Laelius*. It deals mainly with the parts of Aristotelian philosophy, especially rhetoric, and it provides a synopsis of books 8 and 9 of the *Nicomachean Ethics*. The extrinsic prologue introduces material that one should know about 'Dame Philosophy' and Aristotle's ethics before proceeding to *Laelius*, a rhetorical work which teaches ethics. The second prologue (61-66) is intrinsic, that is, it deals with *Laelius* proper.

---

[28] Famiglietti, "Laurent de Premierfait," p. 36.

[29] *Maistre Nicole Oresme. Le livre de ethiques d'Aristote. Published from the Text of MS. 2902, Bibliothèque Royale de Belgique*, ed. A. D. Menut (New York: G. E. Stechert, 1940). See pages 412-95 for books 8 and 9.

[30] Peter F. Dembowski, "Learned Latin Treatises in French: Inspiration, Plagarism, and Translation," *Viator* 17 (1986): 261-62.

[31] Monfrin, "La connaissance de l'antiquité," p. 139. One might also note Jean de Meun's lost late-thirteenth-century translation of Aelred's *Spiritual Friendship* and an anonymous version from around 1300 of selected maxims from Seneca's *Letters to Lucilius*.

The extrinsic preface is a variation of the type C prologue in R. W. Hunt's classification which A. J. Minnis has described in detail.[32] The type C prologue, which had its origins with Boethius or even earlier, was widely used in the twelfth century and later. An unusual feature in Laurent de Premierfait's extrinsic prologue is that he has a great deal to say about the translation itself, which he treats as a literary work in its own right. There he attempts to establish the authority of his version in much the same manner as that used in academic prologues to ancient and medieval Latin works. Under most of the eight standard headings of the type C prologue—title, author, the writer's intentions, the work's form and style, its subject-matter, the branch of philosophy to which it belongs, its usefulness, and the text's order or arrangement—the prefacer turns the discussion from the classical author and text to his own version and his activity as a commissioned translator of ancient moral literature. He notes his own intentions as well as stating Cicero's, he compares the form and style of the original with those of the translation, and in the final two divisions, he writes more about the usefulness of the version itself and its arrangement than about the Latin original. We would now like to show how Laurent de Premierfait adapts the type C divisions in his extrinsic prologue to his own end—the establishment of the authority of his version as a sanctioned and trustworthy text.

As for the title and author, Laurent de Premierfait begins his prologue with a mention of the earlier French translation of Cicero's *On Old Age* which he undertook at the request of Louis II, who, pleased with his work, then ordered him to put *Laelius* into French. The translator not only names himself and his earlier work, but he hints that he is capable and worthy of the present task because of the favorable reception of his previous endeavor. He also implies that the authority, the political power, of the duke and his commission justify the present undertaking (1-2). Near the end of the preface the translator appeals to his patron to defend the version against malicious criticism—that is, to impose the authority of the translation itself (58).

Thirdly, just as Cicero's intention in writing *Laelius* was to satisfy his friend Atticus' request to compose a work on friendship, so Laurent de Premierfait made the translation in order to please the duke and all those

---

[32] Minnis, *Medieval Theory of Authorship. Scholastic Literary Attitudes in the Later Middle Ages*, Middle Ages Series, 2nd ed. (Philadelphia: University of Pennsylvania Press, 1988), pp. 18-27.

who delight in virtuous, ancient teachings (2). What the translator does not state is significant in respect to intention: neither Louis II nor Jean de Berry read Latin or, at least, read it very well. The implication is clear, however, since the translator says that his patron became acquainted with the ancients' virtuous deeds and words through his rendering of *On Old Age*. While not stating here that the translation is meant to make up for the duke's linguistic deficiencies, he writes near the end of this preface of French and foreign courtiers and others at the duke's court who will find the rendering helpful (59). In the Middle Ages a vernacular translation was sometimes offered as a companion to a Latin text for the purpose of learning Latin, just as in the Renaissance Latin versions of Greek works were used for learning to read Greek.

Next, he indicates in regard to form and style that *Laelius* is a dialogue, as is *On Old Age*, and he identifies the principal speakers (2). Later he contrasts the majesty of Cicero's Latin with the meagerness of the translation's French (57-58), and he claims to use in his own discussion of philosophy and summary of the *Ethics* a French idiom so clear and ordinary that the moderately lettered ("les hommes moyennement lettrez") will understand it easily (4). It is apparent, however, from the style of this prologue, excepting the courtly formality of its opening, that Laurent de Premierfait's French is a literary idiom imitative of Ciceronian prose, and his Latinate vocabulary and structures are markedly academic, uncharacteristic of the language of moderately lettered French laymen.

Fifthly, the translator's abstract of *Laelius*' subject-matter leads to his mention of Cicero's debt to the *Nicomachean Ethics* (3-4), and in the sixth place—regarding the branch of philosophy to which *Laelius* belongs—the prefacer outlines the three divisions of Aristotelian philosophy, defines rhetoric, included under the third major division, rational science or dialectics, and notes Cicero's debt to Aristotle's rhetoric (5-10). The lengthy summary of books 8 and 9 of the *Ethics* which follows shifts from the science of rhetoric to Aristotle's treatment of *philia* under the division of ethics (11-56). The key Aristotelian ethical and political model, *philia* between ruler and subject, which figures so prominently in the summary is, of course, absent from Cicero's treatise on Republican *amicitia perfecta*. The Aristotelian model is the basis for the relationship between the duke (or dukes) and the translator described in the opening paragraphs of the prologue: there Laurent de Premierfait emphasizes the duke's status as a highly placed member of the royal family, and he presents himself as a respectful subordinate soliciting his lord's continued benevolence and friendship.

In the prologue's seventh part, which deals mainly with the utility of the translation, he returns to the duke, whose bustling, cosmopolitan court he describes briefly, and he asks for the duke's protection in the face of hostile critics (57-59). Here the models of ruler and subject and of patron and literary protégé converge. He argues the utility of *Laelius* on the grounds that its teachings encourage virtuous conduct, and he localizes the translation's usefulness in the context of the duke's court. He directs his translation at the many Frenchmen and foreigners of various rank who flock to the ducal court and who are moderately learned, that is, who know at least enough Latin to compare Cicero's original with the French version. Although he does not specify, except in the duke's case, the social status of his intended readers at court, he may mean to indicate nobles and bourgeois, too, such as Bureau de Dampmartin, who commissioned the completion of the translation. This part of the introduction has drawn the attention of modern scholars because of the apology for the rendering itself, which, says the translator, some might censure for abasing and trivializing the majesty of the original in the vulgar tongue. He claims, also, that some might blame him for revealing to the uninstructed—that is, lay people—weighty matters or ideas which may lead them into error because of their limited understanding. R. C. Famiglietti suggests that this concern about criticism may explain in part why the translator set his work on *Laelius* aside for a number of years.[33] It is likely, however, that the prefacer, who interrupted his work around the time of his patron Louis II's death, is not expressing a personal attitude here but that his declaration illustrates what one might call the 'defense against envious detractors' topic and the modesty topos commonly found in classical and medieval literature, for example, in the *Decameron*. Nonetheless, in certain cases one cannot dismiss as convention medieval writers' expression of inferiority, indeed, of possible wrongdoing in using the vernacular. A case in point is Boccaccio's agreement with a humanist friend who accused him of prostituting the Muses by turning over their secrets to the unworthy crowd in his 1373-1374 lectures in Italian on Dante's *Divine Comedy*.[34] And

---

[33] Famiglietti, "Laurent de Premierfait," p. 37.

[34] A. J. Minnis, A. B. Scott, and David Wallace, *Medieval Literary Theory and Criticism c. 1100-c. 1375. The Commentary Tradition* (Oxford: Clarendon Press, 1988), p. 374. See Branca, *Boccaccio: The Man and His Works*, pp.

although Marsilio Ficino translated his own 1469 Latin commentary on Plato's *Symposium* into Italian in 1474, he considered Plato's opus, which he rendered into Latin, to be divinely inspired texts of which vernacular translation would amount almost to profanation.

In his argument dealing with the translation's usefulness, Laurent de Premierfait includes the eighth element of the type C prologue by indicating the order or arrangement of the prologues, translation, and Latin text (59). He invites readers to check the accuracy of the translation by comparing it with the original. In following this suggestion, readers would find that the rendering is characterized by a style which approximates the elegance of Cicero's prose and by a very Latinate vocabulary, but the translation does not conform to present-day criteria for accuracy. Quite often the translator glosses the Latin text and expands it considerably. His interpretative amplification is generally helpful for the reader's understanding, but it is more of the nature of explanation and stylistic compensation than of exact translation. The limits of the present study do not permit, however, a detailed stylistic comparison of the rendering and the source text.[35]

The extrinsic prologue has the dual purpose of introducing *Laelius* through its principal philosophical source, the *Nicomachean Ethics*, and of legitimizing the French version. Laurent de Premierfait attempts to achieve this second end by treating his translation formally in the same manner, through a type C *accessus*, used by academics to introduce an authoritative ancient or medieval text in Latin. In the last paragraph another element which aims at legitimizing the version in the medieval Christian reader's eyes is a prayer to Christ, the friend of humankind, to grant the translator knowledge and words in conformity with divine truth and to guide his pen in this endeavor (60). Although he seeks legitimacy for the translation itself as a Christian undertaking, nowhere in his prologues or the rendering does he attempt a Christian interpretation of the ancient text or a reconciliation of classical friendship with *amicitia christiana*.

184-86, on Boccaccio's detractors and his responses.

[35] For a detailed stylistic comparison of Laurent de Premierfait's translation of the *Decameron* (via Antonio di Arezzo's lost Latin version) with the Italian original, see Giuseppe Di Stefano, "Dal *Decameron* di Giovanni Boccaccio al *Livre des cent nouvelles* di Laurent de Premierfait," in *Boccaccio in Europe. Proceedings of the Boccaccio Conference, Louvain, December 1975*, ed. Gilbert Tournoy, Symbolae Facultatis Litterarum et Philosophiae Lovaniensis, Series A, 4 (Louvain: Leuven University Press, 1977), pp. 91-110.

Nonetheless, the extrinsic prologue's prayer and the localization of the commissioned translation in a late-medieval ducal court provide a wholly nonclassical context for *Laelius*. While encouraging an appreciation of ancient wisdom, virtue, and rhetoric through a return to the classical texts, the prologues remain firmly anchored in their own times and academic, courtly, and religious customs.

The intrinsic or second prologue exemplifies the so-called 'Aristotelian' type of academic preface that was commonly used in the thirteenth century and afterwards.[36] This prologue, which introduces *Laelius* from inside, as it were, is centered around the four Aristotelian causes—efficient, material, formal, and final. To summarize this part most briefly, we might note that the efficient cause ("l'efficiente cause," 65) is the author, and the translator names Cicero again (61) and gives a biographical sketch (65). The efficient cause as the productive agent for a literary work can also include the circumstances which prompted the author to compose it. The translator notes two events—a bitter quarrel between two prominent Romans whom all believed to be close friends, and Atticus' request—which prompted Cicero to write *Laelius* (61). The material cause ("la matiere," 65) refers to the literary matter from which the work derives—the *Ethics* (62, 64)—and *Laelius*' subject-matter. The translator defines what is and is not *amicitia vera* (61-65). The formal cause ("la forme," 65) or the literary form is a dialogue, and the translator names the three interlocutors and says a few words about their standing in the Republic (61, 65). He also remarks that Cicero's expression is subtle and concise (61). The final cause ("la cause finale," 66) is the objective at which Cicero aimed in writing and, also, moral or philosophical justification for the work. The translator indicates both a private cause—Cicero's desire to satisfy Atticus' request—and a public one—that the moral treatise might benefit not one but many men (66).

A noteworthy feature of the prologues is that they present *Laelius* in a serious, scholarly manner. Although the prefaces and the translation are intended for the moderately lettered, bilingual lay reader—and, indeed, they are perfectly accessible to the French reader who knows little or no

---

[36] See Minnis' description of the Aristotelian prologue paradigm, *Medieval Theory*, pp. 28-29. For several texts of medieval Latin *accessus* to *Laelius* which resemble the intrinsic prologue, see Elisabeth Pellegrin, "Quelques *accessus* au *De amicitia* de Cicéron," in *Hommages à André Boutemy*, ed. Guy Cambier, Collection Latomus, 145 (Brussels: Latomus, 1976), pp. 274-98.

Latin—they have nothing of the character of a vernacular work of popular-ized philosophy from Latin sources such as Brunetto Latini's encyclopedic *Li livres dou tresor* (see Appendix A.) Laurent de Premierfait is scrupu-lous in treating *Laelius* as a work of great literary and philosophical merit in its own right, in providing an accurate copy of the original, and in defining the treatise's relationship to Aristotle's rhetoric and ethics. As humanistic writings that point to a return to an authentic antiquity via vernacular version, the prefaces are remarkable for the absence of medieval and Christian interference in Laurent de Premierfait's critical interpreta-tion.

The ideals of Republican *amicitia* in *Laelius* and of Aristotle's concord between wise, beneficent ruler and loving subjects at the heart of a peace-ful state presented in the prefaces could not be farther, it would seem, from the political realities of Laurent de Premierfait's time. The protracted internal and international strife that marked early-fifteenth-century French politics—the middle of the Hundred Years War, the reign of a mentally unstable French king, the assassination of the regent, Louis, duke of Or-léans, in 1407, the Cabochian Uprising in 1413, the French defeat at Azincourt in 1415, the bloody civil war between the Burgundian and Ar-magnac factions, a war of which Laurent de Premierfait may have been a civilian fatality—resembles in its intensity and extent the violent political discord of the period during which Cicero wrote *Laelius* and lost his head. In his prefaces Laurent de Premierfait makes no allusion, however, to the vehement political enmity of the Republic's twilight that lies scarcely concealed beneath *Laelius'* surface fiction of the glorious earlier age of Republican heroes. What Laurent de Premierfait does underline is, on one hand, the enduring philosophical friendship between Atticus and Cicero and, on the other, the virtuous duke of Bourbon and his friends at court who share his enthusiasm for learning ("a vous et a voz amis de vostre estude," 5). The philosophical *amistié* of the duke who seeks to know the wisdom and worthy deeds of the ancients in their writings and who attracts men attentive to letters suggests both Aristotle's beneficent-prince model in the first preface's summary and the conclusion to *De amicitia* (27,103-04), where Laelius describes his and Scipio's leisure time spent together in the eager pursuit of knowledge. Laurent de Premierfait's sketch of the courtly *studia humanitatis* represents a late-medieval ideal of virtuous this-worldly pursuits which reanimates in a new context the idealism and op-timism of classical authority. Even though one must consider the prefacer's construction to be for the most part a flattering fiction of courtly life, the eloquent and erudite courtier plays a central role in many fifteenth-century Italian philosophical dialogues—for example, Alberti's *Dell'amicizia.*

In 1441 Leon Battista Alberti (1404-1472) organized an Italian poetry competition, the *Certame coronario*, in Florence on the subject of *la vera amicizia*. At the contest, after which the judges awarded the crown of victory to no one, he recited an Italian poem modeled on Latin hexameters.[37] On the same occasion he offered to the Florentine commune a prose dialogue on true friendship which shortly afterwards he revised and included as the fourth and final book in his collection *I libri della famiglia*, his first major work in the vernacular. As M. Dardano maintains, the author intended for his dialogue *Dell'amicizia* "to demonstrate the stylistic dignity of the vernacular."[38] It is cast as a conversation among several of the most prominent male Alberti elders, members of the family council, who wish to instruct their young kinsmen, Leon Battista and his brother, and it is set in the home of Leon Battista's father Lorenzo in Padua around 1420—that is, during the Alberti family's banishment from Florence, which lasted from 1378 to 1428.[39] The dialogue is most original in that it treats *la vera amistà* according to a familial model—the extended Italian household—which imparts its *virtù* to the contemporary Italian city-state, the successor, more in idea than in fact, to the ancient Roman Republic. *Dell'amicizia* joins family and state through the medium of a true friend whose virtue, wisdom, and love of letters benefit and preserve the family

---

[37] See the sixteen-verse poem in *Leonis Baptistae Alberti opera inedita et pauca separatim impressa*, ed. Hieronymus Mancini, Raccolta di Opere Inedite o Rare di Ogni Secolo della Letteratura Italiana (Florence: J. C. Sansoni, 1890), pp. 236-37. For the other competitors' poems, see *Opere volgari di Leon Batt. Alberti per la più parte inedite e tratte dagli autografi*, ed. Anicio Bonucci (Florence: Tipografia Galileiana, 1843), vol. 1, pp. clxvii-ccxxxiv.

[38] Dardano, "Sintassi e stile nei *Libri della famiglia* di Leon Battista Alberti," *Cultura neolatina* 23 (1963): 223—my translation.

[39] Jean Lacroix, "Panégyrique domestique et projet de société humaniste dans *I libri della famiglia* de Leon Battista Alberti," in *Les relations de parenté dans le monde médiéval*, Senefiance, 26 (Aix-en-Provence: Publications du Centre Universitaire d'Etudes et de Recherches Médiévales d'Aix, 1989), pp. 379-80.

and make him worthy of high office in the state. Leon Battista's family-centered *amicizia* which extends into the state is the moving force in his political program of the emulation in Florence, through the study of ancient letters and the Alberti elders' reliable experience, of the glory, authority, and longevity of the Roman Republic and its distinguished families. In his forward-looking traditional project, Leon Battista offers a perspective in time and place whereby ancient glories serve as backdrop to the glorious present foreground, which promises to replicate itself in future scenes.

In *Dell'amicizia* writing is a civic-minded act. As noted in the first chapter above, an important aspect of the perennial debate in antiquity concerning *amicitia perfecta* was whether it was better practiced within or wholly free from a political context. Paolo Marolda notes that in the first three dialogues of *Della famiglia* there is a similar debate among the Alberti elders, who argue either that virtue is best cultivated actively, in serving both family and state, or that it is brought safely and fully to perfection free from political entanglements. In the fourth dialogue the author decides the question in favor of the family's active service, supported by learning, to the state.[40] Here Leon Battista underlines the writer's responsibility to teach virtue through his own example of erudition and experience as friend to family and state.

As M. Dardano has demonstrated in detail, the syntax and style of *Dell'amicizia* differ markedly from those of the three earlier dialogues in that the author attempted, by way of experiment, to construct in the fourth a new Italian literary language based on classical Latin and the spoken, educated Florentine idiom of his century.[41] Dardano observes that the dialogue's language often tends to the extremes of vernacularism or Latinism, and it is especially unnatural in its imposition of Latin structures on Tuscan. In his attempt to confer a new, if borrowed, dignity to Italian different in nature from Dante's or Boccaccio's idioms through a close—and, frequently, overly close—assimilation to classical Latin, Leon Battista produced a sort of literary Italian in *Dell'amicizia* which ofttimes appears

---

[40] Marolda, "L. B. Alberti e il problema della politica· Il *Fatum et Fortuna* e *I libri della famiglia*," *Rassegna della letteratura italiana* 90 (1986): 30-34 and 39-40.

[41] Dardano, "Sintassi e stile," pp. 215-50. See, also, Ghino Ghinassi, "Leon Battista Alberti fra latinismo et toscanismo: La revisione dei *Libri della famiglia*," *Lingua nostra* 22 (1961): 1-6.

forced.

Dell'amicizia, like the three dialogues which precede it on the subjects of the education of children, marriage, and household management, is largely concerned with practical matters. The author seems to be exclusively attentive to the practice and utility of *amicizia* in the dialogue's first part, where the elder Piero speaks on his personal experiences in the arts of friendship—to wit, the approaches and even ruses which he used to win princes of church and state as *amici*. Little critical attention has been paid, however, to the theory which runs through the dialogue. Leon Battista's formulation of a new and broad-ranging model of *amicizia vera* imposes what seems at first reading an unnatural construction upon the practice of friendship represented in the text, especially when one of the friends is not in the least virtuous. Each of the medieval works studied earlier in this book dealt with one or a few sorts of ideal friendship. The present dialogue illustrates, however, many different sorts of secular *amicizia*—love between prince and courtier, between court and family, paterfamilias and family members, family elders and their young kinsmen, patron and client—all of which are included under the generic label *amicizia*. What the author seems to qualify as 'perfect' and 'true' in his macromodel, his notion of familial *amicizia* as an extensive, indeed, international and intergenerational system, is not the perfection of any one instance or a few kinds of *amicizia* but the perfect interrelatedness of all these sorts among themselves.

As for a definition of *amicizia* which one expects to find in a discussion of the topic, the author and his spokesmen do not even consider defining it until the second part of the dialogue, after Piero's narrative account of his virtuous courtier-prince *amicizia*, in which affection plays a small part or none at all. The erudite elder Adovardo, the main interlocutor along with Lionardo in this second part, broaches the question of defining *amicizia* only to reject the practical importance of a theoretical or learned description: "...I should want a practical man who would teach me how to gain and use friendship rather than to show me how to describe and almost draw it" (p. 276).[42] Nevertheless, Lionardo summarizes the ancients' pre-

---

[42] References within parentheses are to *Liber quartus familie: De amicitia*, in *The Albertis of Florence: Leon Battista Alberti's "Della famiglia,"* trans. Guido A. Guarino, Bucknell Renaissance Texts in Translation (Lewisburg: Bucknell University Press, 1971), pp. 257-326. The Italian original is in L. B. Alberti, *Opere volgari. Volume primo. I libri della famiglia. Cena fami-*

cepts on *amicitia perfecta*: it is "the conjunction of everything human and divine, a reciprocal agreement and love characterized by sincere benevolence and charity," it can exist only between the virtuous, and it is the highest class of *amicizia* (pp. 276-77). Adovardo accepts and, further, praises the ancients' description of *amicitia perfecta* which Lionardo resumes. The problem here is that the classical definition does not correspond to a good number of the practical and literary examples which Leon Battista gives, for they often deal with at least one less than virtuous partner, less than perfect reciprocal agreement on earthly and heavenly matters, less than the highest sort of *amicizia*, or mutual benevolence and generosity that are baldly utilitarian or self-interested rather than sincerely loving. As we shall see, the writer differentiates his family-centered *amicizia vera*, a broad-ranging system of exchange of benefits and honors, from the ethical models and standards of classical tradition, and he offers new measures of virtue based on the family's honor, prosperity, and tradition.

Leon Battista's concept of *amicizia vera*, though it rests on an old-fashioned Aristotelian base, is original and innovative as it 'perfects' the *Nicomachean Ethics* and other classical authorities and refits their teachings to the literary, moral, and political context of mid-fifteenth-century Italy. The speaker Adovardo voices dissatisfaction with the incomplete treatment of virtuous friendship by ancient philosophers and writers: their precepts, "neither very subtle nor very useful" to the experienced man, indicate only the beginnings of an ethical science of *amicizia vera* (p. 277). He is dissatisfied, moreover, with the ancient corpus of writings on *amicitia perfecta* received from the Middle Ages because it is limited to Cicero, Seneca, Aristotelian ethics, and Lucian's *Toxaris*. The interlocutors supplement this limited corpus with two sorts of moral examples—contemporary personal or past familial experiences and ancient Greek writings unknown or scarcely known in Western Europe before Leon Battista's time. As for the latter, Adovardo and Lionardo provide newly recovered book knowledge in scores of citations from Plutarch, Xenophon, Josephus, Herodotus, Plato, Aristotle, Diogenes Laertius, and other Greek writers, and their display of erudition points to the major role that Florence played in the transmission and translation of ancient Greek texts in

---

liaris. Villa, ed. Cecil Grayson, Scrittori d'Italia, 218 (Bari: G. Laterza e Figli, 1960), pp. 263-341.

the author's time. In presenting Greek authorities to "not extremely lettered" Florentine lay readers, Leon Battista's Italian adaptations mark a
third stage of transmission via Latin translation, and they show how
quickly the passage from Greek original to vernacular version sometimes
took place in his century. For example, he adapts in Italian in
Dell'amicizia the Latin translations of Plutarch, Plato, and Aristotle by
his contemporary, the Greek classicist and Florentine chancellor Leonardo
Bruni Aretino (ca. 1370-1444).

Leon Battista's introduction in the vernacular of moral exempla from
ancient Greek texts makes available for the Italian reader a body of knowledge that was lost to Western Europe for almost a millennium. A feature
shared by the 'new' ancient Greek writings which the author fits into the
dialogue is that by and large they escaped the notice of earlier Christian
Latin commentators and adapters. Leon Battista takes advantage of their
relative newness—that is, the absence of a tradition of medieval Christian
interpretation—in applying their lessons to his concept of the modern
Italian family and its relationship with the city-state. The ideological base
of Leon Battista's family-centered *amicizia vera* is Aristotelian and Ciceronian ethics and politics, from which he draws an ideal of the active individual as a family member integrated into a well-functioning state,
which promotes him and his family as much as he and they contribute to
the state's welfare and glory. The author's extensive utilization of the
newly recovered Greeks tends to lend support to his family-centered interpretation of Aristotle and Cicero, and it might be argued that these rather
pristine Greeks contribute to the recovery of a pre-Christian Aristotle and
Cicero, too.

One should note, however, that Albertian *amicizia*, which is secular in
its import, is in no way un-Christian or even halfheartedly Christian. Religion—charity, piety, dutifulness, faith, and reverence—lies at the heart
of Leon Battista's system of familial friendship, of which Adovardo
claims religion to be one of the main supports (p. 282). Yet unlike many
earlier Christian writers, Leon Battista, a churchman, does not conceive of
human friendship, love, family, and the state as flawed counterparts to
heavenly order or oppositional forces to Christian truth. As readers of the
ancients, Leon Battista's spokesmen Adovardo and Lionardo in the dialogue's second major section take a rational approach to religious doctrine, an approach in which religion supports the public and private good.

Another important feature of Leon Battista's 'perfection' of the ancient teachings on *amicitia perfecta* is his idealization of the speakers and himself as models, as trustworthy, faithful familial *amici* who continue and bring near to completion in a new social context ancient philosophy's quest for living well. The successive introduction of four interlocutors—first, the faithful family retainer Buto, then, Piero, the ambitious, successful courtier, lastly, the erudite and worldly-wise Adovardo and Lionardo—traces a social and philosophical ascent from homespun, plebeian humor and common sense, through a practical level of family ethics, economics, and politics in dealing with leaders of state, to, finally, a superior plane of learning, moral reflection, philosophical abstraction, and rhetorical excellence. The author thus constructs a hierarchy of models of familial friendship which culminates with himself, a double for Adovardo and Lionardo, literati seasoned by experience, as perfect benefactor and *amico* to family, state, and the humanities. In the succession of models, the writer represents at each stage a dynamic exchange between a specific friend as individual and a social unit, which in some cases is itself a model of moral excellence. In this interrelationship, the individual *amico* and the social unit, such as the family, or a representative of a unit, such as a prince, reflect and promote one another's concern, virtue, and welfare. Further, the dialogue's *amico vero* is a perfect mediator, a connecting link between family and another sphere of influence. As the virtuous friend of princes, Piero reconciles his friends' ambitions with those of his family, and Adovardo and Lionardo, men of letters, interpret and bring together ancient literature and Alberti family tradition for their kinsmen whom they address. These models describe not the Aristotelian virtuous friend and his alter ego but a singular *amico vero* serving and harmonizing two different realms of authority.

In the following analysis of the textual models of manifold familial *amicizia*, we will identify the types of friends which each of the successive interlocutors exemplifies, and we will determine the specific contribution of that type as an idealized conduit of moral and material benefits to, from, and within the extended family. We will also examine the writer's arguments for a family ethics which justify his identification of the types, some of which are quite lowly, with perfect dutifulness, virtue, and wisdom in *amicizia*. In respect to the dialogue's idealization of its ranked exemplars, we will specify the different, explicit or implied standards of moral excellence that the writer applies to each model. Another consideration is the adaptation and interpretation of ancient literary refer-

ences, most of which have no direct relationship to family or to friendship: how, and how much, does the author transform these references in
fitting them to a contemporary, familial context?

The subject of *la vera amicizia* comes up for discussion among the Alberti elders as they bestow the highest praise upon the aged Buto, a former
family retainer who arrives as the table is being set for the midday meal.
In spite of the great disparity of status between the Alberti gentlemen,
middle-class *cavalieri*, and the perpetually poor Buto, who now earns his
bread at the tables of the more fortunate whom he flatters and entertains
with his plebeian buffoonery, the elders call him their *vero amico* (p.
257). They cite as proof of true friendship his loyalty, benevolence, beneficence, and affection for the Alberti family over several generations. His
amicizia qualifies as true because his unfaltering adherence and service to
the family in its hard times conform to the dictum about a friend in need
which Adovardo cites later (p. 278).

The sketch of the retainer Buto, an outsider who enjoys free access to
the household, combines two traditional types of *amici*, usually friends of
the paterfamilias, which Leon Battista remodels as friends of the whole
family. First, Buto is an ideal client-type who always fulfils his obligation of fidelity to his patron, here the family itself rather than a specific
paterfamilias or other important family member. His gift to the elders of a
small basket of fruit suggests an ancient Roman near equivalent. The basket was associated with Roman clients, to whom the patron usually dis-
tributed money or baskets of food. In the present case, however, the pa-
tron-family provides Buto with a meal, and his small gift may indicate the
relatively modest contribution that he makes to the patron in their mutually supportive relationship. The second model is that of the privileged
outsider, an *amico* as distinct from *parente* or relative, to whom the
household (or, usually, the paterfamilias) grants total confidence and free
access to the domicile. In regard to Buto as client, an influential Italian
household would have many dependents of his kind. In the case of the
privileged outsider, however, the household (or paterfamilias) would permit to very few extramural *amici* the access and familiarity that Buto enjoys.[43]

---

[43] For a discussion of clients and *amici* in fourteenth and fifteenth-century
Tuscan households, see Dominique Barthélemy, Philippe Braunstein, et al.,
Histoire de la vie privée, tome 2, De l'Europe féodale à la Renaissance,
L'Univers Historique (Paris: Seuil, 1985), pp. 169-71.

Buto's buffoonish address to the elders contains several declarations that oppose practice to theory and action to discourse (pp. 257-58). For example, he expresses his self-satisfaction at being unlettered after having listened to former generations of learned Albertis discourse eloquently but mistakenly on true friendship. His oppositional evaluation of theory and praxis and of words and action becomes a central issue later among the interlocutors, who argue for interrelationship rather than opposition. Two of Buto's unsophisticated declarations deserve attention as they relate to other issues in the elders' discussion—namely, authority and gender in true friendship. First, his recognition of a long family tradition of erudite, eloquent discussions on *la vera amicizia* marks the elders present—and, by implication, the author—as authorities on the topic. Following up in a positive manner Buto's unflattering remark about the family's tradition of learning and eloquence, one of the elders does not hesitate to compare the current lunchtime conversation to the philosophical banquets of Plato, Xenophon, and Plutarch (p. 258). In this instance, the present elders' authority in matters of true friendship rests upon Alberti tradition of long date, and it agrees with classical models of literary and philosophical authority.

Secondly, Buto claims to have learned from marital experience that one cannot have true friendship, *certa amicizia*, with one's wife. The elders do not challenge his exclusion of wives from the domain of perfect friendship, nor do they speak of wife or woman in their later arguments. The dialogue's exclusion marks a theoretical distancing from the preceding three dialogues, and especially the second on marriage, to which the husband generally subordinates the interests of male *amicizia*. In the preceding dialogues Leon Battista adopts the marital model from the *Nicomachean Ethics*, which compares the best husband and wife to aristocratic government, in which the better, the husband, rules and entrusts to his spouse domestic responsibilities. The fourth dialogue does not include husband and wife, not even hypothetically in the case of a perfectly harmonious marriage, among the possibilities of unequal but virtuous familial friendship, such as that between the retainer Buto and the Alberti family. The omission of wife and woman from the discussion of familial *amicizia* results largely from the limits within the domicile that Leon Battista assigns to women in the first three dialogues and, also, from the present dialogue's extension beyond the household. Unlike every one of the fourth dialogue's male types, whose influence extends beyond the threshold, woman does not exercise direct power outside Leon Battista's model home. No doubt, belief in male moral superiority explains, too, why the interlocutors, who use 'womanly' to indicate a deficiency in virtue, omit mention of females in regard to virtuous *amicizia*.

The dialogue's first major development is Piero's narrative account of his success in the art of winning princes' favor. His relation illustrates the Alberti males' essential power, *virtù*, to negotiate the exchange of influence between the family and outside centers of authority. In the cases of the three political leaders whom he befriended consecutively—Gian Galeazzo Visconti, duke of Milan, King Ladislaus of Naples, and Pope John XXIII—Piero received something of value from the Alberti family, exchanged it, often through the mediation of other courtiers in the princely households, for the more valuable favor of the prince, the benefits of which he returned to the family. Leon Battista draws Piero as a shrewd man of practice in contrast to Adovardo and Lionardo, who are very learned in addition to being experienced men of the world. Piero offers his narrative as a "domestic example" (p. 262) for the fiction's hearers, the young Leon Battista and his brother, to follow in their future dealings with princes. As a type, Piero may be understood to represent the highest level of familial *amicizia* with extrafamilial, political leaders that the hearers may hope to reach through practical means, a good deal of artful tricks, and family support. As an ethical exemplar, Piero insists upon his constant dutifulness and beneficence to both *amici* whom he serves, family and prince.

Before Piero's narration, the elders debated mostly in abstract terms the relative worth of three factors—wealth, virtuous character, and, thirdly, personal charm and genius—in winning a prince's favor (pp. 259-62). These elements are, of course, part of the stock-in-trade of Aristotelian topics as they relate to utility, virtue, and pleasure in *philia* and its ideal form. They ask Piero to decide which factor is the most important, but instead of judging in favor of one of the three, he argues for the superior value of "our"—that is, the Alberti males'—characteristic diligence and prudence. His practical account illustrates his own perseverance and worldly wisdom and, so, proves his point, but it also offers solutions to three theoretical problems, of which the first two derive from the elders' earlier debate. First, what is the relative worth of wealth, virtue, and charm or genius in winning a prince's friendship? Then, what are the criteria for virtue that apply to *amicizia* with political figures? Lastly, the courtier's problem as mediator of honorable *amicizia* between family and prince: how does he reconcile divergent interests of both parties while providing each with the greatest benefits? The following analysis of Piero's approach to these problems and of the broad-ranging system of *amicizia* as exchange in his account will underline the interlocutors' prescription of familial principles—that is, family ethics, politics, and economics—which offer an original interpretation of an old topic.

While perseverance, prudence, and shrewdness characterize Piero's attempts at winning princes' confidence, it is clear that riches, integrity, and the ability to please as both personal and familial qualities or possessions played essential roles in his success, but to different degrees according to circumstances and the princes' different characters. First, he earned the favor of the avaricious Pope John XXIII, condemned as a simoniac and deposed by the Council of Constance in 1415, when he served as the Albertis' agent in handing over to the pontiff an enormous sum of money which he had demanded of the family (p. 271). In this instance the family's continent-wide banking network amassed the sum needed to satisfy the pope's greed and, at the same time, to whet it so that he accepted Piero's friendship and that of the Albertis in the hope of future gain. Further, to assure the continuity of papal benefits for his family, each time Piero received a favor, he rewarded the pope or his courtiers with a gift.

Then, Piero's relationships of mutual trust and affection with the duke and king show especially the influence of a reputation for integrity as a possession of the Florentine state, the Albertis, and Piero himself. At a first private interview, the warrior duke admits to Piero his admiration for the Florentines because of their virtues, and he has high regard for the Alberti name and reputation for placing Florence's welfare above family interests (pp. 264-65). At the interview Piero demonstrates through his eloquent, self-referential discourse on patriotism that he is worthy of the city's and family's repute, and in subsequent dealings with the duke, Piero "always returned home more firmly established in his good graces and enjoyed greater prestige and a good reputation for virtue among his courtiers" (p. 265). Piero's and the family's patriotism promises the duke future benefits in his primary areas of interest—warfare and its contrary, negotiated friendship between states. Further, Piero tells of the great care which he took in the king of Naples' court to maintain a reputation for integrity by not using or seeming to use the king's favor for unworthy or

unjust ends (p. 270). He claims that even at the vice-ridden curia, the fac-
tious courtiers helped raise him to the highest position because of his
virtues which they recognized (p. 272).

Finally, Piero's relation gives proof of the value of charm and genius in
winning princely *amici*. Most important, vernacular eloquence and ready
speech are absolutely essential. His initial addresses to each of the three
leaders are characterized by prudent observation, a well-developed though
brief argument, an appeal to the hearer's higher feelings, and rhetorical
flourishes of a courtly style, and in each case the hearer receives the address with an immediate declaration of cordial acceptance for him and his
family. Charm of a familial sort, too, enters into play. The grace and elegance (p. 264; "molta gentilezza e leggiadria") of the Tuscan poems of his
relative Antonio Alberti were crucial in his gaining access to one of the
princes. Thus, while Piero claims to argue for the superior value of Albertian diligence and prudence and his own tricks of the courtier's trade, his
three-part narration responds directly by way of practical examples to the
other elders' abstract debate. At the same time, his account redefines their
discussion in expanding its limits from a personal to a familial sort of
friendship in which the prince favors the family as a whole.

Part of the earlier theoretical discussion dealt with the goodness of
friendship with rulers. Lionardo maintained that "princes are idle, do not
practice any honorable professions [*ogni onesto essercizio*], give in to all
their appetites, and are surrounded, not by friends, but by deceivers and
flatterers" and that as wicked men, they favor only the wicked; but
Adovardo contended that there have been virtue-loving rulers and, therefore, good friendship with princes is possible in theory (pp. 259-60). This
question regarding the prince and his court is the topic of the conventional
medieval literary debate pro and contra the courtier's career, a topos which
continued to be in fashion in the Renaissance and later (compare, for example, the anti-courtier tirade at the beginning of novella 1,8 in the *Decameron*.)[44] As another position in this debate, Piero's account demonstrates that some princes are virtuous and, also, that through the application of a specifically familial standard of goodness or *onestà*, even his
amicizia with an incorrigibly vicious leader can be considered honorable.

---

[44] See, also, the discussion of Alberti's Latin works *Pontifex* (1437) and
Momus seu de principe (1447) on the courts of prelates and princes in
Guglielmo Gorni, "Dalla famiglia alla corte: Itinerari et allegorie nell'opera di
L. B. Alberti," *Bibliothèque d'humanisme et Renaissance* 43 (1981): 250-56.

He portrays the duke and the king as good rulers actively engaged in honorable pursuits—military conquest, a source of glory, and hunting, which he commends as a preliminary to military exercises. The utilitarian friendships between the princes and the virtuous courtier, in whom they have confidence, are therefore ethically excellent. On the other hand, he has no illusions about the wickedness of the pope, but he calls that relationship *amicizia*, too, which it is, as with the other two instances, in the sense of a mutually beneficial, self-seeking alliance. In the curia Piero, who dissociates himself as much as possible from evil courtiers, gains from the notoriously wicked pope offices, benefices, and favors for his relatives and friends. In commenting on Piero's *amicizia* with the pope, another elder provides a familial standard of *onestà* which one may apply to Piero's side of the partnership. In his blanket condemnation of prelates, the speaker Giannozzo says: "When it comes to spending money for honest purposes [*alle onestissime spese*], helping their relatives and friends and raising their families to an honorable and prestigious state [*in onorato stato e degno grado*], these prelates show themselves to be inhuman, grasping, hard, and avaricious" (p. 274). 'Honest' and 'honorable,' then, characterize Piero's use of the pope's benevolence to obtain benefits for family and friends. Thus, on Piero's side at least, his utilitarian *amicizia* with the pope was honorable. For his part, Adovardo calls all three instances of princely friendship honorable, pleasurable, and useful (p. 274).

As for the third problem—how is the courtier to mediate *amicizia* between family and prince so that both parties derive the greatest benefits and honor from their association?—Piero's relation provides practical answers and an economical model of the international exchange system operating between the family and princely households. When Lionardo says of one of the duke's intimates who, delighted with Antonio Alberti's verses, aided Piero in gaining audience with the duke, "Learned men state that to join and hold two together you need a third" (p. 266), he might be understood to define the position of Piero as interpreter between the two inner circles of family and rulers' private chambers. Examples show how Piero drew from the continent-wide network of Alberti bankers the funds needed to win the pope's acceptance, and Alberti merchants abroad furnished him with foreign news which he frequently used to gain new favor with the duke (pp. 266-67). A striking illustration of the family agent as a link in an international network of intrafamilial and family-court exchanges is that of Piero's two hunting dogs which saved the king's life and thus gained for Piero immediate access to his intimacy: Piero had received the hounds as a gift from Adovardo's brother in Spain, who received them earlier from the king of Granada in token of that ruler's favor and esteem for his virtues (p. 268).

While Piero receives goods and intangibles from widespread sources within the family and channels them into different courts, he serves simultaneously as the conduit of princely appreciation, which he redistributes throughout the family. As part of the family network and as a type, Piero is but one of many related heads of household or important Alberti bachelors who communicate benefits among themselves; he distributes—and by extension, all the heads of household distribute—princely or other dividends throughout the family network. He poses the principle of the agent's return of benefits to the family (and not to a specific household) in moral terms: "For you know very well it is our duty to help each other gain honor and fortune whenever we can. The friendship of princes in particular is to be gained and used to enhance the good name, prestige, and honor of our relatives and the entire family" (p. 266). Underlying this familial standard of ethical conduct in regard to princes, one can detect the writer's refitting of two principles of ancient *amicitia perfecta* to the collectivity of 'friendly' Alberti households: the principle of joint property of *amici veri* is converted to the shared wealth of heads of household, and the virtuous friend's selflessness in promoting his alter ego is reconfigured to a specific paterfamilias' subordination of his household's interests to those of the family as a whole.

In mediating family-interested *amicizia* with princes, Piero defines his duty to the rulers not to use their influence for unjust or unworthy ends (p. 270). Stated positively, this duty demands that the courtier use the prince's favor to promote to high office only those whose experience and character qualify them for public responsibility (cf. Aristotle's *Politics* 7,4; 1326 b 14-17.) Consequently, Piero advanced only relatives and friends whom he thought likely to serve the best interests of the government and, one supposes, to reflect well on his civic-minded choice. Here, as in his initial audience with the duke, he subordinates his family's and his own interests to the good of the state; or, when viewed in his function as political, economical, and moral mediator, he reconciles the different ambitions of family and court so that they, along with himself, derive the best long-term benefits from their association.

Piero's account would seem to suggest that the elders and the family's resources will one day facilitate the young Leon Battista's advancement in the world. In fact, however, two uncles deprived the youth of his paternal inheritance and left him without resources. Piero's opening remarks about his own lack of funds as an obstacle to gaining access to the duke's inner chambers are perhaps veiled reflections on the hard beginnings of the poor Leon Battista's career. As examples, Piero's dutifulness towards Alberti youths and his intrafamilial, intergenerational benefaction represent the proper ethical attitude and conduct for a family elder.

As with the model client and privileged outsider Buto, one must conjecture a multiplication and extension of the prototypical Piero in order to complete a large and essential part of Leon Battista's macromodel of familial *amicizia*. He is the prototype for a group of adult Alberti males engaged in a branch of the active life, the profession of courtier, a group whose size and geographical distribution determine in large measure the family's public importance. He and other Alberti courtiers and friends in court operate as intermediaries and transmitters in a complex system of communication of authority: all the lines of the network pass from many different and distant courts through the several Alberti courtly interpreters, from which points all lines lead to the many Alberti households in Italy and abroad.

The dialogue's other major development is a learned discussion between Lionardo and Adovardo, who propose to complete the ancients' precepts on *amicitia perfecta*, which Adovardo claims give little more than commonsense observations on the obvious. They intend to provide nothing less than a doctrine of superior authority to that of Aristotle, Cicero, and Seneca on the subject. A prominent feature of their colloquy is the great attention given to its form or architecture. Adovardo prescribes a five-part outline: first, how to gain worthy friends; then, bringing a new friendship to perfection; the proper way in which to end a relationship; reestablishing a friendship that one has broken off; finally, how to retain a man's faithful friendship forever (p. 275). This how-to approach, which would seem to emphasize practice, is in fact most theoretical. In the course of the discussion the interlocutors frequently repeat the five-part outline and mark transitional points between stages (see pages 276, 289, 290, 295, 298, 306, 315, 318, and 325.) This formal division, which underlines the scholarly debate's rhetorical character as reasoned discourse, provides general headings under which fall numerous examples drawn from ancient texts, particularly the newly recovered Greek works mentioned earlier, and from Alberti family experience. Unlike Buto and Piero, Lionardo and Adovardo treat the topic of *amicizia* within such broadly theoretical parameters that they often make no reference to the familial sort. In the last two how-to stages, familial examples are absent, and the copious ancient textual references under these headings are extremely heterogeneous as illustrations of secular friendship in its most varied senses.

The following analysis will be limited to the first three stages and to illustrations of family-related *amicizia* and of the family as a model for various sorts of friendship. It will deal, also, with the extensive use of analogy to give structure and value to the serial groupings of heterogeneous items which appear under the general headings. In each of the five sections, the main speaker Adovardo presents a number of self-contained series of examples in which the individual items derive from essentially different fields of knowledge or experience. Structure itself determines and delimits the sense of the items in a series: the speaker notes an element, often a small one, in the first item, such as a reference from ancient biography, and he proceeds by way of analogy to identify more or less similar elements in any number of essentially unlike successive items. Such serial analogies which make up a great part of the discussion are indicative of the high level of abstraction and, at times, the tenuous coherence of the argument. The analogically structured, self-contained series is, however, the principal means by which the writer validates his family's moral authority in *amicizia vera*: his linking of familial examples to ancient, time-honored references is a strategy whereby he not only completes and updates ancient precepts but also situates several generations of Alberti family experience on a par with ancient textual tradition.

The first connection that the speakers make between the family and ancient philosophical and historical writings deals with authority. In defining the store of creditable knowledge from which the discussants will draw, Lionardo compares a diligent paterfamilias who transmits a lifetime of experience to his kin with the corpus of ancient Greek and Latin works which records the experience of many generations (p. 278). The interlocutors' first lesson to the fictive listeners, the youths Leon Battista and his brother, is to read and revere ancient writings, which are no less authoritative than a seasoned paterfamilias. Yet the speakers do not accept uncritically the authority of ancient texts. They claim that the moral precepts and examples recorded there are only preliminary to practice which confirms or disproves their validity, and they present themselves as experts who know the ancient doctrines on *amicitia* and have verified them empirically. Furthermore, familial exempla validate ancient references by supporting them with experiential proof. Adovardo underlines his role as certifier by introducing each of his six precepts on acquiring friends with "I saw" (p. 282). Here erudition and experience complement one another.

One of Adovardo's serial illustrations of mutually corroborating ancient history, Alberti family lore, and his own experience stresses the moral import of storytelling and of responding to a tale. He recommends as a means of discovering another's thoughts and character telling a story or two about, for example, a lover's ruses or the pursuit of profit and, then, observing the hearer's delight or displeasure (pp. 286-87). As authoritative support for his device for revealing a potential friend's character, he offers a classical exemplum—Brutus and Cassius used a discussion on politics to identify those in whom they could not confide regarding their plot to assassinate Julius Caesar—and a familial, commercial case. The latter, a nonverbal trial, shows the sagacity of past generations of Alberti elders. Adovardo describes a test involving bread crumbs by which Leon Battista's grandfather Benedetto, the most important family leader of his generation, discovered that a seemingly virtuous 'outsider' was a compulsive gambler whom the family could not trust to handle its business affairs (p. 287). In offering his personal observation and two essentially different illustrations from ancient history and family lore, Adovardo completes in a practical manner Cicero's advice in *Laelius* to test potential friends in small as well as large matters. Nonetheless, his illustrations have in themselves nothing to do with Laelian *amicitia perfecta*, and in this case, as with the others which he cites later, the moral perfection or lack of it shown there refer to *amicizia* in a very general sense.

In bringing the first part to a close, Adovardo discusses the use of gifts and good services to draw someone into friendship. He mentions, first, the ancient example of Catiline's gifts tailored to the receivers' tastes and, then, his observations on the family's experience in winning friends. In these two instances, Adovardo (or the writer) radically alters the ethical value of the historical reference in adapting it to family tradition. First, he disregards the negative moral import of the ancient citation—Catiline attempted to attract with gifts not virtuous friends but accomplices in his conspiracy to massacre the Roman senators and usurp the power of the Republic—and he qualifies as exemplary Catiline's skill and prudence in gift-giving. Then, he passes to the Alberti family's exemplary power to

win men of proven virtue as friends. The speaker often effects a similar
conversion of ancient exempla whereby he strips a literary item of its
negative or ambiguous moral value and, then, affirms its positive value as
a model of conduct, which he supports with a familial illustration of
virtù. For example, in his adaptations of the conspirators Brutus and Cassius' stratagem mentioned earlier and the case which will be noted
presently of a Roman leader who skilfully eliminated conspirators, one
observes the same authorial revaluation by which antiquity's morally
doubtful exempla are elevated to a level of ethical excellence comparable
to Alberti family virtue and wisdom.

In the discussion's second stage on how to bring a new friendship to
perfection, Adovardo gives many guidelines of Ciceronian and Aristotelian
provenance: wealthy and influential *amici* are the most useful in helping
one gain the favor of other citizens; those who have proven their loyalty
over a long period are best suited for true friendship; one should prefer a
single or a few true friends to a multitude of common ones; mutual trust,
sincere affection, and good conduct characterize perfect friendship; and of
the three sources and bonds of *amicizia*, pleasure, usefulness, and
"praiseworthy honesty and virtue," the third leads to perfection (pp. 291-
94). The interlocutors fit these commonplaces of ancient *amicitia perfecta*
to the family circle. Adovardo, for his part, domesticates the precepts by
attaching to them *I*, *we*, and *you*—thus he appropriates them as the common property of the familial referents. Then, Lionardo's comments on
Adovardo's instruction point specifically to its application by present and
future family males: "Moved by your words to look into the future..., I
grieve to think there may perhaps be some of our Albertis who do not
know and value the excellent and appropriate precepts you have explained"
(p. 295). He reproaches unnamed Albertis who, in disregard of this doctrine, prefer a multitude of common acquaintances or frequent the wicked,
and as he imagines the ill consequences, he exclaims, "May God spare our
family from such misfortunes!" (p. 296). The interlocutors' fictional ad-
dressee, the speechless youth Leon Battista, will attempt to prevent such
mishaps by recording and transmitting these domesticated precepts on true
friendship and the elder's reproof as a guide for the wise and a corrective
for misguided Alberti males. Thus the two speakers and the writer show
themselves to be model familial *amici* through their prudent and persistent
encouragement of their friendly others—other Alberti males, present and
future—in the pursuit of wisdom and virtue that will assure good fortune

for them and the family. Adovardo's statement of his second duty to a friend—"not to suffer the person to whom I have given my friendship to have any trace of vice or abjectness, but to do my best to help him acquire all virtues and good customs" (p. 296)—coincides with what he demonstrates through his indoctrination to be his moral duty to family.

As types the erudite men of experience Adovardo and Lionardo, spokesmen for the writer, embody the continuity and authority of tradition between past and future Alberti generations: they transmit to the upcoming generation of Alberti males ancient textual exempla and past family wisdom which they augment and update with their own knowledge and experience conveyed in eloquent, reasoned discourse. The continuity of family tradition and, also, the accumulation of wisdom cover four successive generations in *Dell'amicizia*—those of Leon Battista's grandfather, his father, Leon Battista himself, and the Alberti youths to whom the writer addresses *Della famiglia* for their guidance. Here the identity of purpose and similarity in spirit between generations of Alberti kindred counterparts might be interpreted as a familial variant of ancient *amicitia perfecta*'s principle of one soul in two bodies. The dialogue's two distinct versions of Leon Battista—the youth of the dialogue's literary present and the adult writer—demonstrate in abridged form the continuity of tradition and authority through the communication of benefits over time and generations: formerly the recipient of benefits, the writer now performs his duty as family friend in transmitting the same benefits and more to the next generation.

The discussion's third part deals with the proper ways of breaking off a friendship if in spite of encouragement and reproof a partner is unable to correct his vices. This Laelian theme is formulated in terms of civic duty: one has a duty to help a beloved comrade become a better citizen (p. 297). Genuine love of virtue and of country, Adovardo maintains, justifies at times the reduction or discontinuance of intimacy. While considering how serious a comrade's incorrigible vice must be in order to justify estrangement, he characterizes as effeminate the wrongful act of breaking off a friendship for reason of less than the gravest vices: "It is a sign of inconstancy and hateful, womanly fickleness not to know how to persevere in loving one whom you once deemed worthy of your affection. Who will not condemn such a person, for he is guilty ... of ... lack of manly firmness...?" (p. 298). The speaker's negative, feminine-gender designation recalls Cicero's use of *mulierculae* in *Laelius* to indicate moral deficiency.[45] Whereas, however, Cicero specified only treason among justifiable causes, Adovardo indicates a range of vices: treason and complicity with pirates and thieves are intolerable, but one should put up with a friend's relatively harmless though immoderate drinking or concupiscence (p. 303). The speaker's indication of tolerable vices shows just how far the writer's practical standards of good friendship fall below the scaled-down Stoical measure which Cicero proposed. It is worth noting, too, how far these standards depart from Christian orthodoxy. Although the bearable vices mentioned here may not interfere overmuch with good citizenship, they are the capital sins of lust and gluttony.

In treating the duty of preserving benevolence between former friends, a duty which, Adovardo claims, is religious law, he brings in by way of very suitable analogy[46] a Christian authority on family—the pontiffs' writings on the sacrament of matrimony.[47] This is one of only two references to Christian doctrine in the learned discussion (Lionardo refers to the rule of Christian charity, p. 292.) Pontiffs proclaimed that matrimony's primary bond, the sacred, indissoluble contract for two souls to become one "con onestà," remains valid even if the second bond, intimacy for the sake of begetting children, is dissolved in the case of a serious vice or deficiency. Consequently, for religious reasons former spouses are bound to continue their mutual benevolence and keep their earlier confidences secret. By analogy former friends, having broken off intimacy and confidence, are duty-bound to remain benevolent and not to reveal shared secrets (pp. 299-300). In the comparison matrimony serves as the model to which male-to-male *amicizia* conforms. Adovardo follows up this analogy with two ancient textual exempla which demonstrate positively and negatively the prolongation of benevolence and confidentiality in estrangement.

Adovardo teaches proper procedure in discontinuing *amicizia* through a series of examples beginning with the domestic model of a paterfamilias who, burdened by expenses, gradually reduces household expenditures and services (p. 303). The lead item in the series recalls the subject of the

---

[45] For instances in Boccaccio's writings of effeminacy as moral deficiency, see Janet Levarie Smarr, *Boccaccio and Fiammetta*, p. 172.

[46] "Similitudine attissima," p. 312 of the Italian edition.

[47] The author is perhaps referring to the writings on marriage and divorce by the late-twelfth through mid-thirteenth-century popes Innocent III, Honorius III, or Gregory IX.

third dialogue in *Della famiglia* on household management and the authority of the paterfamilias established there. The operative principle in this
item is *masserizia*, economic soundness which is an essential *virtù* that
the father must exercise for the welfare of his household. Earlier, the elder
Giannozzo specified as one of the main vices of priests their complete disregard of *masserizia*.[48] The series that follows, of which most items are
introduced by "similarly," strings together heterogeneous illustrations to
lend support to the precept of removing one's affection by stages: an ancient Roman leader who eliminated one by one many conspirators, removing logs one at a time from the hearth in order to put out a large fire, and
an augmentative variation, raising a tower stone upon stone. The similarity between the ancient reference and the series' predominantly domestic
items is not moral or philosophical but simply numerical.

While functioning as a device for establishing internal coherence, albeit
superficial, in the discourse's subsections, the use of extended analogies
conforms to an intellectual, theoretical worldview. The relationships
among the extremely varied items are patterns of 'harmonies,' of essential
concord, that extend throughout the universe and give a unified sense and
order to particulars. Influenced in part by Latin commentaries on Plato's
Timaeus and Cicero's *Dream of Scipio*, medieval and early-Renaissance
intellectuals sought to uncover universal harmonies, principles of order—
e.g., the laws of astronomy, music, or mathematics—in the seeming disorder of particulars. The present serial analogy of mathematically similar
items illustrates the family intellectual's theoretical view of harmony
among domestic principles, ancient ethics, and a contemporary ethical
code of familial *amicizia*, and as with other examples in the dialogue, it
puts forward the wise, virtuous paterfamilias as the first principle of order.

At the end of Adovardo's address, he and Lionardo comment on its
rhetorical qualities. Adovardo closes his development by stating that he
has exhausted the subject while treating it briefly, and Lionardo praises its
concision, precepts, and copious examples (p. 325). The concluding evaluation of the learned discourse by Adovardo, upon whom Lionardo confers
the title of "excellent master of friendships," might be seen to refer to the
standards of excellence in Cicero's *De oratore*, where it is said that the expert orator, rather than the academic or philosopher, is best qualified to

---

[48] "A' quali, perché pur gli soppedita e sominista la fortuna, sono inconti-
nentissimi, e, senza risparmio o masserizia, solo curano satisfare a' suoi inci-
tati apetiti," p. 282 of the Italian edition.

treat the topic of *amicitia* (1,13,56). Adovardo encourages the application of Ciceronian rhetorical standards to his speech when he distinguishes it from less worthy discourses on the topos by professional philosophers and theoretical descriptions by idle literati (p. 276). The interlocutors' favorable judgment on their own discussion as a work of vernacular rhetoric and erudition calls attention to the Ciceronian ambition of the writer's project—that is, the transfer, or *translatio*, of classical rhetoric and, in part, philosophy to contemporary speakers of Italian. Cicero aspired to recast Greek philosophy and, especially, rhetoric in Latin, which he refashioned and refined for the task, and to define a distinct, ethically superior Roman context for them. In *Dell'amicizia* Leon Battista provides a limited contemporary context—his own family—into which he refits ancient ethical exempla, but his attempt to alter and refine the Tuscan idiom to serve as an authoritative vehicle for moral and rhetorical *virtù* is no less ambitious than Cicero's enterprise. The interlocutors' appreciation of Adovardo's speech is clearly an expression of Leon Battista's self-satisfaction with his dissertation as an illustration of vernacular eloquence and authority.

A number of absences in the dialogue fiction define important areas of discursive power which the author occupies. Notably absent from the colloquy are Leon Battista's father, who is abed seriously ill, and the youth Leon Battista's voice. In a dialogue which praises eloquence and the paterfamilias, the missing voices leave gaps in the fiction which the present activity of writing fills: it is by re-creating the fictional event of the family symposium that the adult writer appropriates for himself the moral voice and eloquence of the best of the previous generation of Alberti elders. The writer reserves the use of one sort of *I*, the author looking back on the event, for transitional sections or descriptions of speakers and circumstances. But the many other *I*'s, the Alberti interlocutors upon whose demonstrated virtues he establishes the authority of his own work, are all in some way doubles for himself. In the present of Leon Battista's composing *Dell'amicizia,* all those other *I*'s are silent—their generation has disappeared—and the writer, their replacement, concentrates them all in his authorial voice. Applying Leon Battista's favored method of analogy, one might compare the multiple personas dialoguing across generations which the writer, the family historio-mythographer, brings back and consolidates in his own voice to the ancient Roman custom of displaying the death masks or busts of distinguished ancestors: thus the exhibitor of masks honors the family and brings honor upon himself. In fact, such displays were fashionable among influential Florentine families in the mid-fifteenth century.[49] While differentiating from one another the many *I*'s referring to the writer and the various elders, Leon Battista underlines the family resemblance, the continuity of the Albertis' *virtù*.

Further, the fiction's substitution of the elders of the family council for the absent father as voices of authority within his household suggests a similar, fatherlike moral authorization in the case of the childless writer. The author positions himself, along with the elders, as an equivalent and surrogate paternal voice, a creditable expert on *amicizia*, and a dutiful family friend in relation to his intended readers, the younger generation of Alberti males, who owe it, almost by filial duty, to heed his counsel.

Finally, we might interpret another conspicuous absence in the dialogue—contemporary Florence, to which Leon Battista presented the work in 1441. This absence suggests a reading of *Dell'amicizia* as a 'to be completed' dialogue between Leon Battista and Florence's leaders, or Signoria, of his day on reaffirming and perfecting an interrupted political friendship. Circumstances explain why the dialogue is not set in Florence of the previous generation, for in 1378 the Albertis, at that time one of the city's most important banking families, were banished. The initial conversation between Piero and the duke alluded to the family's calamities, an oblique way of naming banishment, which Piero blamed, but without resentment, on the unwise Florentine leaders of the day (p. 265). He and the duke implied that the exile and the leaders' imprudence were much less of a misfortune for the family, which continued to prosper, as Piero demonstrated, than for the misguided city, which suffered mishaps. The opposition that Leon Battista sets up in the past between the exiled but self-sufficient Albertis' prosperity and the reversal of fortune of the city that banished them can only mean to suggest, in the present, Florence's continued good fortune after having recalled the family. It is not unreasonable to read the dialogue as an invitation by Leon Battista, the family agent, for a close or closer political association between the present city leaders, most notably the Medicis, who helped organize the *Certame coronario*, and the Albertis schooled in civic virtues. At the dialogue's end Lionardo brings up another topic: how would the "excellent

---

[49] Sharon T. Strocchia, *Death and Ritual in Renaissance Florence*, The Johns Hopkins University Studies in Historical and Political Science, 1 (Baltimore: The Johns Hopkins University Press, 1992), pp. 46-47.

master of friendships" instruct a prince in the art of acquiring *amicizia*, his
citizens' goodwill, and glory (p. 325)? The discussion breaks off here, but
the implication is that Florence's leaders should look to the civic-minded
Albertis and Leon Battista, the current standard-bearer of family tradition,
for the answer. Nevertheless, it is clear, as Paolo Marolda has remarked,[50]
that the mediator's optimism about *la vera amicizia* between family and
city is tempered by a good deal of prudence and political realism regarding
leaders of state, whose virtues and vices highlighted in Piero's narration
are matters of chance.

In spite of their differences in genres, designated audiences, and their ideas
of perfection, these three works have in common several tendencies and
features which set them apart from earlier, medieval idealization of *amicitia* and which offer new and rather consistent views on the topic. One of
their prominent shared features is the formulation of a contemporary ideal
of friendship in terms of a like-minded group within a quasi-institutional
structure instead of the usual pair in medieval fiction or the Christian
trio—that is, two friends joined by God. Although generally compatible
with Christian virtues, the collective like-mindedness, the consensus of
spirit, conduct, and pursuit, is secular, and the writers present the group's
unity, its friendship, as an end in itself. The collective provides the context and the direction for its members' realization of this-worldly objectives. The *Decameron*'s storytellers pursue individually and cooperatively
the goal of providing all with pleasurable, useful, and, at times, virtuous
tales, and the *brigata* marks through its applause or signs of disapproval
its measure of the individual attainment of that objective. In his concluding remarks, the king of the tenth day commends the tales as a whole for
their contributions to the *brigata*'s honorable aims, and he praises the
tellers' collective virtue and brotherly and sisterly *amicizia*. In Laurent de
Premierfait's prefaces, the duke and his *amis* at court are engaged in the
pursuit of a limited secular objective—the nonacademic lay reader's mas-
tery of Cicero's rhetoric and ethics of *amicitia* in the vernacular. Especially ambitious is the shared goal of the family and its individual members in Leon Battista's dialogue—to assure the good fortune and glory of

---

[50] Marolda, "L. B. Alberti," p. 40.

family and state through independent, concerted effort. Although it is certainly not the case that these three writers with ties to the Church deny in any way the traditional values of Christian friendships, they assert the great worth of this-worldly virtues and wisdom as the foundations of communal harmony and living well.

The three writings localize their contemporary groups of friends under a single roof where each self-sufficient unit possesses its own laws, code of conduct, and hierarchy of authority. In the *Decameron* the fictive *brigata* establishes its 'revolving' government—for each of the ten days, a different ruler chosen and authorized by a prescribed system—and its own rules for storytelling and other shared activities. In Filomena's last tale, the conclusion's depiction of the happy, virtuous life of Titus and Gisippus and their wives under one roof mirrors the self-sufficiency and virtuous fraternization of her audience in the country gardens. Leon Battista's father's house where the dialogue takes place is one self-sufficient unit, under the paterfamilias' rule, in a network of similar Alberti family units. The dialogue's gathering in one enclosure of several family leaders from outside represents through unity of place the family's unity of spirit. In his prefaces Laurent de Premierfait emphasizes the continuity of interest in ancient moral philosophy within the court under the duke's direction.

An important shared feature in these works which distinguishes them from earlier, medieval writings on ideals of *amicitia* is their simultaneous representation of two essentially different models of friendship separated by an interval of many centuries: they juxtapose the contemporary group and ancient textual or antique-style *amici veri* for the reader's view. In these Latinizing vernacular works, classical models are appropriate for comparison with the contemporary social group because of the common goal—living well in this world. A radical shift in emphasis in respect to ancient values sets these writings apart from or outside the long literary tradition of Christian friendships which they bypass: in Cicero's formulation of *amicitia perfecta* as complete mutual agreement on matters human and divine, Christian writers beginning with St. Augustine stressed the absolute supremacy of the divine, whereas the present writings, in emphasizing human matters, restrict their views on friendship, ancient and contemporary, to its contributions in pleasure, utility, and moral excellence to life in this world. And fictional chivalric models, although fully inclined to the human side, have little to offer by way of practical comparison with the humanistic writings' circles of urbane friends brought together by their love of letters. In presenting a simultaneous view of ancient and modern friends, the writer provides a general measure of the contemporary group's secular attainment in the ancient models' worldly standards. Titus and Gisippus' magnanimity, eloquence, and *onestà* are the standards of attainment against which Filomena and the *brigata* measure their own virtue in *amistà* and in speech—and, more, against which the author's persona gauges his success in contributing to his readers' pleasure and this-worldly virtue. The pursuit of wisdom and virtue through diligent study which Laelius and Scipio share in Cicero's dialogue is the common measure and aim uniting the duke and his friends in Laurent de Premierfait's introduction. These two works hold up ancient or antique-style models as a mirror in which the contemporary friends see their semblance and like goodness. In the second half of *Dell'amicizia,* however, the self-description of the modern family incorporates systematically the ancients, especially Romans, as literary and philosophical ancestors to whom the Albertis, their continuators and perfecters, are in no way inferior. This twofold construction would seem to represent continuity, rather than juxtaposition, between several successive generations of Alberti 'true friends of the family' and the Romans, with whom the Albertis are in perfect accord on the human side of *amicizia.*

Another common characteristic of the contemporary groups in the three works is that each is centered around a text or text-producer. The physical representation of the groups is significant in that it defines their shared activity, focus, and extension. With each of the *Decameron*'s tales nine of the *brigata*'s members concentrate their attention on the tenth who generates a text, and in *Dell'amicizia* the group's focus changes as the interlocutors, producers of texts, change. The duke and his associates direct their attention to *Laelius* as earlier they did to the translation of *On Old Age*. The group represented in Laurent de Premierfait's prefaces is identical with his readership. In the other two cases, the text-centered circle of friends, who support the speaker, comment upon the text, and quite often praise it, might be understood to depict the author's ideal readership. In *Dell'amicizia* the group consists of two sorts of Alberti males corresponding to the two types of designated readers which Leon Battista identifies in his general preface to *Della famiglia*—learned, practiced Alberti adults and inexperienced youths. The latter would find their model of the receptive listener/reader who interiorizes the text in the writer's portrayal of himself as the adolescent whom the elder interlocutors address.

Along with the focalization upon the text and its production, a shared feature in these humanistic writings which marks them as literary models of new sorts of idealized friendship is the central place there of the author and the activity of writing in relation to his readers, among whom he identifies common interests and pursuits. In each case the writer's establishment of his own authority is essential in validating the joint enterprise of his readership. For Laurent de Premierfait's readers, the authority of the Latin *Laelius* is of course not problematic, but the translation is, for the validity of the common pursuit of the readers at court depends upon the translator's interpretation. In his prefaces he places himself in central view by writing about his activity as translator and by assuming the teacher's voice to interpret for his lay readers philosophical and literary matters of which they should be aware in the bilingual text. His arguments, too, for the reliability of his vernacular version, along with the duke's endorsement of his past and present endeavors, are essential in establishing his expertise and right not just in face of detractors but, more importantly, in his courtly readers' eyes. In *Dell'amicizia* the writer is doubly central to the readers' view: the author behind the personas of the masterful interlocutors addresses his fictive disciple—himself. In this master-disciple dialogue, the writer's authority is more than a question of a convincing display of erudition, worldly experience, and rhetorical excellence; his authority has the sense of the right to command, as with the paterfamilias. The elder Adovardo's precepts, for example, are not suggestions that the Alberti youths may choose to follow, they are authorial imperatives. Here the author not only validates his family's common pursuit of perfecting *amicizia*, he orders it. In the *Decameron* the merging of virtuous friend and excellent orator in Filomena's last novella and, also, in the character Filomena as demonstrated in her telling might be interpreted to represent the central role of the writer as the readers' source of pleasure, utility, and virtue. Sometimes Boccaccio's persona defends his moral authority in addresses to his readership composed, he claims, of noble-minded ladies, and in his epilogue he argues that his readers' character and benevolence or ill will determine whether his stories have beneficial or injurious moral effects (p. 830). The benevolent sharing of writing and reading between the author and his audience is reflected, with a shift to simulated speaking and listening, in the *brigata*'s production and reception of tales. In the *Decameron*, as in *Dell'amicizia,* the author's arguments for the moral value of his writing are at the same time a validation of his literary friends' high-minded reading.

Laurent de Premierfait's description of his vernacular readership at court is hardly specific, while Leon Battista's designation of Alberti males and Boccaccio's of noble ladies of leisure are overly specific, for they do not represent the much broader range of vernacular readers at which Leon Battista aimed in offering his dialogue to Florence or that Boccaccio knew to be his actual readership. (It goes without saying that Boccaccio's persona's conventional address of medieval love literature—the lover-author writes to unnamed honorable and amorous ladies-readers—includes male readers in a kind of voyeuristic complicity in the literary sport.) Although the writers are thorough in detailing the benefits which they offer their designated audiences, they say very little about what 'the friends of Boccaccio,' one might say, or 'of Leon Battista' do as readers. What does it mean to be a vernacular reader, and what are the characteristics that these writers expect of their ideal readership?

Around the time of these writings, there were definite signs of positive changes in attitude towards the reading of vernacular literature. It was only in the fourteenth century that Italian literature and, at the end of the century, French began to be read with anything approaching the serious consideration that had formerly been reserved for Latin works. Dante's interpretations of his own writings in Italian mark a beginning, but Boccaccio's unfinished commentaries and public lectures in Italian near the end of his life on Dante's *Divine Comedy*[51] clearly indicate that the reading and interpretation of vernacular literature were serious matters for the citizens of Florence. Boccaccio's critical comments demonstrate, too, that an informed reading of Dante requires no less erudition than that needed to interpret Virgil, for example. The first prose commentary in French on a French work, the anonymous verse romance *Les échecs amoureux* (ca. 1370-1380), dates from around 1400. This encyclopedic commentary, probably written by Evrart de Conty, a physician to Charles V, for whom he translated into French from Latin the pseudo-Aristotelian *Problemata*,[52]

---

[51] Italian text: *Tutte le opere di Giovanni Boccaccio*, vol. 6: *Esposizioni sopra la "Comedia" di Dante*, ed. Giorgio Padoan, I Classici Mondadori (Milan: A. Mondadori, 1965).

[52] Françoise Guichard-Tesson, "Evrart de Conty, auteur de la *Glose des Echecs amoureux*," *Le moyen français* 8-9 (1983): 111-48. Partial edition: *L'harmonie des sphères. Encyclopédie d'astronomie et de musique extraite du commentaire sur "Les échecs amoureux" (XVe s.) attribué à Evrart de Conty*, ed. R. Hyatte and Maryse Ponchard-Hyatte, Studies in the Humanities, 1 (New

provides a thorough, scholarly interpretation of the romance, particularly in regard to classical mythology, the seven liberal arts, and French literature itself. In *Dell'amicizia* the depiction of Adovardo and Lionardo as readers and interpreters of ancient literature for Italian speakers suggests the high level of erudition required of the ideal reader for a thorough appreciation of Leon Battista's vernacular work, a level of learning which the author in fact identifies near the end of his general preface in the adult Albertis among his designated readers. The rather high standards of literacy that these three humanists set for the lay reader in order for her or him to enjoy the full benefits of their written work would seem to correspond to the recent changes in attitudes towards vernacular literature.

We have already discussed the ethical measures proposed in the humanistic texts. To close we might note several of the attitudes and moral qualities that the three writers attribute to or ask of contemporary readers. From these texts a new—or, rather, renewed—model of ideal literary friendship emerges in which the author and his lay readers share beliefs, pursuits, and ethical goals that derive from classical notions of *amicitia perfecta* based upon the practice of *virtus*, 'manly' virtues and the orator's persuasive ethical power. In Filomena's tale of Gisippus and Titus, the speaker makes of Boccaccio's readers at least four demands, mainly required beliefs, which for the most part new for the period and which the other two writers sometimes make, too, or even intensify. First, she asks her audience—in other terms, the readers—to believe in the efficacy of reason, human ingenuity, and *virtù* in governing their own destiny. Leon Battista demands the same of the younger Albertis among his readership, but he asks them not only to believe, as he does, that mortals are entirely capable of rising above Fortune through virtue, reasoning, and diligent effort but, also, to will such power for themselves: "Let us recognize that virtue, valiant deeds, and manly customs are within the reach of mortals if they desire them" (preface, p. 32). Leon Battista pushes his demands beyond belief in and will to possess *virtù* in requiring his readers to accept the duty of employing their acquired virtues actively in order to bring the family prosperity, longevity, and glory.

Secondly, the pride in being Italian that the 'Greek-bashing' Filomena encourages in her tale and expects of her audience—and which Boccaccio expects of his—becomes with Leon Battista almost a century later an ab-

York: Peter Lang, 1985).

solute requirement of patriotism. He asks his readers to believe—and to act upon the belief—that they are the continuators and perfecters of the ancient Romans and, not the least, of their military might. To Cicero's essential love of country and of glory, Leon Battista adds duty to family to the requirements for his friends and readers. In Laurent de Premierfait's prefaces, 'French pride' in his readers and, especially, his patron, one of France's most distinguished military leaders during Charles V's reign in the wars against the English, is understood no less in the national than in the linguistic sense.

Thirdly, Filomena's address to the *brigata* strongly suggests among her listeners—and Boccaccio's readers—not only moral similarities but solidarity in recognizing shared problems and overcoming them through joint effort, through the combined *virtù* of rhetorical excellence and excellent *amistà*. Together her two protagonists overcome Love's tyranny and social opposition, and so, too, the *brigata*'s ten members work jointly through the friendly, virtuous production and reception of tales to confront their common problems—love and the plague, with the gloomy spirits and social disorder that both tend to produce. Solidarity among readers to achieve a common goal is apparent in Laurent de Premierfait's prefaces, where members of the court, under the duke's leadership, seek to learn the ancients' teachings in the vernacular. Along with belief in the efficacy of group action, solidarity among writer and readers as familial 'true friends' in promoting one another's and the group's interests is a central dynamic principle in Leon Battista's dialogue.

On the other hand, although the idea of solidarity among vernacular writers and readers is somewhat new, the three works share an old political agenda—support of the status quo and respect for patriarchal authority. Titus and Gisippus' actions and arguments through most of the novella subvert the right to arrange marriage which belongs to the family and the paterfamilias. But in the novella's conclusion Titus, the new Roman head of household, gives, as is his right, his sister to Gisippus in marriage. In his preface Boccaccio's persona identifies the principal shared problems of his female readers: "forced to follow the whims, fancies, and dictates of their fathers, mothers, brothers, and husbands," they are constrained to a life of idleness and longing for love, and they are not permitted the freedom outside the home by which men may drive away love's melancholy (pp. 46-47). A present-day reader might imagine possible consolidated attempts on the part of women in Boccaccio's time to overcome this socially imposed burden and its consequences, but the author's recommendation is for women of leisure to put up with the existing situation and to pass their abundant 'free' time profitably and pleasurably in reading or sewing (p. 47). He would have one understand that his female reader converts his writing and her leisure into her delight, profit, and virtue. That the fictive narrator of novella 10,8 is female would appear to subvert the exclusive maleness of the tale's voices of authority in rhetoric as well as in perfect friendship, and it might seem to suggest that Boccaccio's female readers can, like Filomena, do other than while away the idle hours with book or needle. But, again, the female narrator's voice is wholly supportive of the male *amicizia* and privilege that her tale confirms. In Laurent de Premierfait's prefaces the rather new idea, which dates from the reign of Charles V, of a united effort on the part of French princes, courtiers, and court writers to appropriate in the vernacular the ancients' authority is a single item in the larger agenda of consolidated support of the duke's political and moral influence which the prefaces underwrite. Leon Battista's appeals to family solidarity for the continuing renovation of perfect friendship demand of readers an unquestioning respect for the paterfamilias' authority, without which family and state fall. In the conclusion to his general preface, he demands of his young readers more than acceptance of paternal authority; he asks them to love it in the *auctor*: "Pay heed to what our fathers, most learned, erudite, and refined men, thought ought to be done and reminded us to do for our family. Read my work and love me" (p. 34).

Lastly, belief in vernacular eloquence, the worthy successor of Latin. In spite of the writer's modest claim in the fourth day's prologue to have employed in earlier tales a homespun, unassuming style (p. 325), Filomena's reasoned eloquence asks readers to accept the new fashioned Florentine vernacular—Boccaccio's literary version of it—as equal in sublimity and authority to classical rhetoric which her telling feigns to be in the mouths of Titus and Gisippus. Her failure to note which language—Latin or Greek or both—her antique-style friends and orators spoke is perhaps not an inadvertent omission: contemporary readers would recognize only that they, "our equals," spoke Filomena's tongue. Laurent de Premierfait's comparison of his own common French prose, meager, deficient, even insignificant, with Cicero's grand and grave Latin (paragraphs 57-58) is but an expression of the modesty topos which he does not expect his readers to take at face value—the expected response is praise. He explains in the second preface that *Laelius* is primarily a work of rhetoric which

teaches ethics. Readers must trust that the vernacular rendering approaches
the original in eloquence, that it translates, not betrays, the original's
primary philosophical characteristic and end, elevated, reasoned language
as the persuasive conveyor of truth—otherwise, a French summary of the
treatise's ethical content would have sufficed. Leon Battista asks his readers to accept the vernacular eloquence of his Latinizing interlocutors, interpreters of the ancient Romans' wisdom and virtue, as the successor of
Latin rhetoric and its perfection. His innovative Italian, a hybrid of Florentine and Latin, as the written expression of the sacred laws of friendship
and the paterfamilias' consecrated right commands readers' belief, even
reverence. In these vernacular arts of perfecting friendship, the designated
readers would not only see in the text their own moral reflection cast in a
most favorable light, they would also 'hear' a language like their own yet
more refined in the writer's version. For a new age of model friends—
women, lovers, courtiers, merchants, even clerics—quite different from
any that the ancients had imagined, each version elevates the shared
tongue of writer and reader in dignity and offers a new, authoritative vehicle for the expression of moral character and the means of imposing it. In
emphasizing the importance of language and rhetoric in the best friendship, the three humanistic writers ask lay readers to believe that excellent
speaking and writing in the vernacular are essential components of the virtuous life.

A NOTE ON DIDACTIC WORKS AND TRANSLATIONS
OF THE THIRTEENTH CENTURY

The thirteenth century produced numerous treatises, allegories, and compendia, primarily in Latin, on the topics of ideal, ordinary, and bad friendships as well as translations and commentaries on Aristotle's *Nicomachean Ethics*. In the first half of the century, Cicero's *Laelius*, Seneca's *Letters to Lucilius*, and a broad range of Biblical, ancient Greek, and Latin works of all periods are most frequently cited as authorities, while the second is dominated by the *Nicomachean Ethics*.

First, Boncompagno da Signa's Latin prose *Amicitia*, composed in 1205, is cast as a debate in which the Body argues that friendship does not exist, and the Soul contends that friendship is no earthly thing. The Body asks the Soul thirty questions about *amicitia*, and they call in Reason to judge their debate. Boncompagno describes in separate chapters twenty-six different types of friends, good, ordinary, and bad: *amicus propter amicum, fidelis, par, dominabilis, subicibilis, realis, vocalis, transcursibilis, conditionalis, ymaginarius, umbratilis, sophisticus, superstitiosus, retrogradus, fortunae, mercalis, venativus, versipellis, fucatus, voluptuosus, orbatus, futilis, ventosus, vitreus, amicus propter inimicum, ferreus*. Brunetto Latini, discussed below, adapts several of these types in his *Favolello*. Boncompagno lists some European and Middle Eastern notables from around 1200 as illustrations, mostly of the bad types, and he localizes his treatise in time and place through frequent references to the Crusades and Italian cities. See *"Amicitia" di Maestro Boncompagno da Signa*, ed. Sarina Nathan, Miscellanea di Letteratura del Medio Evo, 3 (Rome: Presso La Società, 1909).

Albertano da Brescia's Latin prose treatise *De dilectione Dei et proximi et aliarum rerum et de forma honestae vitae*, from 1238, is in the form of a master-to-disciple address in which Albertano offers moral advice to a certain Vincenzio. The part of the treatise dealing with friendship is by and large a compendium of *Laelius* and *The Letters to Lucilius* with frequent allusions to Proverbs and Ecclesiasticus, Ovid, Sallust, Cassiodorus, Martial, the *Disticha Catonis*, and other Latin sources. Albertano was perhaps influenced in part by a near-contemporary treatise, Andreas Capellanus' Latin prose *De amore, de arte honeste amandi et de reprobatione inhonesti amoris* (around 1185); see Andreas Capellanus, *On Love*, ed. and trans. P. G. Walsh (London: Duckworth, 1982), p. 1. We might note that *Laelius* is one of the minor sources for *De amore*, where in book 1 excellence of character, along with courteous speech and manners, makes a man worthy of a woman's love and where Andreas argues against the possibility of true love between husband and wife on the authority of *Laelius*. Albertano admonishes Vincenzio to avoid friendship with bad men—the foolish, avaricious, cupidinous, proud, perverse, loquacious, and wrathful—and then speaks on good friendship's usefulness, tests, laws, and preservation. See the Italian translation: *Tre trattati d'Albertano giudice da Brescia: Il primo della dilezion d'Iddio, e del prossimo, e della forma dell' onesta vita: Il secondo della consolazione, e de' consigli: Il terzo delle sei maniere del parlare, scritti da lui in lingua latina, dall'Anno 1235. in fino all'Anno 1246. e traslatati ne' medesimi tempi, in volgar fiorentino* (Florence and Mantua: Stamperia di S. Benedetto, 1732).

Vincent of Beauvais's encyclopedic compilation in Latin, the *Speculum majus*, from around 1254, contains in its second major section, the *Speculum doctrinale*, several chapters on *amicitia* (book 5, chapters 82-93) which are made up of Latin quotations from numerous Biblical, ancient Greek, and Latin sources from all periods: Proverbs, Tobias, Aristotle, Plato, Theophrastus, Seneca's letters and plays, Ovid, Quintilian, the *Disticha Catonis*, Valerius Maximus, Quintus Curtius, Symmachus, Sidonius, Pliny, Prudentius, Claudianus, Terence, Gauthier de Châtillon's *Alexandreis*, Boethius, Sallust, Arator, Horace, Plautus, Sedulius, Varro, Petronius, Martial, Tibullus, etc., along with generous excerpts from *Laelius* and *De officiis*. See *Bibliotheca mundi. Vincenti Burgundi ex ordine praedicatorum venerabilis episcopi Bellovacensis speculum quadruplex, naturale, doctrinale, morale, historiale. In quo totius naturae historia, omnium scientiarum encyclopaedia, moralis philosophiae thesaurus, temporum & actionum humanarum theatrum amplissimum exhibetur*, 4 vols. (Douai: B. Bellerus, 1624), vol. 2, cols. 450-56. The third section, the *Speculum morale*, is an early-fourteenth-century addition.

As noted in chapter one, an anonymous translator put part of book 8 of the *Nicomachean Ethics* into Latin at the end of the twelfth or the beginning of the thirteenth century. An important work before the completion

of the Latin versions of the last books of the *Ethics* is Hermannus Allemanus' Latin translation from Arabic in 1240 of the Middle Commentary,
a paraphrase with comments and glosses, on the ten books of the *Ethics*
by the Spanish Arab Averroes (Ibn Rushd) from 1177. See *Aristotelis
opera cum Averrois commentariis*, 10 vols. (Frankfurt am Main: Miner-
va, 1962; reprint of the Venice 1562-1574 Juntas edition), vol. 3. The
original Arabic text of the Middle Commentary which Hermannus Allemanus used is lost, but there exists a Hebrew rendering of it by Samuel
ben Judah of Marseilles from 1321. Hermannus Allemanus also translated
into Latin in 1243-1244 under the titles *Compendium alexandrinum*,
Translatio alexandrina, or *Summa alexandrina* an Arabic version of an
anonymous Greek summary of the ten books of the *Ethics*. The latter text
in Latin served as a principal source for Brunetto Latini's French prose *Li
livres dou tresor* (see below.)

Around 1246-1247 Robert Grosseteste translated all of the *Nicomachean
Ethics* from Greek to Latin. See the editions of Grosseteste's version and
its late-thirteenth-century revision: *Ethica nicomachea. Translatio Roberti
Grosseteste Lincolniensis sive liber ethicorum, A. recensio pura*, ed. R.-
A. Gauthier, Aristoteles Latinus, 26, nos. 1-3, fasc. 3 (Leiden: E. J. Brill,
1972), and *Ethica nicomachea. Translatio Roberti Grosseteste Lincolniensis sive liber ethicorum, B. recensio recognita*, ed. R.-A. Gauthier, Aristoteles Latinus, 26, nos. 1-3, fasc. 4 (Leiden: E. J. Brill, 1973). Around
the same time Grosseteste translated into Latin from Greek the commentary on book 1 of the *Ethics* by Eustratius (end of the eleventh century or
beginning of the twelfth), the anonymous scholia on books 2-4, an
anonymous exposition of book 7, the commentary on book 8 by Aspasius (early second century A.D.; Grosseteste completed Aspasius' unfinished work), and Michael of Ephesus' interpretations, written before 1040,
of books 9 and 10. For Grosseteste's versions of the commentaries on
books 8 and 9, see *Aristotelis over vriendschap, boeken VIII en IX van de
"Nicomachische Ethiek" met de commentaren van Aspasius en Michaël in
de latijnse vertaling van Grosseteste*, ed. Wilifried Stinissen, Vanhan-
delingen van de Koninklijke Vlaamse Academie voor Wetenschappen, Letteren en Schone Kunsten van België, Klasse der Letteren, 45 (Brussels:
Paleis der Academiën, 1963). The sentence-by-sentence explanations of
Aspasius and Michael of Ephesus, who were philosophy professors, may
have been given as lectures.

Albertus Magnus and Thomas Aquinas produced Latin commentaries on the *Nicomachean Ethics* in Grosseteste's or other thirteenth-century Latin versions. Albertus Magnus (ca. 1200-1280) wrote a line-by-line explication (between 1248 and 1252) apparently intended for lectures and a summary (before 1261). Both texts incorporate the Greek commentaries in Grosseteste's translation and Averroes' Middle Commentary in Hermannus Allemanus' Latin version, and they include references to Avicenna (Ibn Sina), Cicero, St. Anselm, Plato, and other Aristotelian works. See editions: *Sancti doctoris ecclesiae Alberti Magni ordinis fratrum praedicatorum opera omnia*, vol. 14, parts 1 and 2: *Super ethica commentum et quaestiones*, ed. Wilhelmus Kübel (Monasterii Westfalorum: Aschendorff, 1968-1972), and *Alberti Magni Ratisbonensis episcopi ordinis praedicatorum opera omnia*, vol. 7: *Ethicorum libri X*, ed. Auguste Borgnet (Paris: L. Vivès, 1891).

Thomas Aquinas (1225-1274) is thought to have completed in 1271-1272 his line-by-line commentary on the *Nicomachean Ethics*, which he may have begun as early as 1261. See *Sancti Thomae de Aquino opera omnia iussu Leonis XIII P.M. edita*, vol. 47, parts 1 and 2: *Sententia libri ethicorum*, ed. R.-A. Gauthier (Rome: Ad Sanctae Sabinae, 1969). Aquinas attended Albertus Magnus' lectures in Cologne between 1248 and 1252, and he knew of Albertus Magnus' written explication but probably not his summary. Among modern scholarship on Aquinas' interpretation of the *Ethics*, one might note James McEvoy's comparison of Aelred of Rievaulx's and Aquinas' concepts of excellent friendship in *"Philia* and *Amicitia*: The Philosophy of Friendship from Plato to Aquinas," *Sewanee Mediaeval Colloquium Occasional Papers* 2 (1985): 16-21, and Vernon J. Bourke's "The *Nicomachean Ethics* and Thomas Aquinas," in *St. Thomas Aquinas, 1274-1974, Commemorative Studies* (Toronto: Pontifical Institute of Mediaeval Studies, 1974), vol. 1, pp. 239-59. Although R.-A. Gauthier, the commentary's editor, finds nothing new or distinctive there in regard to a medieval Christian interpretation of Aristotle's ethical friendship, Harry V. Jaffa sees in Aquinas' treatment of *amicitia* what he believes to be significant equivocations and a reordering of Aristotelian virtues according to Christian doctrine; see Jaffa, *Thomism and Aristotelianism. A Study of the Commentary by Thomas Aquinas on the "Nicomachean Ethics"* (Chicago: University of Chicago Press, 1952), especially chapter 6, "Magnanimity and the Limits of Morality," pp. 116 ff. The fact that Aquinas does not cite here Averroes' Middle Commentary on the *Ethics* is perhaps significant in that he was an opponent of Averroism. On the other hand, Averroes' text, although important in itself as a commentated summary, is unremarkable as a guide to Aristotelian ethics.

Around the time that Albertus Magnus and Aquinas composed their learned commentaries in Latin, the encyclopedic works in French and Italian by the Florentine Brunetto Latini (ca. 1220-1294 or 1295) provided to popular audiences summaries of Aristotelian natural, ethical, and rhetorical sciences along with adaptations of several Latin compendia and information on such varied subjects as ancient and medieval history and fiction, cosmography, geography, real and imaginary beasts, and politics. Brunetto Latini composed two redactions of his major work, the French prose *Li livres dou tresor*, during his exile in France, which began in 1260, and after his return to Italy around 1267. See *Li livres dou tresor par Brunetto Latini*, ed. P. Chabaille, Collection de Documents Inédits sur l'Histoire de France, 1re Série, Histoire Littéraire (Paris: Imprimerie Impériale, 1863), and *Li livres dou tresor de Brunetto Latini*, ed. Francis J. Carmody, University of California Publications in Modern Philology, 22 (Berkeley: University of California Press, 1948). The first half of the *Tresor*'s second book (chapters 2-49 in Carmody's edition) is a summary of the ten books of the *Nicomachean Ethics* which Latini adapted from the *Compendium alexandrinum* in Hermannus Allemanus' Latin version. This part gives no living, historical, or legendary examples and refers to no authority other than the *Ethics* except for the rare allusion to the Bible. See chapters 43-45 (Carmody's edition) for Latini's treatment of books 8 and 9 of the *Ethics*. The other half of the second book, which deals with virtues and a few vices, includes adaptations of several medieval Latin compendia: Guillaume Perrault's *Summa aurea de virtutibus*, Guillaume de Conches's *Moralium dogma philosophorum*, Albertano da Brescia's *Ars loquendi et tacendi*, Martin of Dumium's *De quattuor virtutibus cardinalibus*, and Isidore of Seville's *Sententiae*; it contains five chapters (102-06 in Carmody's edition) on *amistié* and perfect friendship which cite Cicero, Proverbs, Seneca, Jerome, Ambrose, Boethius, Sallust, Lucan, and the legendary lives of Aristotle and Merlin. Latini's contemporary Bono Giamboni translated the *Tresor* into Italian prose; see *Il tesoro di Brunetto Latini volgarizzato da Bono Giamboni*, ed. Luigi Carrer, Biblioteca Classica Italiana di Scienze, Lettere, ed Arti, Classe 2, 1 and 2 (Venice: Gondoliere, 1839). The part of Bono Giamboni's *Tesoro* that corresponds to the first half of book 2 of Latini's *Tresor*—i.e., Giamboni's Italian translation of Latini's French adaptation of Hermannus Allemanus' Latin rendering of an Arabic version of an anonymous Greek summary of the *Nicomachean Ethics*—was published separately: *Etica d'Aristotile compendiata da Ser Brunetto Latini e due leggende di autore anonimo*, ed. Francesco Berlan (Venice: Società dei Bibliofili, 1844).

Latini's Italian poems *Il tesoretto* (1265 or 1266) and *Il favolello* or *Favoletto* (after 1282) treat in the form of an allegorical dream vision some of the same ethical subjects found in his French prose *Tresor*. See *Il tesoretto e il favolello*, ed. B. Wiese, Bibliotheca Romanica, 94 and 95, Bibliotheca Italiana (Strassburg: Heitz and Mündel, [1909]), and *Il tesoretto (The Little Treasure)*, ed. and trans. Julia Bolton Holloway, Garland Library of Medieval Literature, Series A, 2 (New York: Garland, 1981)—the latter publishes the verses that correspond to the concluding section of the *Tesoretto* in Wiese's edition as a separate poem, *La penetenza*. In the *Tesoretto* the part related to book 2 of the *Tresor* begins at verse 1125, where the personified virtues of Prudence, Temperance, Fortitude, and Justice appear. *Il favolello*, which has no apparent relationship to the *Tresor*, is introduced at the end of the *Tesoretto* (or the *Penetenza* in Holloway's text). In this short poem dedicated to Latini's friend, the poet Rustico di Filippo, Ptolemy, "master of astronomy and of philosophy," offers advice on friendship and repeats commonplaces about *verace amistade*, which he contrasts to love, and he describes a half dozen types of true and false friends, such as *l'amico di ferro* and *l'amico di vetro*, which come from Boncompagno da Signa's extensive listing in *Amicitia*.

LAURENT DE PREMIERFAIT'S PREFACES TO HIS
TRANSLATION OF CICERO'S *LAELIUS*

Laurent de Premierfait's French translation of Cicero's *Laelius de amicitia* survives in fourteen manuscripts. The following English translation of his two unpublished prefaces is based on the French text in MS. Paris, Bibliothèque Nationale, fonds français 1020, folios 44r-55v, which I collated with MSS. fonds français 126 and 24283 in the same library.

Within brackets are included words necessary to complete the sense of the French text. Paragraph markers in the base manuscript have been followed only when they indicate a logical division.

Here begins the translator's first prologue to the book *On True Friendship*.

1 To his most excellent, glorious, and noble prince, Louis, uncle to the king of France, duke of Bourbon, count of Clermont and Forez, lord of Beaujeu, grand chamberlain and peer of France, [in order to] use rightly and well your authority and temporal power, [may you have] desired victory over your manifest and secret enemies, increased good character and virtues, and the entire fulfillment of your best wishes; and [may] I, Laurent de Premierfait, your clerk and servitor, be worthy of benevolence and friendship in your sight, [my] lord and prince. It is a great commendation and a specific sign of a good and noble heart when it receives such pleasure and satisfaction from its virtuous deeds that, passing from one virtue to another, consequently it pursues and brings into action all virtues and each in agreement with itself. For thus, just as a swallow's arrival at the end of February is not a sure sign that winter is past and springtime come, so the single product of a sole virtue does not provide sure proof that a man is virtuous; rather, many deeds and various works performed in conformity with virtue are required.

2 I have made these remarks because you, most excellent, noble, and glorious duke and prince, not long ago ordered me to put into the French language the book *On Old Age* which Tullius composed and wrote for his friend Atticus, a noble citizen of Rome, which book I, obeying your command, translated the least poorly that I could—and you received this [work] which I presented you very kindly and with joyful heart, as it seemed to me by the exterior signs which show the heart's secrets—and [also] because you, having become acquainted through the text of the said book with the praises and recommendations of the good elders and their virtuous deeds and words of which alone (and not of others) one should speak and write, ordered me for your sake and for all who take delight in good and approved teachings to turn my hand to putting into French another work by Tullius called *On True Friendship*, which he also wrote at the said Atticus' behest and dedicated to him. This book *On True Friendship* is [composed] in the same manner of discourse as the work *On Old Age*. For in *On Old Age* Tullius imagined that the two noble youths Scipio and Laelius question the old and wise Cato, and he responds to their questions with examples and arguments, as you know. And in the present book *On True Friendship* Tullius imagines that Fannius and

Scaevola, noble and wise Romans, question Laelius, a very sage Roman who enjoyed a most good and great friendship with Scipio Africanus, and the said Laelius answers Fannius' and Scaevola's questions. If you ask me why Tullius wrote these two books in dialogue form—that is, there are two who question a sole respondent—know that Tullius will explain the reason to you in his prologue translated hereinafter.

3 Then Tullius, as he says, considered that the immortal gods have granted men several gifts and many favors, among which the gift of wisdom is most great and exceedingly precious, and after wisdom the second greatest present is the boon of true friendship, which is very similar to the gift of wisdom, for just as the sage neither modifies nor changes his will because of any consideration of temporal things, but always lives in the same manner and [acts the same] towards all, so the true friend, whether in prosperity or in adverse fortune, always loves him with whom he united once in friendship, just as is apparent in Tullius' argument and by that which Aristotle, preeminent in natural and moral philosophy, argues on friendship in books eight and nine of the [*Nicomachean*] *Ethics* as a rational [or dialectical] philosopher who is able and knows how to explain all seemingly marvelous things. And in this book Tullius discusses friendship as an advisor who admonishes [all] to pursue [the course of] friendship.

4 I wish to specify and include in my prologue two things worth noting. Firstly, I will indicate the divisions of philosophy and explain certain words so that it will be quite clear what and how each of the two wrote on friendship. Aristotle, a Greek, was not instructed by Tullius, a Latin. But Tullius, as he says, read and studied the works of Aristotle, who wrote in the time of Alexander the Great. And Tullius wrote in the time of Julius Caesar or shortly after his death. And in saying these things, I will employ such clear and ordinary language that moderately lettered men will understand me completely and quickly. Secondly, I will summarize briefly all or the greater part of the conclusions or views which Aristotle put forth and asserted in the two books of the *Ethics* noted above.

5 Now I come to the sectioning of the body of Dame Philosophy within which is included the present book written by Tullius, an orator and philosopher. I divide her into sections so that one may understand immediately within which part of philosophy are to be placed and included the present book and the one on old age, which you have chosen for honorable reasons as [works with which] you and your friends [who share] your eagerness [for learning] are to be well acquainted. For since you are a duke and prince belonging to France's ruling royal lineage of which the glorious name is praised and known throughout the seven climes of the world, you and all those who are of such a [high] degree of lordship and power as yourself should at all times willingly frequent old age, which of its very name signifies the concept of wisdom and, also, friendship, the companion of virtue which nurtures and maintains cities and republics which are divided into three classes of men, among whom, by the grace of God, you, as is well deserved, are of the highest and first degree of lordship and nobility, which of old took and even today takes its rightful beginning and proper origin from the name of philosophy.

6 Philosophy is the love of knowledge which teaches the truth of divine and human matters in the constant study of living well. Therefore, he seems ignoble and worthless who chooses [to have as] his [friends] men ignorant of the sciences and devoid of any virtue.

7 Philosophy is sectioned into three parts. The first is called ethics, which disposes and turns men's minds to good character and virtues. The second part is called natural science, by which one seeks and explains the causes of phenomena occurring in nature. The third part is called rational science [or dialectics], which teaches the proper measure and right manner of words arranged in reasoned arguments. In these three parts of philosophy lies and resides all knowledge of earthly and celestial things, without which no one, not even because of ripe old age, should be called a perfect man. For the soul which is adorned with neither virtues nor sciences is just like a fine, polished panel on which there is no painting.

8 In rational philosophy is included rhetorical science, which long ago was first translated from Greek into Latin and established in sure and concise rules by certain Latin authors, of whom one was Tullius, a noble philosopher and the leader in eloquence in the Latin language, who in his *Rhetoric* admits freely that Aristotle, foremost among philosophers and a Greek rhetorician, was a great aid to him while he was writing *The Art of Rhetoric* in the Latin language, whereby one can conclude that Aristotle was a giant in rhetoric, and Tullius, too, who wrote after him. But in order to see further, Tullius climbed on Aristotle's shoulders.

9 This Tullius was called an orator because he had a most perfect knowledge of the fair rhetorical art. Rhetoric is the invaluable science of speaking well [which is] necessary in civil questions concerning things and persons so as to perform just and good acts. One calls an orator a

good man who knows how to speak wisely in accordance with the rules of the science of rhetoric. The goodness of the orator consists in four things—namely, in natural skill, learning, [his] life, and [his] character. Whoever possesses fully within himself these four things is a man of eloquence.

10 Skilfully wrought eloquence resides in five things—to wit, in determining rightly in one's mind the truth of matters, in ordering well the things which one has ascertained, in expressing them in a harmonious arrangement of words, in proving [one's point] clearly, and in having a good memory. This rhetorical art of which Tullius was the leader in the Latin language comes to a man through three means—namely, through natural skill, the instruction that one receives from wise men, and the practice of speaking or writing frequently in Latin or another language.

11 It is not necessary to speak further about the three parts into which I divided philosophy a moment ago, for I wish [now] to summarize briefly all or the greater part of the two aforementioned books of the *Ethics* insofar as it concerns the subject of friendship.

12 Aristotle says: Friendship is divided into three sorts because it originates for reason of pleasure or for gain or on account of upright character which are or seem to be in the person who loves and in the loved one. Friendship is a virtue of the heart and mind, or, at least, it never exists without virtue. It is very much necessary to human life. No man should choose to live without friends, even though he might possess all other worldly goods. Rich men, princes, and powerful lords especially need to have friends, for I do not see what the advantage of such riches and dominion might be if one has no friends whom he can benefit, which is a very praiseworthy thing among men. And, further, if Fortune were to withdraw her support from the rich and powerful, they could save or protect neither themselves nor their possessions if they had no friends. The greater the abundance of goods that men receive from Fortune, the less secure they are and the more they need friends. Some say that a man needs to fall back on his friends only when he experiences poverty or some other harsh and foul strokes of Fortune. Yet I say that young men need friends to keep them from doing evil, and the aged, too, need friends who will be attentive to them and direct them in old age.

13 Friendship is so powerful that it holds cities and citizens together, and those who make civil laws pay greater attention to preserving friendships among men than to preserving justice, for if men in cities and provinces are friends among themselves, there is indeed neither need nor use for the exercise of justice among them, but it is fitting for just men to be friends with one another, for a similar thing recognizes its likeness. So it is, thus, that both justice and friendship are virtues.

14 Many men are benevolent towards those whom they have never seen.

15 Men who love one another wish for their partner good things in proportion to [the goodness of] their reciprocal love.

16 Those motivated by profit love for reason of a particular possession, and those who inclined to pleasure love because of a thing which pleases them. Friendships for reason of profit and pleasure are accidental and contingent, for when the pleasure or profit comes to an end, so does the motive for which they became friends. Old men love mainly with an eye to profit, for the aged do not seek at all to make friends for pleasure but for profit alone. Young men become friends lightly, and lightly they break off their friendship, for it is interrupted when their pleasure ceases. Men cannot know if they are friends with one another before they have eaten a good deal of salt together. Men should not accept anyone in friendship nor should they deem themselves friends before it is clear that they are equally friendly towards one another, for man's will is fickle, and friendship is firm and permanent. Those who are friends with a view to profit separate when the profit is ended. The bad are friends for pleasure and profit.

17 Only the friendship of good men is firm and immutable, for they love on account of themselves, without any other cause than that they are good. Different and distant places [of habitation] never cause friendship to dissolve, but they do not permit friends to do what they are obliged to do.

18 The aged and servile men are not at all friendly with a view to pleasure, since the reason for their pleasure is insufficient.

19 One cannot have a constant friendship with melancholic men or disagreeable persons, for he cannot stay with them for the space of a day. And thus by nature a man flees from sadness and seeks a pleasurable thing. There is nothing that does so much to make a man befriend another and the other him as does living together.

20 A thing is likeable and desirable which because of itself is good and pleasurable, and for this reason people love gold or jewels or books and things which have no soul. Brute beasts gladly recognize those who like them because these persons are well disposed towards them.

21 Friendship occurs less among crabbed men and the aged inasmuch as

they are [typically] rather unlettered and hardly eloquent, for conversation
and eloquence are likeable things which promote friendships. Youths become friends straightaway by conversing together, but old men do not.

22 It is not an easy thing to please exceedingly a single man or, by
some stroke of luck, several men together. Friends must try one another
out, and so it must needs be that friendship comes about through their
getting accustomed to one another, for friendship between men is made or
undone through their similarity or their difference from one another.

23 According to friendship's ordering, in the first place each wishes
well for himself.

24 He is a flatterer who is more than an excellent friend—that is, he
who acts or speaks beyond what the code of friendship demands is no
longer a friend, rather he is a flatterer.

25 It is a greater thing to love someone than to be loved by him.

26 Equality and resemblance engender friendship, and especially the resemblance in things consistent with virtue which are a source of friendship. Good men should not suffer their friends to commit sin or provide
them the means by which they may sin. Bad men love only for a brief period because they delight in their common wickedness.

27 Men who enter into friendship with an eye to profit make use of reciprocal exchanges, and when one [such] friend needs something, he gives
another thing because he desires ardently to possess that which he needs.

28 The possessions of men who love one another should be held in
common, for friendship resides in communality of possessions. Brothers
and those who are raised together have their goods in common, and consequently they love one another, but [for] other men [it is] not [so], because
their possessions are separate and divided. Particular governments were
formed on earth because men brought their persons and goods together in
common, and afterwards men initiated and entered into friendships because
of such sharing.

29 A tyrant does not have friendship inherently, for he is heedful only
of what is profitable to himself, but the king has friendship inherently,
for he is attentive to what is profitable to his subjects. He is not a king
who does not possess self-sufficiency as a consequence of his own virtue
and if he is not superior in all good things to other men. Evil in earthly
lordship is true tyranny, and a bad king is, properly speaking, a tyrant,
and therefore friendship is impossible in his case. A father's sharing with
his children contains in itself the form and likeness of the kingdom. And

accordingly the poets called Jupiter "father of the gods and men," for he
divided and shared out himself and his goods in proper measure among
those in his kingdom, for which he was greatly loved. The dominion of
the king over his people aims at being in accordance with friendship in
the same manner as the rule of the father over his children. When women
rule as heirs to kingdoms, such lordship is not in accordance with virtue,
but it favors riches and power, and, therefore, friendship is absent.

30 Friendship which is in agreement with justice must be apportioned
according to each act of kindness of the one who loves and the beloved.
But the king or other [lords] should [show their] friendship towards their
subjects by granting them more goods and favor than their friendship merits. If the king is good, he loves and is beneficent to his subjects, and
thus he takes care of them so that they may do well, just as the shepherd
cares for his flock. In tyranny there is very little or no friendship. When
nothing is shared between a lord and his subject, there will be no friendship or justice, either. All friendship consists in sharing and reciprocal
beneficence in conformity to justice.

31 Fathers and mothers love their children because they are a part of
their own flesh. And children love their fathers and mothers because they
are descended from them. Parents love their children more than children do
the parents because parents know with greater certainty those whom they
engender than those engendered do their begetters. Parents love their children as themselves, for those who are begotten by them are like a self-
same thing, joined and not separated [from the procreators]. But children
love their parents because they are born of them, which is a degree of re-
moval. Children have great advantage in becoming friends with their wet
nurses and those near to them in age, for those alike in age love one another, and [so, too, do] those who are brought up together and [raised] in a
similar manner. Sons and daughters are friends with their parents, and men
are friends with the gods, and children are friends with their teachers, for
parents benefited their children because they brought them up, and the
gods [benefited men] because they brought them into being, and teachers
gave them instruction for living well. Men and women do not live together solely for the love of having children but for the love of acquiring
those things necessary for life by helping one another. Children are a
shared possession for both father and mother, and consequently they have
in common friendship with them.

32 Barren women do not have lasting love of children, for friendship

which comes through the lover's choice is measured according to the quality of the beloved. Since, therefore, the sterile woman cannot have children, she cannot choose friendship with them.

33 In the choice of friendship the principal means are virtue and good conduct—that is to say, he who wishes to choose a friend should note if he is virtuous and easy to get along with and inclined to sharing.

34 The good friend's property is dispensed to his poor and necessitous friends to satisfy their needs. Honor is the reward of virtues and benefits— that is to say, for one who is unable to do more, it is sufficient to honor his virtuous friend and whoever benefits him.

35 Aristotle says: He is not honored who never benefited or contributed to the shared goods [of friends]. Such a man cannot usually be honored or [shown a sign of] love by receiving resources from the shared goods. One renders a shared thing to whoever is beneficial in respect to that which is shared. And a shared thing is nothing other than honor. Friendship requires only that a man do what is possible, without regard to the station or importance of his friend. In all friendships one does not take into account the station and importance of friends as he does in the case of honors that he pays to the gods and mothers and fathers, for it is enough for friends to do what they can, but a man can never suitably repay the gods and parents.

36 Many allow themselves to be loved, but they do not wish to love another.

37 Aristotle says: Since we have said enough about friendship in our eighth book, in this ninth we will speak of the characteristics of friendship and how one may make it last.

38 Whoever wishes to preserve friendship in the administration of government must compensate every cobbler for his shoes, weavers for making of a piece of cloth, and other craftsmen for their handiworks according to what each deserves. A rich Greek promised a harper that the better he played, the greater would be the reward that he received afterwards. The next morning the harper requested of the man what he had promised, and the wealthy man told him that he had given him pleasure for pleasure, because the delight that the harper had taken in the rich man's promise was sufficient payment to the harper in return for the pleasure that he had given the wealthy man by playing the harp well.

39 In this manner it is proper for the man who wishes to preserve friendship to reciprocate in equal measure and kind. When a man observes that his friend is indigent, on account of his friendship with him he should give, without regard to repayment, the things of which he has urgent need.

40 A vintner taught his children to honor a person who knew any kind of trade, and, also, he instructed them that in order to preserve friendship, the more someone seemed to them to know of the worthy sciences, the more esteem he should have [in their eyes].

41 Without infringing [the laws of] friendship, one can rightly call before a magistrate for [legal] action because of their extravagant promises those who, their hand stretched out, receive money in order to do something and, afterwards, do not carry out what they said [they would]. It is not possible to repay exactly [in kind] those who teach a certain science, for one cannot suitably requite the gift of philosophy with money. The value of the money and the worth of the science cannot match one another. In order to maintain friendship it is sufficient to return the benefit received according to the condition of those to whom it was given. It is not fitting in accordance with friendship that one render to each exactly what he gave, for the son should not give back to his father all the goods that he received from him, since one does not offer all [his] sacrifices to Jupiter, but he makes offerings to other, lesser gods, too.

42 Friendship requires that a man repay in a general manner what he owes his friend, but there is a difference depending upon whether the friend is upright or [morally] deficient. And, most surely, it is proper to lean to the side of righteousness, for not everything is worthy of being loved, but only that which is good and upright. It is just, in accordance with friendship, to accuse him who deceives another, and [it is even] more just than accusing those who corrupt or counterfeit public currency, because it is not fitting for your friend to be someone who loves wickedness or who resembles bad men [in character]. He is a friend who is benevolent and beneficent because of his love of virtue, and, above all, according to [the dictates of] friendship, each is benevolent towards himself.

43 Two things preserve friendship—namely, delight in remembering the things which the friends have done and the good hope that they have regarding the things which they will do in the future. When men have committed themselves to friendship, sadness and delight will have the same effect on one and the other, because friends share their [good and bad] fortune. One should behave as openly with his friend as [he would] with himself, for two friends are a single thing. Only the actions of virtue such as friendship and justice are not accompanied at all by penitence or displeasure, but bad and vicious acts are full of repentance and regret. Therefore friendship is equity, for it is virtue in action. The evil man is not at all a friend to himself, because in him there is nothing worthy of friendship.

44 Benevolence is similar to friendship if they exist together, but, nonetheless, benevolence is not friendship. Benevolence is extended to men with whom one is acquainted only through hearsay, and so benevolence is concealed within one's will, but friendship is the opposite [because it is overt], as was said earlier.

45 Besides friendship, there is another manner of loving which is called *amacion*, which comes [into being] through the habit of seeing a person frequently or of thinking often about the graces that he possesses and of fixing there one's desire. Benevolence comes quickly and suddenly to a person's mind on account of seeing in another some pleasing good, such as skill at singing, writing, wrestling, dancing, combat, and other exceptional gifts. Benevolence is the beginning of friendship just as sight is the beginning of physical pleasure.

46 Men enter into friendship in order to benefit one another. And as for those things pertaining to the soul and to physical existence, there are three which engender friendship—namely, benevolence, agreement, and beneficence. Those who perform good deeds are called benefactors. Those to whom one is beneficent are called beneficiaries. Benefactors, then, love the beneficiaries more than beneficiaries do their benefactors. And it is [a sign of] greater friendship to give than to receive. Every craftsman loves his own handiwork more than his work loves him. Accordingly, human as well as animal parents love their children more than children do their parents. Poets love their own verses as much as parents love their children. Just as the father proves through the children whom he engendered that he had in himself the potential to do this, so the poet through the verses which he composed shows that there were in his soul the skill and potential to make such verses. The virtuous endeavor of the present moment is pleasant for friends, and hope, too, for the future is pleasurable, and so is the memory of a virtuous undertaking in the past. All men and animals, too, love more those things which are accomplished through a relatively great deal of effort, and for this reason mothers love their children more than fathers do. And this same thing which is present in mothers in respect to their children occurs with benefactors in respect to beneficiaries, for it requires a greater effort to do good than to receive a benefit. Consequently, there is greater friendship in the benefactor than in the beneficiary.

47 It is proper to love one's friend superlatively and more than any other thing whatsoever. From the true friend come all the benefits of friendship which are showered on the friends, and from them they reach others. The friend is a single soul with his comrade's, and the possessions and troubles of friends are shared. In friendship there should be equality between one and the other, and two friends are as close as are the knee and the leg. The man who is a dear friend to another is just like a city in respect to the citizens or like any other community of people, for the city defends the citizen and the citizen, the city. The people, too, preserve the law, and the law likewise preserves the people. When any friend of the commonweal does a good deed, he finds someone who helps him, and likewise he aids others.

48 Every friend who exercises good judgment chooses the good for himself, and every virtuous friend yields to judgment which is guided by reason.

49 Beneficence is characteristic of a good and virtuous man. And although it is better to be beneficent to one's friends than to others, even though they may be just as honorable, nevertheless, it is not fitting that one benefit friends alone, rather one should be useful to outsiders as well.

50 He is not a virtuous man who chooses to have for himself [alone] all the goods of nature and of fortune, for the possession of such goods is not joyful without companionship—that is, without a friend—because a man should be political—that is, willing to share and apt to live with companions—and in this lies his felicity. A fortunate man in this world needs to have friends so that he may aid them and be aided by them if his good fortune turns sour. A delightful and pleasant life [together] is sufficient for beginning friendship with someone, without there being any other pleasure beyond this.

51 If we wish, we are never disappointed in entering into friendship with others, for we can observe and get to know neighbors and those familiar with us better than ourselves. The deeds and words of virtuous friends are delightful to good friends who know one another well and hold each other in high esteem. The solitary man who lives entirely within himself leads a hard and dangerous life, for he can hardly be very useful to himself [in the event of urgent need]. And thus he lives in manifest peril, for if he leans towards or falls into vice or penury, he has no friend to lift him up or help him. A virtuous friend delights in his heart because of his partner's good deeds, and he grieves because of bad ones as well, for a good musician delights in sweet melodies, and he is afflicted and irritated by cacophony. The virtuous friend chooses naturally a virtuous comrade, and then the goodness of the one becomes better because of the other's goodness. The life of a friend is a natural good shared by the friends, and it is delightful to feel in oneself the good which is there. And thus life is a gift of nature that one should choose and desire, especially in good men. By this, accordingly, I conclude that in the same manner that one of the two friends desires naturally that he himself live, he desires likewise that his companion may live thus.

52 It is neither advisable nor good to enter into friendship with many different men, for it is burdensome to aid and provide for several friends if through ill fortune or some other circumstance they should fall from their [usual] standing. And perhaps your life and also your finances would not permit [you] to provide for them and raise them again.

53 If you have more friends than is fitting for your own private life, such friends, who are overabundant and too numerous, keep and hamper you from living well. And, furthermore, it is not possible to frequent and live with several friends inasmuch as many men have diverse and different manners [of comportment and tastes]. Therefore, it is not possible for a friend to divide and share himself out among several friends who, perchance, will want to be with him at the same moment, when they happen to be in different locations. And, moreover, it is difficult to be joyful and sing and to feel grief and weep in intimacy with several of one's friends. And for this reason it is likely that a man who has many friends will disappoint all of them together, no matter how hard he may try to accommodate himself to all of them.

54 Friendship demands a superabundant power of loving. This superabundance can exist solely in respect to a single friend or at most a very few. We have seen that it is not at all fitting for you to be a friend to several men. According to the law of friendship, poor, unfortunate men need friendship and support, and fortunate, wealthy men need friends so that they can live with them and benefit them. The presence of friends is delightful and pleasant just as much in adversity as in [times of] good fortune. Sad and troubled friends are greatly relieved when their comrades grieve and lament with them, for the presence of grieving and condolent friends is a mixture, and sorrow which is shared out among many seems lessened in each.

55 To see and hear one's friends in person is delightful, and thus it is of great aid to the unfortunate friend so that he will not be distressed because of his misfortune. He who is a friend gives comfort and consolation through his gaze and, also, through his speech, but let the friend be affable and kind, for he is acquainted with the sort of things by which his comrade is delighted or saddened. Every friend is careful not to be a cause of sadness or displeasure for his comrades. Therefore, if you have several friends, you should in all things follow the best one in virtue. You must summon needy friends promptly and quickly to share with you your goods and wealth, because the good friend should be a benefactor and aid during his needy friend's hard times, for it is the characteristic of a friend to be beneficent chiefly to those who are in need.

56 Of the four things which are sources of friendship, the principal one is living and residing together. The four sources of friendship are beneficence, benevolence, agreement, and living together. The friendship of bad men is evil, for their sharing is bad, and thus they have no [moral] strength in themselves, and bad men who come together make one another worse.

57 After you have heard [expressed] before you, most noble duke and excellent lord, the conclusions and principal judgments from the text by Aristotle, who as a Greek philosopher wrote in this manner to a greater extent and better than any man whose teachings the Latins read, I, with the aid of Our Lord Jesus Christ, the true friend of men in Whom are stored all the treasures of wisdom, wish to proceed to the translation of the book *On True Friendship*, which was composed and written by Tullius, a noble and excellent orator, for of all those whose books are known, Tullius spoke the best on true friendship in his function as orator, who while exhorting [his readers] to do a certain thing presents persuasive arguments at one moment and exempla at another. And since some who see this book translated into the French language will say, as I suppose, that the majesty and gravity of its words and judgments are much abased and trivialized by my common language, which because of its poverty of words is meager and deficient, and that, therefore, I ought not to have undertaken or completed this translation, to them I answer that in view of the command from such a great and excellent lord as yourself and whereas one should by all means open the path to understanding those books of which the teachings incline towards virtues and good conduct which lead men to the true port of salvation, I was authorized to translate this book licitly, without just blame, especially inasmuch as others in the same manner undertook the publication of the holy books of the Bible literally in the vulgar tongue, which is a very perilous thing for the ears of lay people, since they may value less the divine mysteries contained in the canonized books, for just as those who are begotten outside and against the ordinance of divine laws or who are otherwise marked by crimes or corrupt and bad character should neither serve nor have right of entry or dignity in God's church, likewise men without learning and those not instructed in the divine sciences should neither read nor hear on their own the sacred books in which the Spirit of God, through the mouths of holy men, revealed and disclosed the divine mysteries pertaining to Itself and the church, Its consecrated friend and wife.

58 Wishing, therefore, to proceed to my main work offered as a gift, I entreat and ask you to bear patiently my ignorance and insignificance in comparison with this book composed wisely and nobly written in the Latin language; to read it several times and ponder in our hearts the gravity of its judgments and the majesty of its words, for given the subtlety that the author employed in this book, it is very unlikely that slightly and moderately lettered or clever men could understand this or any other artfully written book immediately at a single reading or hearing; and to defend my cause as your very own against the envious who without just or probable grounds might attempt in malice to challenge this, your work, which I have woven and loomed to the best of my ability.

59 And since to your court and presence, as to those of other princely lords, hasten and flock, for urgent as well as honorable motives, many men of various estates and from foreign countries, of whom some read and understand the French language and others, Latin, I have placed at the beginning of your volume and after this prologue the text of all the book, [which is] very accurate and divided according to the form and manner which I employed in the book *On Old Age*. And, furthermore, [I have done this] so that one may know readily if the sense of the Latin corresponds to the French there which I derived from it.

60 Because of my apparent want and the legitimate desire that I have to put into this endeavor a good beginning, a better middle, and an excellent conclusion which can come from no other but Him Who, without having given less generously of them, possesses all His gifts of grace, I pray and ask of [Our] God Jesus Christ, friend of humankind, that through His superabundant friendship by which He loves all who wish to love Him, He enrich my soul with knowledge unadulterated by error and my mouth with words consonant with good conduct without derogating divine law and that He guide my pen diligently [so that it will] write without listless sloth.

Here is the second prologue by Laurent, translator of Tullius, author of the book *On True Friendship*, which he dedicates and addresses to his friend Atticus, a noble Roman citizen. And in this work Tullius, paramount in all Latin eloquence, proceeds by dialogue, just as he does in his book *On Old Age*.

61 Tullius' artful and concise expression in this book *On True Friendship* is conveyed in dialogue form. That is to say, in this work there are two [*sic*] men who speak—namely, Gaius Laelius, a noble and sage Roman in discussion with Gaius Fannius and Scaevola, noble and wise Roman elders who answer very subtly the said Laelius' questions with ethical reasoning and exempla. And this book shows quite clearly that earlier two Roman citizens—namely, Quintus Pompeius and Publius Sulpicius, nobles and very close friends who had long lived intimately together—after a period of time developed a mutual hatred and mortal dissension. For this reason there arose a very great outcry among the Romans then living to whom it did not seem right that in the hearts of noble and wise men there should occur such a contrary and sudden change as that from very great friendship to great and mortal hatred. Since, therefore, Atticus, a noble Roman and close friend of the said Tullius, observed that from very sure friendship between men often came discord and quarreling, he asked Tullius if one should at any rate desire friendship and if it were the case that one should seek friendship by all means. Atticus asked what the characteristics and nature of friendship are so that Tullius might consequently remove [all] doubt. [For these reasons] he wrote and composed this book or work on friendship. In it Tullius' intention and thought are solely to speak on and deal with true friendship by explaining its origin and preservation, that is to say, how friendship is engendered and maintained between men.

62 It is true that Aristotle, preeminent among the Peripatetic philosophers, who are the most renowned of all, discussed friendship in very
subtle arguments and concise conclusions in his book the *Ethics*. And
this sort of discourse is appropriate for a man concerned with logic, but
not for an orator, as is Tullius. Consequently, in this prologue I leave
aside all the arguments set forth by Aristotle save one which states that
friendship is perfected by and made up of three things—to wit,
benevolence, agreement, and beneficence. From these three things is taken
and derived the description of true friendship—that is to say, true
friendship is a wish for good things directed towards someone solely for
the sake of him who is loved, wherefore the lover and the beloved have a
similar desire for good things.

63 This book by Tullius speaks only about true friendship, and one
should not expect it to deal with feigned friendship, which, properly
speaking, is not friendship at all but a fiction, for pretended friends join
and attach themselves to other men for reason of gain and hope of profit.
They simulate a true thing which is false, and outwardly they feign friend
ships.

64 One finds three sorts of friendships. [The first] is natural and true and
is founded on the good of uprightness, of which Tullius speaks in his
book as an orator, for whom it is appropriate to deliberate prudently on
the things about which he speaks. Consequently, it is abundantly clear
that Tullius never intended for his work to supersede the conclusions
which Aristotle proved or argued persuasively in the ninth book of the
Ethics. The second [sort of] friendship is natural and not true, and this
friendship combines profit and pleasure. The third [sort of] friendship is
neither natural nor true, and it is founded solely on profit, such as that
among merchants and those who pursue the scent of worldly gain, that is
to say, lucre.

65 Therefore, the subject-matter of the present book to which Tullius
mainly directs his attention consists of the commandments of true friendship which are recorded in this work. The form of the book is a discourse
cast as a dialogue wherein Laelius engages in discussion with Gaius Fannius and Scaevola, a Roman augur, for according to the distinctions of offices or rank, Scaevola as augur had the chief voice among the Romans.
But the efficient cause of this book was Tullius, surnamed Cicero, who
descended from the lineage of the very ancient chieftains of the Volscians,
also called the Tuscans. Tullius was a very important Latin author on elo-

quence, and in his time he was a very good citizen and consul of the city of Rome.

66 The final cause for which this book was written is twofold, for one [part] is private and the other is public. The private reason for writing this book was that Tullius wished to satisfy and comply with the honorable petition and request of Atticus, a wise and kind man most learned in ethical, natural, and, also, dialectic philosophy. But the public end for which this work was written is so that in composing this volume at the behest of one man—namely, Atticus—Tullius might profit not merely one but many. This book is subject to moral philosophy, which is called ethics, and at its beginning should be written this heading: "Here begins the proem to the book *On True Friendship* composed by Tullius, surnamed Cicero, and this proem extends as far as the paragraph [beginning] 'Gaius Fannius,' at which paragraph Tullius' proposition begins and is continued as far as the paragraph [beginning] 'Sed quoniam amici[tia]e,' at which paragraph Tullius begins the subject-matter which is developed through reasoning and exempla up to the end of the book."

SELECT BIBLIOGRAPHY

Chapter One
Editions and translations

Apuleius. *De Platone et eius dogmate*. In *Apulei Platonici Madaurensis opera quae supersint, III, de philosophia libri*. Edited by P. Thomas. Bibliotheca Teubneriana. Rev. ed. Stuttgart: Teubner, 1970.

Aristotle. *The Nichomachean Ethics*. Translated by H. Rackham. Loeb. Rev. ed. 1934. Reprint ed., Cambridge, Mass., and London: Harvard University Press and William Heinemann, 1947. All the Loeb Classics editions listed here give facing Greek-English or Latin-English texts.

———. *On Sophistical Refutations, On Coming-to-be and Passing-away..., On the Cosmos*. Translated by E. S. Forster and D. J. Furley. Loeb. Cambridge and London: Harvard University Press and W. Heinemann, 1955. *On Coming-to-be and Passing-away* is *On Generation and Corruption*.

———. *The Works of Aristotle Translated into English*. Vol. 9: *Ethica nicomachea..., Magna moralia..., Ethica eudemia, De virtutibus et vitiis*. Translated by W. D. Ross, St. George Stock, and J. Solomon. Oxford: Clarendon Press, 1925.

Les *"Auctoritates Aristotelis," un florilège médiéval. Etude historique et édition critique*. Edited by Jacqueline Hamesse. Philosophes Médiévaux, 17. Louvain: Publications Universitaires, 1974.

Aulus Gellius. *The Attic Nights of Aulus Gellius*. Translated by John C. Rolfe. Loeb. 3 vols. New York and London: G. P. Putnam's Sons and W. Heinemann, 1927-1928.

Cicero. *De officiis*. Translated by Walter Miller. Loeb. 1913. Reprint ed., New York and London: G. P. Putnam's Sons and W. Heinemann, 1928.

———. *Laelius de amicitia*. In *De senectute, De amicitia, De divinatione*. Translated by William Armistead Falconer. Loeb. 1923. Reprint ed., Cambridge and London: Harvard University Press and W. Heinemann, 1946.

———. *Letters to Atticus*. Translated by E. O. Winstedt. Loeb. 3 vols. 1912-1918. Reprint ed., Cambridge, New York, and London: Harvard University Press, G. P. Putnam's Sons, and W. Heinemann, 1928-1945.

Cornelius Nepos. *The Book of Cornelius Nepos on the Great Generals of Foreign Nations*. In *Lucius Annaeus Florus, Epitome of Roman History. Cornelius Nepos*. Translated by E. S. Forster. Loeb. Cambridge and London: Harvard University Press and W. Heinemann, 1929.

Diogenes Laertius. *Lives of Eminent Philosophers*. Translated by R. D. Hicks. Loeb. 2 vols. New York and London: G. P. Putnam's Sons and W. Heinemann, 1925.

Epictetus. *The Discourses as Reported by Arrian, The Manual, and Fragments*.

Translated by W. A. Oldfather. Loeb. 2 vols. Cambridge and London: Harvard University Press and W. Heinemann, 1925-1926. See following entry.

Epicurus. *Principal Doctrines. Vatican Sayings.* In *The Stoic and Epicurean Philosophers. The Complete Extant Writings of Epicurus, Epictetus, Lucretius, Marcus Aurelius.* Edited by J. Oates [and translated by Cyril Bailey et al.] New York: Random House, 1940.

Fragmenta philosophorum graecorum. Vol. 2: *Pythagoreos, sophistas, cynicos et Chalcidii in priorem Timaei platonici partem commentarios continens.* Edited and translated by G.-A. Mullachius. Scriptorum Graecorum Bibliotheca, 120. Paris: A. Firmin-Didot, 1867. Facing Greek-Latin texts.

Plato. *Plato with an English Translation.* Vol. 5: *Lysis, Symposium, Gorgias.* Translated by W. R. M. Lamb. Loeb. 1925. Reprint ed., Cambridge and London: Harvard University Press and W. Heinemann, 1961.

Pliny the Younger. *Letters.* Translated by William Melmoth and revised by W. M. L. Hutchinson. Loeb. 2 vols. 1915. Reprint ed., Cambridge and London: Harvard University Press and W. Heinemann, 1935-1961.

Plutarch. *The Life of Cicero.* Translated by J. L. Moles. Warminster, Eng.: Aris and Phillips, 1988. Facing Greek-English texts.

Seneca. *Ad Lucilium epistulae morales.* Translated by Richard M. Gummere. Loeb. 3 vols. New York and London: G. P. Putnam's Sons and W. Heinemann, 1918-1925.

———. *De beneficiis.* Translated by John W. Basore. In *Seneca in Ten Volumes, III, Moral Essays.* Loeb. 1935. Reprint ed., Cambridge and London: Harvard University Press and W. Heinemann, 1975.

Valerius Maximus. *Actions et paroles mémorables.* Translated by Pierre Constant. Classiques Garnier. 2 vols. Paris: Garnier Frères, [1935]. Facing Latin-French texts.

———. *Valerii Maximi factorum et dictorum memorabilium libri novem, cum Julii Paridis et Januarii Nepotiani epitomis.* Edited by C. Kempf. Bibliotheca Teubneriana. 1888. Reprint ed., Stuttgart: B. G. Teubner, 1966.

Walter of Burley. *"Gualteri Burlaei liber de vita et moribus philosophorum" mit einer altspanischen Übersetzung der Eskurialbibliothek.* Edited by Hermann Kunst. Bibliothek des Litterarischen Vereins in Stuttgart, 177. Tübingen: H. Laupp, 1886.

Xenophon. *Memorabilia and Œconomicus.* Translated by E. C. Marchant. Loeb. Cambridge and London: Harvard University Press and W. Heinemann, 1938.

Zeno of Citium and Cleanthes. *The Fragments of Zeno and Cleanthes, with Introduction and Explanatory Notes.* Translated by A. C. Pearson. London: C. J. Clay and Sons, 1891. Greek and English texts.

Studies

Baron, Hans. "Cicero and the Roman Civic Spirit in the Middle Ages and the Early Renaissance." *Bulletin of the John Rylands Library* 22 (1938): 72-97.

Bloomer, W. Martin. *Valerius Maximus and the Rhetoric of the New Nobility.* London and Chapel Hill: The University of North Carolina Press, 1992.

Bollack, Jean. "Les maximes de l'amitié." In *La pensée du plaisir. Epicure: Textes moraux, commentaires.* Le Sens Commun. Paris: Les Editions de Minuit, 1975. Pp. 565-82.

Bolotin, David. *Plato's Dialogue on Friendship. An Interpretation of the "Lysis," With a New Translation.* Ithaca and London: Cornell University Press, 1979.

Bourke, Vernon J. "The *Nicomachean Ethics* and Thomas Aquinas." In *St. Thomas Aquinas, 1274-1974, Commemorative Studies.* Toronto: Pontifical Institute of Mediaeval Studies, 1974. Vol. 1, pp. 239-59.

Braxator, R. F. *Quid in conscribendo Ciceronis Laelio valuerint Aristotelis ethicon nicomachorum de amicitia libri.* Diss. Halle, 1871.

Brown, Peter, Evelyne Patlagean, Michel Rouche, Yvon Thébert, and Paul Veyne. *Histoire de la vie privée, tome 1, De l'Empire romain à l'an mille.* L'Univers Historique. Paris: Seuil, 1985.

Brun, Jean. *Le stoïcisme.* 8th ed. Paris: Presses Universitaires de France, 1980.

Brunt, P. A. "*Amicitia* in the Late Roman Republic." *Proceedings of the Cambridge Philological Society* 11 (1965): 1-20.

Cooper, John M. "Aristotle on the Forms of Friendship." *The Review of Metaphysics* 30 (1977): 619-48.

———. "Friendship and the Good in Aristotle." *The Philosophical Review* 86 (1977): 290-315.

Dugas, L. *L'amitié antique d'après les moeurs et les théories des philosophes.* Paris: Félix Alcan, 1894.

Earl, Donald. *The Moral and Political Tradition of Rome.* Ithaca: Cornell University Press, 1967.

Farrington, Benjamin. *The Faith of Epicurus.* New York: Basic Books, 1967.

Fraisse, Jean-Claude. *Philia. La notion d'amitié dans la philosophie antique.* Paris: J. Vrin, 1974.

Glidden, David K. "The *Lysis* on Loving One's Own." *Classical Quarterly,* n. s., 31 (1981): 39-59.

Gold, Barbara K. *Literary Patronage in Greece and Rome.* Chapel Hill: University of North Carolina Press, 1987.

Hellegouarc'h, J. *Le vocabulaire latin des relations et des partis politiques sous la République.* Collection d'Etudes Anciennes. 2nd ed. Paris: Les Belles Lettres, 1972.

Heyblutt, Gustav. *De Theophrasti libris peri philias.* Diss. Bonn, 1976.

Hicks, R. D. *Stoic and Epicurean.* 1910. Reprint ed., New York: Russell and

Russell, 1961.

Hutter, Horst. *Politics as Friendship. The Origins of Classical Notions of Politics in the Theory and Practice of Friendship.* Waterloo, Ontario: Wilfred Laurier University Press, 1978.

Inwood, Brad. *Ethics and Human Action in Early Stoicism.* Oxford: Clarendon Press, 1985.

Kidd, I. G. "Moral Actions and Rules in Stoic Ethics." In *The Stoics.* Edited by John M. Rist. Major Thinkers Series, 1. Berkeley: University of California Press, 1978. Pp. 247-58.

Kilpatrick, Ross S. *The Poetry of Friendship. Horace, Epistles I.* Edmonton: University of Alberta Press, 1986.

McEvoy, James. "*Philia* and *Amicitia*: The Philosophy of Friendship from Plato to Aquinas." *Sewanee Mediaeval Colloquium Occasional Papers* 2 (1985): 1-23.

Minar, Edwin L., Jr. "Pythagorean Communism." *Transactions and Proceedings of the American Philological Association* 75 (1944): 34-46.

Minio-Paluello, L. "Henri Aristippe, Guillaume de Moerbeke et les traductions latines médiévales des *Météorologiques* et du *De generatione et corruptione* d'Aristote." *Revue philosophique de Louvain* 45, nos. 6-7 (May-Aug. 1947): 206-35.

Muckle, J. T. "Greek Works Translated Directly into Latin Before 1350." *Mediaeval Studies* 4 (1942): 33-42, and 5 (1943): 102-14.

Pelzer, Auguste. "Les versions latines des ouvrages de morale conservés sous le nom d'Aristote en usage au XIIIᵉ siècle." *Revue néo-scolastique de philosophie* 23 (1921): 316-41 and 378-412.

Price, A. W. *Love and Friendship in Plato and Aristotle.* New York: Oxford University Press, 1989.

Reynolds, L. D., editor. *Texts and Transmission. A Survey of the Latin Classics.* Oxford: Clarendon, 1983.

——, and N. G. Wilson. *Scribes and Scholars. A Guide to the Transmission of Greek and Latin Literature.* 2nd ed. Oxford: Clarendon, 1974.

Rose, Valentinus. "Die Lücke im Diogenes Laertius und der alten Übersetzung." *Hermes* 1 (1886): 367-97.

Sansen, Raymond. *Doctrine de l'amitié chez Cicéron. Exposé—Source—Critique—Influence.* Diss. Paris IV, 1972.

Singer, Irving. *The Nature of Love.* Vol. 1: *Plato to Luther.* 2nd ed. Chicago: University of Chicago Press, 1984.

Steinmetz, Fritz-Arthur. *Die Freundschaftslehre des Panaitios nach einer Analyse von Ciceros "Laelius de amicitia."* Palingenesia, 3. Wiesbaden: Franz Steiner, 1967.

Sullivan, Francis A. "Cicero and *Gloria*." *Transactions and Proceedings of the American Philological Association* 72 (1941): 382-91.

Tracy, Theodore, "Perfect Friendship in Aristotle's *Nicomachean Ethics*." *Illinois Classical Studies* 4 (1979): 65-75.

Voelke, André-Jean. *Les rapports avec autrui dans la philosophie grecque d'Aristote à Panétius*. Bibliothèque d'Histoire de la Philosophie. Paris: J. Vrin, 1961.

White, Peter. "*Amicitia* and the Profession of Poetry in Early Imperial Rome." *Journal of Roman Studies* 68 (1978): 74-92.

Wiseman, T. P. "*Pete nobiles amicos*: Poets and Patrons in Late Republican Rome." In *Literary and Artistic Patronage in Ancient Rome*. Edited by Barbara K. Gold. Austin: University of Texas Press, 1982. Pp. 28-49.

Chapter Two

Editions and translations

Abelard, Peter, and Heloise. *The Letters of Abelard and Heloise*. Translated by Betty Radice. Harmondsworth, Eng.: Penguin, 1974.

Aelred of Rievaulx, St. *De spirituali amicitia*. In *Ælredi Rievallensis opera omnia, I, opera ascetica*. Edited by A. Hoste and C. H. Talbot. Corpus Christianorum, Continuatio Mediaevalis, 1. Turnhout, Belgium: Brepols, 1971. Pp. 281-350.

——. *The Mirror of Charity*. Translated by Elizabeth Connor and introduced by Charles Dumont. Cistercian Fathers Series, 17. Kalamazoo, Michigan: Cistercian Publications, 1990.

——. *Spiritual Friendship*. Translated by Mary E. Laker and introduced by Douglas Roby. Cistercian Fathers Series, 5. Kalamazoo: Cistercian Publications, 1977.

Ambrose, St. *Duties of the Clergy*. In *St. Ambrose, Select Works and Letters*. Translated by H. De Romestin. Vol. 10 of *A Select Library of Nicene and Post-Nicene Fathers of the Christian Church, Second Series*. Grand Rapids, Michigan: W. B. Eerdmans, 1955. Pp. 1-89.

Augustine, St. *Agostino di Ippona. L'amicizia cristiana. Antologia dalle opere e altri testi di Ambrogio di Milano, Gerolamo e Paolino di Nola*. Edited by L. F. Pizzolato. Civiltà Letteraria di Grecia e di Roma, Autori, Series Latina, 31. Turin: Paravia, 1973.

——. *The Confessions of St. Augustine*. Translated by J. G. Pilkington. New York: Liveright, 1943.

——. *The Rule of Saint Augustine. Masculine and Feminine Versions*. Translated by Raymond Canning. London: Darton, Longman, and Todd, 1984.

Bernard of Clairvaux, St. *The Letters of St. Bernard of Clairvaux*. Translated by Bruno Scott James. Chicago: Henry Regnery, 1953.

——. *Treatises II: The Steps of Humility and Pride. On Loving God*. Translated by M. Ambrose Conway. Cistercian Fathers Series, 13. Kalamazoo: Cistercian Publications, 1973.

——. *Treatises III: On Grace and Free Choice. In Praise of the New Knighthood*. Translated by Conrad Greenia. Cistercian Fathers Series, 19. Kalamazoo: Cistercian Publications, 1977.

Cassian, St. John. *The Conferences*. Translated by Edgar C. S. Gibson. In *Sul-

pitius Severus, Vincent of Lerins, John Cassian. Vol. 11 of *A Select Library of Nicene and Post-Nicene Fathers of the Christian Church, Second Series.* New York: The Christian Literature Company, 1894. Pp. 291-545. Conference 16 is on pp. 450-60.

Daniel, Walter. *The Life of Ailred of Rievaulx.* Edited and translated by F. M. Powicke. London: Thomas Nelson and Sons, 1950. Facing Latin-English texts.

Dante Alighieri. *The Divine Comedy of Dante Alighieri.* Translated by Allen Mandelbaum. Vol. 1: *Inferno.* Vol. 2: *Purgatorio.* Vol. 3: *Paradiso.* Toronto: Bantam, 1982-1986. Facing Italian-English texts.

Francis of Assisi, St. *Writings and Early Biographies. English Omnibus of the Sources for the Life of St. Francis.* Edited by Marion A. Habig and translated by Raphael Brown, Benen Fahy, et al. Chicago: Franciscan Herald Press, 1973.

——, and St. Clare. *Francis and Clare. The Complete Works.* Translated by Regis J. Armstrong and Ignatius C. Brady. The Classics of Western Spirituality. New York: Paulist Press, 1982.

The Life of Christina of Markyate, A Twelfth Century Recluse. Edited and translated by C. H. Talbot. Oxford: Clarendon Press, 1959. Facing Latin-English texts.

The Little Flowers of St. Francis. First Complete Edition. An Entirely New Version with Twenty Additional Chapters. Also, The Consideration on the Holy Stigmata, The Life of Brother Juniper. Translated by Raphael Brown. Garden City, N. Y.: Image Books, 1958.

Peter of Blois. *Un traité de l'amour du XIIᵉ siècle: Pierre de Blois.* Edited by M. M. Davy. Paris: E. de Boccard, 1932.

The Quest of the Holy Grail. Translated by P. M. Matarasso. Harmondsworth, Eng.: Penguin, 1969.

La queste del Saint Graal, roman du XIIIᵉ siècle. Edited by Albert Pauphilet. Classiques Français du Moyen Age, 33. Paris: Champion, 1923.

Thomas Aquinas, St. *Basic Writings of Saint Thomas Aquinas.* Edited by Anton C. Pegis. 2 vols. New York: Random House, 1945.

——. *On Charity (De caritate).* Translated by Lottie H. Kendzierski. Mediaeval Philosophical Texts in Translation, 10. Milwaukee: Marquette University Press, 1960.

Studies

Benson, Robert L., Giles Constable, and Carol D. Lanham, eds. *Renaissance and Renewal in the Twelfth Century.* Cambridge: Harvard University Press, 1982.

Benton, John F. "The Correspondence of Abelard and Heloise." In *Culture, Power and Personality in Medieval France.* Edited by Thomas N. Bisson. London: Hambleton Press, 1991. Pp. 487-512.

——. "A Reconsideration of the Authenticity of the Correspondence of Abelard and Heloise." In *Petrus Abaelardus (1079-1142): Person, Werk und Wirkung.* Edited by Rudolf Thomas. Trierer Theologische Studien, 38. Trier: Paulinus Verlag, 1980. Pp. 41-52.

Bouton, Jean de la Croix. "La doctrine de l'amitié chez saint Bernard." *Revue d'ascétique et de mystique* 29 (1953): 3-19.

Brooke, Christopher N. L. *The Medieval Idea of Marriage.* New York: Oxford University Press, 1989.

Brooke, Rosalind B., and Christopher N. L. Brooke. "St Clare." In *Medieval Women.* Edited by Derek Baker. Studies in Church History, Subsidia 1. Oxford: Basil Blackwell, 1978. Pp. 275-87.

Brown, Peter. *The Making of Late Antiquity.* Cambridge: Harvard University Press, 1978.

Delhaye, Philippe. "Deux adaptations du *De amicitia* de Cicéron au XIIᵉ siècle." *Recherches de théologie ancienne et médiévale* 15 (1948): 304-31.

[Diederich], Mary Dorothea. "Cicero and Saint Ambrose on Friendship." *The Classical Journal* 43 (1948): 219-22.

Dronke, Peter. *Women Writers of the Middle Ages. A Critical Study of Texts from Perpetua († 203) to Marguerite Porete († 1310).* Cambridge: Cambridge University Press, 1984.

Fiske, Adele M. *Friends and Friendship in the Monastic Tradition.* CIDOC Cuaderno 51. Cuernavaca, Mexico: Centro Intercultural de Documentación, 1970.

Fleming, John V. *An Introduction to the Franciscan Literature of the Middle Ages.* Chicago: Franciscan Herald Press, 1977.

Gilson, Etienne. *The Mystical Theology of Saint Bernard.* Translated by A. H. C. Downes. New York: Sheed and Ward, 1940.

Hagendahl, Harald. *Augustine and the Latin Classics.* Studia Graeca et Latina Gothoburgensia, 20, nos. 1 and 2. 2 vols. Göteborg, Sweden: Elanders Boktryckeri Aktiebolag, 1967.

Holdsworth, Christopher J. "Christina of Markyate." In *Medieval Women.* Edited by Derek Baker. Studies in Church History, Subsidia 1. Oxford: Basil Blackwell, 1978. Pp. 185-204.

Hoste, Anselme. "Le traité pseudo-augustinien *De amicitia.* Un résumé d'un ouvrage authentique d'Aelred de Rievaulx." *Revue des études augustiniennes* 6 (1960): 155-60.

Leclercq, Jean. "L'amitié dans les lettres au Moyen Age." *Revue du Moyen Age latin* 1 (1945): 391-410.

——. *Monks and Love in Twelfth-Century France. Psycho-Historical Essays.* Oxford: Clarendon Press, 1979.

Matarasso, Pauline. *The Redemption of Chivalry. A Study of the "Queste del Saint Graal."* Histoire des Idées et Critique Littéraire, 180. Geneva: Droz, 1979.

McGuire, Brian Patrick. *Friendship and Community: The Monastic Experience 350-1250.* Cistercian Studies Series, 95. Kalamazoo: Cistercian Publications, 1988.

McNamara, Jo Ann. "Chaste Marriage and Clerical Celibacy." In *Sexual Practices and the Medieval Church.* Edited by Vern L. Bullough and James Brundage. Buffalo, N. Y.: Prometheus Books, 1982. Pp. 22-33.

McNamara, Marie Aquinas. *Friendship in Saint Augustine.* Studia Friburgensia, New Series, 20. Fribourg, Switzerland: The University Press, 1958.

Meilaender, Gilbert. *Friendship. A Study in Theological Ethics.* Notre Dame: The University of Notre Dame Press, 1981.

Morris, Colin. *The Discovery of the Individual 1050-1200.* New York: Harper and Row, 1972.

O'Sharkey, Eithne. "Punishments and Rewards of the Questing Knights in *La queste del Saint Graal.*" In *Rewards and Punishments in the Arthurian Romances and Lyric Poetry of Mediaeval France. Essays Presented to Kenneth Varty on the Occasion of His Sixtieth Birthday.* Edited by Peter V. Davies and Angus J. Kennedy. Arthurian Studies, 17. Cambridge, Eng.: D. S. Brewer, 1987. Pp. 101-17.

Pétré, Hélène. *Caritas. Etude sur le vocabulaire latin de la charité chrétienne.* Spicilegium Sacrum Lovaniense, Etudes et Documents, fasc. 22. Louvain: Spicilegium Sacrum Lovaniense, 1948.

Testard, Maurice. *Saint Augustin et Cicéron.* 2 vols. Paris: Etudes Augustiniennes, 1958.

Vansteenberghe, [E.] "Amitié." In *Dictionnaire de spiritualité ascétique et mystique. Doctrine et histoire.* Edited by Marcel Viller, F. Cavallera, and J. de Guibert. Paris: Gabriel Beauchesne et Ses Fils, 1937. Vol. 1, cols. 500-29.

———. "Deux théoriciens de l'amitié au XIIe siècle: Pierre de Blois et Aelred de Riéval." *Revue des sciences religieuses* 12 (1932): 572-88.

Wadell, Paul J. *Friendship and the Moral Life.* Notre Dame: The University of Notre Dame Press, 1989.

Ward, Benedicta. *Miracles and the Medieval Mind. Theory, Record and Event, 1000 to 1215.* Middle Ages Series. Philadelphia: University of Pennsylvania Press, 1982.

Chapter Three

Editions and translations

Ami and Amile, Translated from the Old French. Translated by Samuel Danon and Samuel N. Rosenberg. York, South Carolina: French Literature Publications Company, 1981.

Ami et Amile, chanson de geste. Edited by Peter F. Dembowski. Classiques Français du Moyen Age, 97. Paris: Honoré Champion, 1969.

Andreas Capellanus. *On Love.* Edited and translated by P. G. Walsh. London: Duckworth, 1982. Latin text and translation.

"Anglonormannische Texte im MS. Arundel 220 des Britischen Museums."

Edited by John Koch. *Zeitschrift für romanische Philologie* 54 (1934): 20-56.

Eilhart von Oberge. *Tristrant*. Translated by J. W. Thomas. Lincoln, Nebraska: University of Nebraska Press, 1978.

Gottfried von Strassburg. *"Tristan," Translated Entire for the First Time, With the Surviving Fragments of the "Tristran" of Thomas*. Translated by A. T. Hatto. Harmondsworth, Eng.: Penguin, 1960.

Guillaume de Lorris and Jean de Meun. *Le roman de la rose*. Edited by Ernest Langlois. Société des Anciens Textes Français. 5 vols. Paris: Firmin Didot and Librairie Ancienne Honoré Champion, 1914-1924.

Lancelot, roman en prose du XIIIe siècle. Edited by Alexandre Micha. Textes Littéraires Français, 247, 249, 262, 278, 283, 286, 288, 307, and 315. 9 vols. Paris and Geneva: Droz, 1978-1983.

Robert, Friar. *The Saga of Tristram and Isönd*. Translated by Paul Schach. Lincoln: University of Nebraska Press, 1973.

Le roman de Tristan en prose. Edited by Renée L. Curtis. Arthurian Studies, 12, 13, and 14. 3 vols. Cambridge, Eng.: D. S. Brewer, 1985.

Le roman de Tristan en prose, tome I. Edited by Philippe Ménard. Textes Littéraires Français, 353. Geneva: Droz, 1987.

Thomas. *Les fragments du "Roman de Tristan," poème de XIIe siècle*. Edited by Bartina H. Wind. Textes Littéraires Français, 92. Geneva: Droz, 1960.

Studies

Allen, Peter L. *The Art of Love. Amatory Fiction from Ovid to the "Romance of the Rose."* Middle Ages Series. Philadelphia: University of Pennsylvania Press, 1992.

Baumgartner, Emmanuèle. "Le personnage de *Kahedin* dans le *Tristan en prose*." In *Mélanges de langue et de littérature du Moyen Age et de la Renaissance offerts à Jean Frappier*. Publications Romanes et Françaises, 112. 2 vols. Geneva: Droz, 1970. Vol. 1, pp. 77-82.

Blakeslee, Merritt R. "The Authorship of Thomas's *Tristan*." *Philological Quarterly* 64 (1985): 555-72.

Bouchard, Constance B. "The Possible Nonexistence of Thomas, Author of *Tristan and Isolde*." *Modern Philology* 79 (1981): 66-72.

Brody, Saul Nathaniel. *The Disease of the Soul. Leprosy in Medieval Literature*. Ithaca and London: Cornell University Press, 1974.

Bruce, James Douglas. *The Evolution of Arthurian Romance From the Beginnings Down to the Year 1300*. 2nd ed. 2 vols. Baltimore: The Johns Hopkins University Press, 1928.

Burrell, Margaret. "The Participation of Chrétien's Heroines in Love's Covant." *Nottingham French Studies* 30, no. 2 (1991): 24-33.

Calin, William. *The Epic Quest: Studies in Four Old French Chansons de geste*. Baltimore: The Johns Hopkins University Press, 1966.

Chênerie, Marie-Luce. "L'aventure du chevalier enferré, ses suites et le thème des géants dans le *Lancelot*." In *Approches du "Lancelot en prose." Etudes recueillies par Jean Dufournet*. Collection Unichamps, 6. Paris: Honoré Champion, 1984. Pp. 59-100.

Cropp, Glynnis M. *Le vocabulaire courtois des troubadours de l'époque classique*. Publications Romanes et Françaises, 135. Geneva: Droz, 1975.

De Combarieu du Gres, Micheline. *L'idéal humain et l'expérience morale chez les héros des chansons de geste, des origines à 1250*. Etudes Littéraires, 3. 2 vols. Aix-en-Provence: Publications de l'Université de Provence, 1979.

Denomy, A. J. "An Inquiry into the Origins of Courtly Love." *Mediaeval Studies* 6 (1944): 175-260.

Frappier, Jean. "La 'Mort Galehaut.'" In *Histoire, mythes et symboles*. Publications Romanes et Françaises, 137. Geneva: Droz, 1976. Pp. 137-47.

———. "Le personnage de Galehaut dans le *Lancelot en prose*." In *Amour courtois et table ronde*. Publications Romanes et Françaises, 126. Geneva: Droz, 1973. Pp. 181-208.

Hume, Kathryn. "Structure and Perspective: Romance and Hagiographic Features in the Amicus and Amelius Story." *Journal of English and Germanic Philology* 69 (1970): 89-107.

Grimbert, Joan Tasker. "Love, Honor, and Alienation in Thomas's *Roman de Tristan*." *The Arthurian Yearbook* 2 (1992): 77-98.

Hunt, Tony. "The Significance of Thomas's *Tristan*." *Reading Medieval Studies* 7 (1981): 41-61.

Jones, George Fenwick. "Friendship in the *Chanson de Roland*." *Modern Language Quarterly* 24 (1963): 88-98.

Kay, Sarah. "Seduction and Suppression in *Ami et Amile*." *French Studies* 44 (1990): 129-42.

Kelly, Douglas. "*En uni dire* (*Tristan* Douce 839) and the Composition of Thomas's *Tristan*." *Modern Philology* 67 (1969-1970): 9-17.

Kennedy, Elspeth. *Lancelot and the Grail: A Study of the Prose "Lancelot."* Oxford: Clarendon Press, 1986.

Legros, Huguette. "*Ami et Amile*: Compagnonnage épique et/ou amitié spirituelle." *Bien dire et bien aprandre* 6 (1988): 113-29.

———. "Le vocabulaire de l'amitié, son évolution sémantique au cours du XIIe siècle." *Cahiers de civilisation médiévale* 23 (1980): 131-39.

Lot, Ferdinand. *Etude sur le "Lancelot en prose."* Bibliothèque de l'Ecole des Hautes Etudes, Sciences Historiques et Philologiques, fasc. 226. Rev. ed. Paris: Librairie Ancienne Honoré Champion, 1954.

Makida, Geneviève. "La religion dans *Ami et Amile*." In *"Ami et Amile," une chanson de geste de l'amitié. Etudes recueillies par Jean Dufournet*. Collection Unichamp, 16. Paris: Honoré Champion, 1987. Pp. 39-50.

Marchello-Nizia, Christiane. "Amour courtois, société masculine et figures du pouvoir." *Annales. Economies—Sociétés—Civilisations* 36 (1981): 969-82.

Markale, Jean. *Lancelot et la chevalerie arthurienne*. Paris: Imago, 1985.

Mathew, Gervase. "Ideals of Friendship." In *Patterns of Love and Courtesy. Essays in Memory of C. S. Lewis*. Edited by John Lawlor. London: Edward Arnold, 1966. Pp. 45-53.

Micha, Alexandre. *Essais sur le cycle du Lancelot-Graal*. Publications Romanes et Françaises, 179. Geneva: Droz, 1987.

Mickel, Emanuel. "The Question of Guilt in *Ami et Amile*." *Romania* 106 (1985): 19-35.

Pauphilet, Albert. Review of *Etude sur le "Lancelot en prose,"* by F. Lot. *Romania* 45 (1918-1919): 514-34.

Payen, Jean-Charles. "Le *Tristan en prose*, manuel de l'amitié: Le cas Dinadan." In *Der altfranzösische Prosaroman. Funktion, Funktionswandel und Ideologie am Beispiel des "Roman de Tristan en prose."* Edited by Ernstpeter Ruhe and Richard Schwaderer. Beiträge zur Romanischen Philologie des Mittelalters, 12. Munich: Wilhelm Fink, 1979. Pp. 104-21.

Reiss, Louise Horner. "Tristan and Isolt and the Medieval Ideal of Friendship." *Romance Quarterly* 33 (1986): 131-37.

Robreau, Yvonne. *L'honneur et la honte. Leur expression dans les romans en prose du Lancelot-Graal (XIIe-XIIIe siècles)*. Publications Romanes et Françaises, 157. Geneva: Droz, 1981.

Roubaud, Jacques. *La fleur inverse. Essai sur l'art formel des troubadours*. Paris: Ramsay, 1986.

Suard, François. "Le merveilleux et le religieux dans *Ami et Amile*." In *De l'étranger à l'étrange ou la 'conjointure' de la merveille (en hommage à Marguerite Rossi et Paul Bancourt)*. Senefiance, 25. Aix-en-Provence: Publications du Centre Universitaire d'Etudes et de Recherches Médiévales d'Aix, 1988. Pp. 449-62.

Subrenat, Jean. "Les tenants et aboutissants du duel judiciaire dans *Ami et Amile*." *Bien dire et bien aprandre* 6 (1988): 41-56.

Sweetser, Franklin P. "L'amour, l'amitié et la jalousie dans le *Lancelot en prose*." *Travaux de littérature* 2 (1989): 23-29.

Vesce, Thomas E. "Reflections on the Epic Quality of *Ami et Amile: Chanson de geste*." *Mediaeval Studies* 35 (1973): 129-45.

Wack, Mary Frances. *Lovesickness in the Middle Ages: The "Viaticum" and Its Commentaries*. Middle Ages Series. Philadelphia: University of Pennsylvania Press, 1990.

Zink, Michel. "Lubias et Belissant dans la chanson d'*Ami et Amile*." *Littératures* 17 (1987): 11-24.

Chapter Four
Editions and translations

Alberti, Leon Battista. *The Albertis of Florence: Leon Battista Alberti's "Della famiglia."* Translated by Guido A. Guarino. Bucknell Renaissance Texts in Translation. Lewisburg, Pennsylvania: Bucknell University Press, 1971.

————. *Leonis Baptistae Alberti opera inedita et pauca.* Edited by Hieronymus Mancini. Raccolta di Opere Inedite o Rare di Ogni Secolo della Letteratura Italiana. Florence: J. C. Sansoni, 1890.

————. *Opere volgari.* Vol 1: *I libri della famiglia. Cena familiaris. Villa.* Edited by Cecil Grayson. Scrittori d'Italia, 218. Bari: G. Laterza e Figli, 1960.

Boccaccio, Giovanni. *The Decameron.* Translated by G. H. McWilliam. Baltimore: Penguin, 1972.

————. *Tutte le opere di Giovanni Boccaccio.* Vol. 4: *Decameron.* Edited by Vittore Branca. I Classici Mondadori. Milan: A. Mondadori, 1976.

Cicero. *De oratore. De fato. Paradoxa stoicorum. De partitione oratoria.* Translated by E. W. Sutton and H. Rackham. Loeb. 2 vols. 1942. Reprint ed., Cambridge and London: Harvard University Press and W. Heinemann, 1967.

Studies

Baratto, Mario. *Realtà e stile nel "Decameron."* Vicenza: Neri Pozza, 1970.

Barthélemy, Dominique, Philippe Braunstein, Philippe Contamine, Georges Duby, Charles de La Roncière, and Danielle Régnier-Bohler. *Histoire de la vie privée, tome 2, De l'Europe féodale à la Renaissance.* L'Univers Historique. Paris: Seuil, 1985.

Battaglia, Salvatore. *La coscienza letteraria del medioevo.* Collana di Testi e di Critica, 2. Naples: Liguori, 1965.

Bergin, Thomas G. *Boccaccio.* New York: Viking Press, 1981.

Blackbourn, Barbara L. "The Eighth Story of the Tenth Day of Boccaccio's *Decameron*: An Example of Rhetoric or a Rhetorical Example?" *Italian Quarterly* 27 (1986): 5-13.

Bozzolo, Carla. "Le 'Dossier Laurent de Premierfait.'" *Italia medioevale e umanistica* 22 (1979): 439-47.

————. "La lecture des classiques par un humaniste français: Laurent de Premierfait." In *L'aube de la Renaissance.* Edited by D. Cecchetti, L. Sozzi, and L. Terreaux. Bibliothèque Franco Simone, 18. Geneva: Slatkine, 1991. Pp. 67-81.

Branca, Vittore. *Boccaccio: The Man and His Works.* Translated by Richard Monges and Dennis J. McAuliffe and edited by D. J. McAuliffe. New

York: New York University Press, 1976.

Brownlee, Kevin, and Walter Stephens, eds. *Discourses of Authority in Medieval and Renaissance Literature*. Hanover, New Hampshire, and London: University Press of New England, 1989.

Cavallini, Giorgio. *La decima giornata del "Decameron."* Biblioteca di Cultura, 172. Rome: Bulzoni, 1980.

Chavy, Paul. "Les premiers translateurs français." *The French Review* 47 (1974): 557-65.

Dardano, M. "Sintassi e stile nei *Libri della famiglia* di Leon Battista Alberti." *Cultura neolatina* 23 (1963): 215-50.

Deligiorgis, Stavros. *Narrative Intellection in the "Decameron."* Iowa City: University of Iowa Press, 1975.

Dembowski, Peter F. "Learned Treatises in French: Inspiration, Plagarism, and Translation." *Viator* 17 (1986): 255-69.

Di Stefano, Giuseppe. "Dal *Decameron* di Giovanni Boccaccio al *Livre des cent nouvelles* di Laurent de Premierfait." In *Boccaccio in Europe. Proceedings of the Boccaccio Conference, Louvain, December 1975.* Edited by Gilbert Tournoy. Symbolae Facultatis Litterarum et Philosophiae Lovaniensis, Series A, 4. Louvain: Leuven University Press, 1977. Pp. 91-110.

———. *Essais sur le moyen français*. Ydioma Tripharium, Collana di Studi e Saggi di Filologia Romanza Diretta da Alberto Limentani, 4. Padua: Liviana, 1977.

Dombroski, Robert S., editor and translator. *Critical Perspectives on the "Decameron."* London: Hodder and Stoughton, 1976.

Famiglietti, R. C. "Laurent de Premierfait: The Career of a Humanist in Early Fifteenth-Century Paris." *Journal of Medieval History* 9 (1983): 25-42.

Gadol, Joan. *Leon Battista Alberti. Universal Man of the Early Renaissance.* Chicago: University of Chicago Press, 1969.

Gathercole, Patricia M. "The Manuscripts of Laurent de Premierfait's Works." *Modern Language Quarterly* 19 (1958): 262-70, and 23 (1962): 225-28.

Ghinassi, Ghino. "Leon Battista Alberti fra latinismo e toscanismo: La revisione dei *Libri della famiglia.*" *Lingua nostra* 22 (1961): 1-6.

Gorni, Guglielmo. "Dalla famiglia alla corte: Itinerari e allegorie nell'opere di L. B. Alberti." *Bibliothèque d'humanisme et Renaissance* 43 (1981): 241-56.

Hauvette, Henri. *De Laurentio de Primofato (Laurent de Premierfait) qui primus Joannis Boccacii opera quaedam gallice transtulit ineunte saeculo XV.* Paris: Hachette, 1903.

Hollander, Robert. *Boccaccio's Two Venuses*. New York: Columbia University Press, 1977.

Hunt, R. W. "Introductions to the *Artes* in the Twelfth Century." In *Studia mediaevalia in honorem admodum Reverendi Patris Raymundi Josephi Martin*. Bruges: De Tempel, 1948. Pp. 85-112.

Jarzombek, Mark. *On Leon Baptista Alberti. His Literary and Aesthetic Theo-

ries. Cambridge: MIT Press, 1989.

Kennedy, George A. *The Art of Rhetoric in the Roman World, 300 B.C.-A.D. 300*. Princeton: Princeton University Press, 1972.

Kirkham, Victoria. "The Classic Bond of Friendship in Boccaccio's Tito and Gisippo (*Decameron* 10.8)." In *The Classics in the Middle Ages*. Edited by Aldo S. Bernardo and Saul Levin. Medieval and Renaissance Texts and Studies, 69. Binghamton, N. Y.: Center for Medieval and Early Renaissance Texts and Studies, 1990. Pp. 223-35.

Lacroix, Jean. "Panégyrique domestique et projet de société humaniste dans *I libri della famiglia* de Leon Battista Alberti." In *Les relations de parenté dans le monde médiéval*. Senefiance, 26. Aix-en-Provence: Publications du Centre Universitaire d'Etudes et de Recherches Médiévales d'Aix, 1989. Pp. 373-93.

Lee, A. C. *"The Decameron." Its Sources and Analogues*. 1909. Reprint ed., New York: Haskell House, 1972.

Lucas, Robert H. "Mediaeval French Translators of the Latin Classics to 1500." *Speculum* 45 (1970): 225-53.

Marolda, Paolo. "L. B. Alberti e il problema della politica: Il *Fatum et Fortuna* e *I libri della famiglia*." *Rassegna della letteratura italiana* 90 (1986): 29-40.

Marsh, David. *The Quattrocento Dialogue. Classical Tradition and Humanist Innovation*. Harvard Studies in Comparative Literature, 35. Cambridge: Harvard University Press, 1980.

May, James M. *Trials of Character. The Eloquence of Ciceronian Ethics*. Chapel Hill and London: North Carolina Press, 1988.

Mazzotta, Giuseppe. *The World at Play in Boccaccio's "Decameron."* Princeton: Princeton University Press, 1986.

Michel, Paul-Henri. *Un idéal humain au XVe siècle: La pensée de L. B. Alberti*. Paris: Les Belles Lettres, 1930.

Minnis, A. J. *Medieval Theory of Authorship. Scholastic Literary Attitudes in the Later Middle Ages*. Middle Ages Series. 2nd ed. Philadelphia: University of Pennsylvania Press, 1988.

Monfrin, Jacques. "La connaissance de l'antiquité et le problème de l'humanisme en langue vulgaire dans la France du XVe siècle." In *The Late Middle Ages and the Dawn of Humanism Outside Italy. The Proceedings of the International Conference, Louvain, May 11-13, 1970*. Edited by G. Verbeke and J. Ijsewijn. Mediaevalia Lovaniensa, Series 1, 1. Louvain: University Press, 1972. Pp. 131-70.

Olson, Glending. *Literature as Recreation in the Later Middle Ages*. Ithaca: Cornell University Press, 1982.

Pellegrin, Elisabeth. "Quelques *accessus* au *De amicitia* de Cicéron." In *Hommages à André Boutemy*. Edited by Guy Cambier. Collection Latomus, 145. Brussels: Latomus, 1976. Pp. 274-98.

Ponte, Giovanni. *Leon Battista Alberti, umanista e scrittore*. Genoa: Tilgher, 1981.

Purkis, G. S. "Laurent de Premierfait. First French Translator of the *Decameron.*" *Italian Studies* 4 (1949): 22-36.

Santinello, Giovanni. *Leon Battista Alberti. Una visione estetica del mondo e della vita.* Facoltà di Magistero dell'Università di Padova, 5. Florence: G. C. Sansoni, 1962.

Scaglione, Aldo D. *Nature and Love in the Late Middle Ages.* Berkeley and Los Angeles: University of California Press, 1963.

Seigel, Jerrold E. *Rhetoric and Philosophy in Renaissance Humanism. The Union of Eloquence and Wisdom, Petrarch to Valla.* Princeton: Princeton University Press, 1968.

Simone, Franco. *Il rinascimento francese. Studi e ricerche.* Biblioteca di Studi Francesi, 1. Turin: Società Editrice Internazionale, 1961.

Smarr, Janet Levarie. *Boccaccio and Fiammetta: The Narrator as Lover.* Urbana and Chicago: University of Illinois Press, 1986.

Sorieri, Louis. *Boccaccio's Story of Tito e Gisippo in European Literature.* Comparative Literature Series. New York: Institute of French Studies, 1937.

Strocchia, Sharon T. *Death and Ritual in Renaissance Florence.* The Johns Hopkins University Studies in Historical and Political Science, 1. Baltimore: The Johns Hopkins University Press, 1992.

Wilson, N. G. *From Byzantium to Italy: Greek Studies in the Italian Renaissance.* Baltimore: The Johns Hopkins University Press, 1992.

INDEX

BRILL'S STUDIES
IN
INTELLECTUAL HISTORY

1. POPKIN, R.H. *Isaac la Peyrère (1596-1676)*. His Life, Work and Influence. 1987. ISBN 90 04 08157 7
2. THOMSON, A. *Barbary and Enlightenment*. European Attitudes towards the Maghreb in the 18th Century. 1987. ISBN 90 04 08273 5
3. DUHEM, P. *Prémices Philosophiques*. With an Introduction in English by S.L. Jaki. 1987. ISBN 90 04 08117 8
4. OUDEMANS, TH.C.W. & A.P.M.H. LARDINOIS. *Tragic Ambiguity*. Anthropology, Philosophy and Sophocles' *Antigone*. 1987. ISBN 90 04 08417 7
5. FRIEDMAN, J.B. (ed.). *John de Foxton's Liber Cosmographiae (1408)*. An Edition and Codicological Study. 1988. ISBN 90 04 08528 9
6. AKKERMAN, F. & A. J. VANDERJAGT (eds.). *Rodolphus Agricola Phrisius, 1444-1485*. Proceedings of the International Conference at the University of Groningen, 28-30 October 1985. 1988. ISBN 90 04 08599 8
7. CRAIG, W.L. *The Problem of Divine Foreknowledge and Future Contingents from Aristotle to Suarez*. 1988. ISBN 90 04 08516 5
8. STROLL, M. *The Jewish Pope*. Ideology and Politics in the Papal Schism of 1130. 1987. ISBN 90 04 08590 4
9. STANESCO, M. *Jeux d'errance du chevalier médiéval*. Aspects ludiques de la fonction guerrière dans la littérature du Moyen Age flamboyant. 1988. ISBN 90 04 08684 6
10. KATZ, D. *Sabbath and Sectarianism in Seventeenth-Century England*. 1988. ISBN 90 04 08754 0
11. LERMOND, L. *The Form of Man*. Human Essence in Spinoza's *Ethic*. 1988. ISBN 90 04 08829 6
12. JONG, M. DE. *In Samuel's Image*. Early Medieval Child Oblation. (in preparation)
13. PYENSON, L. *Empire of Reason*. Exact Sciences in Indonesia, 1840-1940. 1989. ISBN 90 04 08984 5
14. CURLEY, E. & P.-F. MOREAU (eds.). *Spinoza. Issues and Directions*. The Proceedings of the Chicago Spinoza Conference. 1990. ISBN 90 04 09334 6
15. KAPLAN, Y., H. MÉCHOULAN & R.H. POPKIN (eds.). *Menasseh Ben Israel and His World*. 1989. ISBN 90 04 09114 9
16. BOS, A.P. *Cosmic and Meta-Cosmic Theology in Aristotle's Lost Dialogues*. 1989. ISBN 90 04 09155 6
17. KATZ, D.S. & J.I. ISRAEL (eds.). *Sceptics, Millenarians and Jews*. 1990. ISBN 90 04 09160 2
18. DALES, R.C. *Medieval Discussions of the Eternity of the World*. 1990. ISBN 90 04 09215 3
19. CRAIG, W.L. *Divine Foreknowledge and Human Freedom*. The Coherence of Theism: Omniscience. 1991. ISBN 90 04 09250 1
20. OTTEN, W. *The Anthropology of Johannes Scottus Eriugena*. 1991. ISBN 90 04 09302 8
21. ÅKERMAN, S. *Queen Christina of Sweden and Her Circle*. The Transformation of a Seventeenth-Century Philosophical Libertine. 1991. ISBN 90 04 09310 9
22. POPKIN, R.H. *The Third Force in Seventeenth-Century Thought*. 1992. ISBN 90 04 09324 9
23. DALES, R.C & O. ARGERAMI (eds.). *Medieval Latin Texts on the Eternity of the World*. 1990. ISBN 90 04 09376 1
24. STROLL, M. *Symbols as Power*. The Papacy Following the Investiture Contest. 1991. ISBN 90 04 09374 5

25. FARAGO, C.J. *Leonardo da Vinci's 'Paragone'*. A Critical Interpretation with a New Edition of the Text in the *Codex Urbinas*. 1992. ISBN 90 04 09415 6
26. JONES, R. *Learning Arabic in Renaissance Europe*. Forthcoming. ISBN 90 04 09451 2
27. DRIJVERS, J.W. *Helena Augusta*. The Mother of Constantine the Great and the Legend of Her Finding of the True Cross. 1992. ISBN 90 04 09435 0
28. BOUCHER, W.I. *Spinoza in English*. A Bibliography from the Seventeenth-Century to the Present. 1991. ISBN 90 04 09499 7
29. McINTOSH, C. *The Rose Cross and the Age of Reason*. Eighteenth-Century Rosicrucianism in Central Europe and its Relationship to the Enlightenment. 1992. ISBN 90 04 09502 0
30. CRAVEN, K. *Jonathan Swift and the Millennium of Madness*. The Information Age in Swift's *A Tale of a Tub*. 1992. ISBN 90 04 09524 1
31. BERKVENS-STEVELINCK, C., H. BOTS, P.G. HOFTIJZER & O.S. LANKHORST (eds.). *Le Magasin de l'Univers*. The Dutch Republic as the Centre of the European Book Trade. Papers Presented at the International Colloquium, held at Wassenaar, 5-7 July 1990. 1992. ISBN 90 04 09493 8
32. GRIFFIN, JR., M.I.J. *Latitudinarianism in the Seventeenth-Century Church of England*. Annoted by R.H. Popkin. Edited by L. Freedman. 1992. ISBN 90 04 09653 1
33. WES, M.A. *Classics in Russia 1700-1855*. Between two Bronze Horsemen. 1992. ISBN 90 04 09664 7
34. BULHOF, I.N. *The Language of Science*. A Study in the Relationship between Literature and Science in the Perspective of a Hermeneutical Ontology. With a Case Study in Darwin's *The Origin of Species*. 1992. ISBN 90 04 09644 2
35. LAURSEN, J.C. *The Politics of Skepticism in the Ancients, Montaigne, Hume and Kant*. 1992. ISBN 90 04 09459 8
36. COHEN, E. *The Crossroads of Justice*. Law and Culture in Late Medieval France. 1993. ISBN 90 04 09569 1
37. POPKIN, R.H. & A.J. VANDERJAGT (eds.). *Scepticism and Irreligion in the Seventeenth and Eighteenth Centuries*. 1993. ISBN 90 04 09596 9
38. MAZZOCCO, A. *Linguistic Theories in Dante and the Humanists*. Studies of Language and Intellectual History in Late Medieval and Early Renaissance Italy. 1993. ISBN 90 04 09702 3
39. KROOK, D. *John Sergeant and His Circle*. A Study of Three Seventeenth-Century English Aristotelians. Edited with an Introduction by B.C. Southgate. 1993. ISBN 90 04 09756 2
40. AKKERMAN, F., G.C. HUISMAN & A.J. VANDERJAGT (eds.). *Wessel Gansfort (1419-1489) and Northern Humanism*. 1993. ISBN 90 04 09857 7
41. COLISII, M.L. *Peter Lombard*. 2 volumes. 1994. ISBN 90 04 09859 3 (Vol. 1), ISBN 90 04 09860 7 (Vol. 2), ISBN 90 04 09861 5 (Set)
42. VAN STRIEN, C.D. *British Travellers in Holland During the Stuart Period*. Edward Browne and John Locke as Tourists in the United Provinces. 1993. ISBN 90 04 09482 2
43. MACK, P. *Renaissance Argument*. Valla and Agricola in the Traditions of Rhetoric and Dialectic. 1993. ISBN 90 04 09879 8
44. DA COSTA, U. *Examination of Pharisaic Traditions*. Supplemented by SEMUEL DA SILVA's *Treatise on the Immortality of the Soul*. Tratado da immortalidade da alma. Translation, Notes and Introduction by H.P. Salomon & I.S.D. Sassoon. 1993. ISBN 90 04 09923 9
45. MANNS, J.W. *Reid and His French Disciples*. Aesthetics and Metaphysics. 1994. ISBN 90 04 09942 5
46. SPRUNGER, K.L. *Trumpets from the Tower*. English Puritan Printing in the Netherlands, 1600-1640. 1994. ISBN 90 04 09935 2
47. RUSSELL, G.A. (ed.). *The 'Arabick' Interest of the Natural Philosophers in Seventeenth-Century England*. 1994. ISBN 90 04 09888 7
48. SPRUIT, L. Species intelligibilis: *From Perception to Knowledge*. Volume I: Classical Roots and Medieval Discussions. 1994. ISBN 90 04 09883 6

49. SPRUIT, L. Species intelligibilis: *From Perception to Knowledge*. Volume II. (in preparation)
50. HYATTE, R. *The Arts of Friendship*. The Literary Idealization of Friendship in Medieval and Early Renaissance Literature. 1994. ISBN 90 04 10018 0

DATE DUE

			Printed in USA